Damascus Diary

Damascus Diary

An Inside Account of Hafez al-Assad's Peace Diplomacy, 1990–2000

Bouthaina Shaaban

LYNNE RIENNER PUBLISHERS

BOULDER
LONDON

Published in the United States of America in 2013 by
Lynne Rienner Publishers, Inc.
1800 30th Street, Boulder, Colorado 80301
www.rienner.com

and in the United Kingdom by
Lynne Rienner Publishers, Inc.
3 Henrietta Street, Covent Garden, London WC2E 8LU

© 2013 by Lynne Rienner Publishers, Inc. All rights reserved

Library of Congress Cataloging-in-Publication Data
Shaaban, Bouthaina.
Damascus diary : an inside account of Hafez al-Assad's peace diplomacy,
  1990–2000 / Bouthaina Shaaban.
       p. cm.
Includes bibliographical references and index.
ISBN 978-1-58826-863-1 (alk. paper)
1. Syria—Politics and government—1971–2000. 2. Assad, Hafez,
  1930–2000. 3. Middle East—Politics and government. I. Title.
DS98.4.S53 2013
956.05'3—dc23
                                                    2012025115

British Cataloguing in Publication Data
A Cataloguing in Publication record for this book
is available from the British Library.

Printed and bound in the United States of America

 The paper used in this publication meets the requirements
of the American National Standard for Permanence of
Paper for Printed Library Materials Z39.48-1992.

5 4 3 2 1

*To my late parents,
Mr. Younis Shaaban and Mrs. Abla Al Ali,
who taught me how to love, forgive, and work for peace*

Contents

Foreword, Fred H. Lawson ... ix
Acknowledgments ... xiii

    Introduction ... 1
1. The Road to Madrid ... 9
2. Blessed Are the Peacemakers ... 39
3. The Rise of Bill Clinton ... 61
4. Syria's Honeymoon with Clinton's America ... 79
5. The Deposit That Never Was ... 95
6. Rabin's Assassination and the Long Road to Nowhere ... 117
7. The Legacy of Yusuf al-Azma ... 129
8. The April Understanding ... 137
9. The Not-So-Secret Lauder Talks ... 157
10. The Shepherdstown Debacle ... 171
11. The Man Who Did Not Sign ... 187
    Epilogue ... 199

Appendixes

    1: Letter from George H. W. Bush to Hafez al-Assad,
       May 31, 1991   203
    2: Letter from Bill Clinton to Hafez al-Assad, May 27, 1993   207
    3: Letter from Bill Clinton to Hafez al-Assad, July 4, 1993   211
    4: Letter from Bill Clinton to Hafez al-Assad,
       September 4, 1993   213
    5: Letter from Bill Clinton to Hafez al-Assad,
       December 2, 1993   215
    6: Letter from Bill Clinton to Hafez al-Assad,
       October 12, 1999   217
    7: Minutes of the Telephone Conversation Between
       Bill Clinton and Hafez al-Assad, January 18, 2000   219

Chronology of Key Events   223
Cast of Characters   229
Bibliography   231
Index   235
About the Book   245

Foreword

Fred H. Lawson

HOW SYRIAN FOREIGN POLICY ACTUALLY GETS MADE REMAINS largely unknown. Scholars and journalists alike assume that since the country's last coup d'état in November 1970 the president has dominated the policymaking process, if not drawn up and conducted foreign affairs all by himself. Even observers who enjoy close personal relations with Syria's successive leaders imply that no real discussion or bargaining takes place among members of the political elite about matters of diplomacy and national security. But we are not really sure, because insider accounts of policymaking in Damascus have been nonexistent, in any language.

Into this void comes Bouthaina Shaaban's memoir of her years as personal interpreter and external relations adviser to Hafez al-Assad, who was president of Syria from March 1971 until his death in June 2000. Shaaban's story is primarily the improbable tale of an ambitious, energetic, even starstruck high school graduate from an obscure village who brings herself to the attention of the country's new leader during his first visit to the military academy in Homs. Remarkably, the president takes note of the bold young woman and promises to assist her in pursuing a university education. Her father, not sure what to make of his daughter's brashness and extremely suspicious that anything will come of her endeavor, stays home when she is abruptly summoned to the Presidential Palace for an audience. Thanks to her audacity, the regulations that govern financial assistance to university applicants from poor backgrounds are immediately amended; she enters the English literature program at Damascus University and leaves her home ground far behind.

As personal interpreter to President Hafez al-Assad, Shaaban finds herself involved in a succession of closed-door meetings, sometimes with only her patron and a US president, secretary of state, or special envoy in the room alongside her. Her accounts of such encounters must therefore be considered authoritative, and she on occasion explicitly contrasts her own recollections with those that have been recorded by US officials. It does not matter so much which version turns out to be true; the divergent reports underscore significant differences of perception and interpretation as much as they do disagreements over facts. Shaaban's narrative is no more or less colored by political interest or concern for the writer's historical legacy than are the public memoirs that have been composed by the United States.

In addition to her own memory, Shaaban relies on unpublished minutes, letters, and background papers culled from the archives of the Syrian presidency and the Foreign Ministry in Damascus. Such documents have never before been exploited, and they provide assessments of events and personalities that constitute a truly Syrian perspective on international affairs. Again, whether the viewpoint is right or wrong, or better or worse than that of the US Department of State, is beside the point. Much more than any analysis that might be constructed by outside scholars and diplomats, no matter how learned and astute, Shaaban's memoir really does constitute a view from Damascus.[1]

And what does it show? First, it hints that there is indeed some sort of process behind foreign policymaking in Syria. In May 1994, US secretary of state Warren Christopher arrived in Damascus, carrying a provisional offer from Israeli prime minister Yitzhak Rabin to withdraw from the Golan and dismantle Israeli settlements over a period of five years. President al-Assad told Christopher that he would give an answer the following day, and during the next twenty-four hours he sat down with three senior figures—Foreign Minister Faruq al-Shar', Minister of Defense Mustafa Tlas, and Chief of the General Staff Hikmat Shihabi—to work out a suitable response. Shaaban notes that the Syrian president, "contrary to what the Americans thought, was a very consensual leader who was very careful to consult with his top officials before reaching a strategic decision of such magnitude." One wishes that other examples of high-level policymaking had been incorporated into the text, and that they spelled out the alternatives that got advanced, weighed, and rejected during the course of deliberations.

Second, Shaaban's account belies the usual notion that Hafez al-Assad was a stone-faced, "taciturn" statesperson.[2] The posters that cluttered the walls of Damascus throughout the 1990s, which often displayed a broadly beaming president, turn out to be right: the Eternal Leader possessed a keen sense of humor. When Secretary of State James Baker remarked that Damascus's announcement that Syria was going to attend the 1991 Madrid conference had shifted the spotlight away from Mikhail Gorbachev's triumphant arrival at the summit of the Group of 7 industrial states, al-Assad adroitly responded, "We actually did that on purpose to create some problems for Gorbachev." Not all quips were so light-hearted. When Baker subsequently joked that "face to face" talks with Israeli officials would be better than "back to back" negotiations, the Syrian president retorted, "All that is missing is [for you to add] 'and smiling.'"

By the late 1990s, a great deal of attention was accorded to President al-Assad's physical condition. US officials went out of their way to look for signs that might indicate whether or not the Syrian leader was slowing down or losing his edge. Shaaban dismisses such speculation as baseless, even fundamentally wrong-headed. Yet, she shows that the sharp-witted negotiator who bantered so easily with Baker had turned prickly by the time he met President Bill Clinton in Geneva in March 2000. Clinton offered nothing new, merely reiterating well-worn Israeli proposals concerning the future of the Golan. Irritated, al-Assad turned to his trusted translator and growled, "What are they talking about? Territorial swaps? That part of [Lake Tiberias] is ours and has always been ours. I myself used to swim in it, with my colleagues, before the [June 1967] war. How can we give that up?" When Clinton tried to present the case that Israel was offering to give back "90 percent of the Golan," and that a better deal might never come along again, Shaaban notes that "it was no use; President al-Assad was no longer listening." The session then deteriorated markedly, with al-Assad grousing, "I neither 'understand' [Clinton's problems as intermediary] nor do I want to understand. That is not my job. I'd better leave."

Bouthaina Shaaban's memoir can be read on several different levels. Anyone interested in the opportunities available to women in Baath Party–ruled Syria is likely to be intrigued by details that specialists in Middle Eastern diplomacy will find irrelevant, if not distracting. On the whole, however, we are fortunate to have this initial glimpse into ways that Baathist Syria perceived and dealt with the outside world. May it presage the publication of more detailed and systematic insider accounts, as other high-ranking Syrian officials find themselves increasingly free to tell their own stories.

Notes

1. Itamar Rabinovich, *A View from Damascus* (London: Vallentine Mitchell, 2008).

2. See, as only one recent example, David W. Lesch, *Syria: The Fall of the House of Assad* (New Haven: Yale University Press, 2012), 19.

Acknowledgments

THIS BOOK COULD NOT HAVE BEEN COMPLETED WITHOUT A long list of people who made it happen. I start out by thanking members of my family—my two daughters, Nahed and Nazek, my son, Rida, my husband, Khalil Jawad, and the newest addition to my family, my grandson, Najem E. Alsaleh—who were, and remain, my true and loved partners in everything I have ever produced and every word I have ever written. Without them, I wouldn't be the woman I am today. They have made me stronger, wiser, and more capable of carrying on when times seemed rough, either in Syria or the wider Arab world. Our dining table in Damascus was the scene of the daily lengthy discussions we have had for years, covering everything about the trials and tribulations of peacemaking in the Middle East. We hoped together, were discouraged together, and looked back on ten years of the peace process together, bitterly regretting how Israel had missed a golden opportunity at making peace with Syria.

I would also like to thank Syrian historian Dr. Sami Moubayed, who offered his expertise on modern Syrian affairs, authenticating and reviewing historical documents related to the peace process. My appreciation also goes to all the peacemakers of the world, regardless of the final achievement, be it big or small. The most important conclusion I derived from this long experience is that working for peace is a holy duty that we should pursue in every conflict because the alternative is so ugly and inhuman.

I would like to thank all those responsible for the archives of the Ministry of Foreign and Expatriates Affairs and of the Presidential Palace, especially Dr. Iskandar Louka. Their patience and generous help was an invaluable treasure, as they tolerated endless hours that I spent reviewing minutes, letters, handwritten documents, and transcripts of telephone calls.

I also would like to thank my editor, Mrs. Loulou Brown, who worked with me tirelessly on this book since its inception. My thanks also go to Ms. Lynne Rienner and all those working at Lynne Rienner Publishers, especially my project editor, Ms. Lesli Brooks Athanasoulis, who made the production of this book a work of joy. Last but not least, I would also like to extend my deep appreciation to my assistant, Mrs. Raghad al-Mahrous, who worked with me on the book minute-by-minute and day-by-day.

—Bouthaina Shaaban

Damascus Diary

Introduction

IN THE SUMMER OF 1971, I MET PRESIDENT HAFEZ AL-ASSAD for the very first time, completely unaware that one day, more than twenty years later, I would work with him for the last ten years of his life. I was an eighteen-year-old girl from a small village near Homs who had finished her baccalaureate exams, ranking first within the entire Homs province, and was preparing to go to college. He was Syria's charming, charismatic, and powerful new president, having been elected to office a few months earlier in March 1971. Assad had launched his famous "Correction Movement" in November 1970, toppling hard-liners within the ruling Baath Party. He served as prime minister for four months, after which he ran for presidential office and won with a landslide victory in early 1971.

The following story, which I have often talked about in television interviews, speaks volumes about my special relationship with President Assad, why he appreciated me, and why I considered him to be such an inspiring father figure—not only to me, but to the Syrian nation as a whole. He is the kind of leader who shows up once in a lifetime and is to Syrians what Winston Churchill is to the British, Ataturk is to the Turks, and Gamal Abdul Nasser is to the Egyptians. I always saw similarities between him—as a historical leader—and South Africa's Nelson Mandela, who is also one of my icons and role models in life.

During the summer of 1971, President Assad had passed legislation that provided grants to top-level students, who could then enroll at state-run universities. However, the legislation was flawed. Despite the fact that I had scored the highest grade point average in Homs and the fourth in the whole of Syria, I did not qualify for a grant and thus would not be able to attend Damascus University as my father could not afford it. I decided, with no doubt in my mind whatsoever, that I wanted to meet the president and explain to him what was wrong with the decree he had just issued. My father could not send me to university without the grant, but the decree stated that I could only enroll at a two-year college. This did not at all accord with my ambition, which was to obtain a PhD in English literature.

My father thought my idea was insane and shook his head in disbelief that his beloved daughter wanted to meet Syria's new strongman, Hafez al-Assad. Nevertheless, he gave me a generous amount of money to help me on my journey. I took the bus, all alone, from our village, al-Masoudieh, down to Homs where President Assad was supposed to be visiting the Military Academy that summer. It was my first trip outside the village, and in retrospect I now tend to agree with my father that my endeavor was indeed bold and more than a little crazy.

Before going to the academy, I tried to talk with the city's governor, telling him that I was number one in the entire province and that I therefore deserved a grant to enroll at university. "If you can't help me," I warned him, "then I'm going to see the President of the Republic." The governor told me that the president was due to visit the city's Military Academy the following morning and offered to take me to see him if I dropped by his office at 10 A.M. sharp. I arrived at 9:30 A.M., but my heart sank when I realized that the governor had already left his office for an audience with President Assad.

I left depressed, thinking how right my father seemed to be—it was indeed crazy to aim so high. I remember walking from the governor's office to the bus station and realizing that I was in a dilemma about whether to take that day's bus to my village or to stay for an extra day and try to find another way to reach the president. I understood that none of the people I knew or had recently met with were ready to make a very brave decision to help save my future. My initial hunch had been right; only President Hafez al-Assad would be able to help me and change the decree. The problem remained, though, as to how in the world I could reach him. I remember that my neck became stiff as I walked with my head bent downward, in deep thought about my academic future. Then when I looked up, I saw a minibus with a big name on it: "Samoura." I gazed hard at the name and said to myself that wherever that minibus was going, I would ride in it. A minute later, a man near it yelled, "Kullieyyeh" (military collegc). I took the minibus, and to my surprise it traveled out of town to a forlorn place in the middle of nowhere. This was its last stop. I felt like staying on the bus and returning to Homs, but instead I plucked up courage and got out.

The huge iron door of the Homs Military Academy was closed, with three fully armed military officers standing beside the door. The sentry guard posted outside looked at me with raised eyebrows, surprised that a girl of my size and age was standing amid a colorful array of oversized men in uniforms decorated with stars, stripes, and large war medals. "I want to meet President Hafez al-Assad," I said, strongly articulating my words, which were definitely beyond my years. He turned me away with the brush of a hand, falling just short of saying, "Shut up before anybody hears you!" I begged him, in fact insisted, claiming that if he let me through, my meeting the president might change my entire life. Eventually the young sentry guard sympathized with my request and indicated that I should walk into the military complex. He then asked me not to tell anybody how I got into the building. What I recall more than anything else was how large the premises were; they stretched for miles, having housed and trained many generations of Syrian officers since the 1940s. Needless to say, I got lost and had to ask for directions as to where the president might be found. I was told that he would be having lunch at noon, "around the swimming pool."

I waited patiently beneath the burning sun around the pool, to find President Assad approaching at midday, accompanied by Air Force commander Naji Jamil, wearing a white military uniform. Heavy security formed a chain around the president, and his top lieutenants surrounded them. I rushed up to Assad but was prevented from getting close to him by security. With his back turned toward me and without looking at me, one of the security officials hit me with his elbow, and I almost fell to the floor. President Assad then signaled to his security officials to stand back and asked me to step forward. I ran toward him so quickly that my head crashed rather violently into his chest. I was embarrassed but didn't want to lose such a precious moment. Ignoring the collision, I began to speak politely, carefully articulating my words: "President Assad, I am Bouthaina Shaaban, from al-Masoudieh village. I got my baccalaureate, ranking first in Homs and fourth in Syria, but your recent decree has not done me justice. My father cannot afford to send me to university, and my future is therefore in your hands!" Young as I was, I thought that al-Masoudieh was the center of the universe and that by inserting its name into my plea I would immediately attract the president's attention. Young people do crazy things, I now say to myself as I look back at that episode forty years later. The president looked at me and smiled. "Don't worry, my daughter; you will get what you want!" he said. I was told to go home and wait to hear from the Presidential Palace.

The call from Assad's office came much sooner than I expected—in fact, the very next day. We did not have a telephone where we lived, so the Presidential Palace phoned the village chief's office, asking that I come to Damascus the following morning for an audience with the president. I prepared for the long trip to the Syrian capital, which I also took by bus, wearing clothes in loud, red colors that I vividly remember. It was my first trip ever to Damascus, and, needless to say, I was very excited about seeing the capital of my country and meeting the president yet again, this time at the Presidential Palace. Yet again, my father was uneasy about the trip and doubtful about the consequences.

I arrived at the Muhajreen Palace, located on the slopes of Mount Qassiun, with a panoramic, splendid view of Damascus. President Assad had set up base there shortly after coming to power. Various Syrian presidents had used the palace since the 1940s, and it remained Assad's base until 1978, when he moved to another one that was far less extravagant, located at Rawda Square. The president's director of protocol, Khalil al-Saadawi, said that I had no more than ten minutes to tell my story, from A to Z, to the president. I nodded—I would have accepted any condition just to meet Hafez al-Assad again. All I needed, I said to myself, were two minutes.

Assad walked into the room where I was seated, tall and charming as I had seen him two days earlier at the Military Academy. He was wearing a blue suit and radiated power and confidence, as he often did on TV. He began by inquiring about my particular problem and then asked questions about my village, including whether we had electricity and phone lines. I answered no to each of his questions, prompting him to extend the meeting by a good forty minutes. He was clearly eager to know why Syrian villages in the second half of the twentieth century were still living in darkness. While sitting with him, all I could say to myself was, "Bouthaina, you must be crazy! He is the president of the Republic. Why in the world does he need to sit here and listen to your stories?" The meeting ended cordially, and before walking out, he asked me to pass by whenever I happened to be in Damascus.

While I was being driven back home on the bus, the driver tuned into Damascus Radio. The first item of news was that President Assad had amended his earlier decree related to grants given to high achievers. I felt a shiver down my spine—the president of the republic had not waited a day to change the law; he must have signed the new decree right after I'd walked out of his office! I wanted to tell everybody on the bus: "Did you hear that? The president has changed the law because of *me*!" But I managed to contain myself and waited until I'd reached al-

Bouthaina Shaaban (seventh from left) while a freshman at Damascus University, pictured with President Hafez al-Assad in 1971.

Masoudieh before I began to shout with joy, where family and friends were already celebrating, coining the new law "Bouthaina's decree"!

As a result of the change in the law, I enrolled at Damascus University that summer, where I studied English literature. Along with a group of classmates, who had also benefited from the decree, I paid yet another visit to the Presidential Palace to thank the president for granting us the opportunity to complete our university education. I then did my MA and PhD studies in the UK, where I also studied English literature.

Many years later, when I was a professor at Damascus University and adviser at the Ministry of Foreign Affairs, Foreign Minister Farouk al-Shara asked me to ride with him in his car "for an important meeting." That was strange, since Shara had never previously asked me to accompany him on any such meeting. While en route, he told me that the president's interpreter had been taken ill and that Hafez al-Assad needed someone to translate for him because he was receiving a delegation of US members of Congress. I was overcome with fear as I thought of standing by the president's side at an official meeting. A million ideas went through my head: *What if I made a mistake? What if I stuttered? Would he remember me? What if I disappointed him?*

When we walked in, Assad greeted us without indicating whether he recognized me from our previous meeting twenty years earlier. It would be a miracle if he did, I said to myself, given how many people he must meet every day. I was just another Syrian citizen, one of an enormous number of Syrian citizens whom he had met during the early months of his first term in office. I was very agitated, and this clearly showed on my face. President Assad, always the gentleman, patted me on the shoulder and said, "Don't be afraid. If we make a mistake, we'll just repeat what we are saying. It's no big deal." By saying, "If *we* make a mistake," he was actually politely saying, "If *you* make a mistake."

When the meeting ended and right after his American guests had left, President Assad turned to me and said, "What would have happened to us if we had not sent you to university? We would have sat here today without an interpreter!" He had remembered me! It was remarkable for a man of his standing and power to be so thoughtful, sharp, and considerate. It was—and remains—one of the most memorable days in my life because it was right there and then (as he confided to me much later) that I earned the president's trust and respect, from that day in 1991 until his passing on June 10, 2000.

President Assad took pride in me as a university professor and a writer and always treated intellectuals and writers with great respect. During ten years of serving as his interpreter, I had a hunch that he was hoping I would record the true events of this period. He never said anything to me, but any time a mention was made of posterity or how he was going to be remembered, he would cast a very meaningful look at me. He often spoke about future generations, stressing that he wanted them to embrace and defend the decisions he was making. Once he died, I started to recall his remarks about posterity and how his eyes shone when they looked at me in connection with remarks made about this issue, although I stress again he never, ever mentioned it directly to me. I remember I appeared on television with our well-known novelist Colette Khoury, and he later said to me that he'd seen me on TV with Colette and that I seemed to be a good match for her, even though she was much older than I was. Here again, I felt he was celebrating me as a writer for the same reasons mentioned above: his admiration for men and women of letters, seeing them as invaluable to Syria.

About a year after his death, I saw him in a dream. He said to me, "Bouthaina, why have you still not written about the period when you worked with me?"

I replied, saying, "Because I didn't know where to start and what kind of book I should write. Do I have to write about your childhood, your youth, your family, or your career?"

He said, "No, no! You don't have to write about all that. Four chapters would be enough." He explained that they should focus on Syria and the West, his relationship with the West, his role in the peace process, and finally, "Hafez al-Assad and Bill Clinton."

I understood that he wanted me to write the truth about him and to dispel the huge misconceptions in the West about his reputation and his role in the peace process and also the misconceptions of Bill Clinton's role, whom he trusted completely. Thus I decided to write my own impression of the Syrian-Israeli peace process, especially after reading what US and Israeli participants had already written. I felt I owed it to my country and to students interested in the Middle East to provide them with a Syrian perspective that has been recorded to the best of my ability, as I witnessed and best remember it.

From 1991 until 2000, I was dedicated to bringing peace to our region and putting an end to the Arab-Israeli conflict. I had to live the heartache of leaving my family, including my two daughters. In 1995, I gave birth to my son, Rida, and took a trip to Washington, D.C., when he was only two months old. I took him to a nursery and talked to "Mama Nadia," as we called her. I kissed him and explained that I was leaving him in my endeavor to try to ensure he lived in a better and more peaceful world. Both he and I were crying. I said to him, even though, of course, I knew he wouldn't understand, "Please don't think that I'm a bad mother leaving you here; it's for a better future for you and for all other children that I'm leaving you today." His tears still hurt me even today and the beautiful eyes of Nahed and Nazek beseeching me not to leave them are forever stuck in my memory. I was hoping I would be able to tell them I left them to make their world and that of their children a happier and more peaceful one, but sadly, for reasons elaborated in this book, peace between Syria and Israel was not achieved. What a waste! Not only the waste of efforts of very many people, who sacrificed years of their lives for this endeavor, but also what a waste of the lives of people who are still being killed, uprooted, or displaced on account of the lack of peace in the region. My only consolation is that I have devoted all the time required and have used up all my energy needed for a noble cause. I hope that current and future generations will never give up and will try again and again to make peace, just as our greeting always starts with "As-sal mu 'alaykum"(Peace be upon you). Peace is the most precious commodity for us humans. Enemies of peace are enemies of humanity, whereas those who try to make peace know that even if they fail, someone else will pick up the torch. Thus, "Blessed be the peace makers," whether or not they succeed.

The important thing is to keep trying and never give up.

1

The Road to Madrid

IT WAS IN CAIRO ON A HOT SUMMER DAY THAT WE WERE HIT by news that was to completely revamp the Arab world as a whole and become a turning point in modern world history. In my capacity as adviser to Syrian foreign minister Farouk al-Shara, I had traveled to Egypt to attend the nineteenth Islamic Conference of Foreign Ministers of the forty-five-member Organization of the Islamic Conference (OIC). This was shortly before I became private interpreter to President Hafez al-Assad. At the time I was a professor in the English Department at Damascus University, teaching romantic poetry. Nusrat Bhutto, the strong-minded former first lady of Pakistan (wife of Zulfikar Ali Bhutto and mother of Benazir Bhutto) was on the panel with two other speakers when somebody slipped a note into her hand on that fateful day, August 2, 1990. "Saddam Hussein has invaded Kuwait!" I will never forget the expression of shock on her face—and that of everybody else in the room—as we tried to digest the magnitude of what had happened.

There were various accounts of the reasons behind that invasion, which five months later famously led to what is now known as the Gulf War. Iraq had accused Kuwait of stealing Iraqi oil through slant drilling, but many cited Saddam's inability to repay the $14 billion borrowed from the Kuwaitis, originally to finance his eight-year war with Iran, as reason for his invasion. (Kuwait had been his principal ally during the Iran-Iraq War, providing money and logistical support. One account blamed US ambassador April Glaspie for encouraging Saddam to carry out his attack, saying that Washington would consider this an internal dispute and would not interfere.[1] The reasons notwithstanding, the Iraqi army rolled into Kuwait at 2:00 A.M. on August 2, catching the Kuwaitis completely off guard. The emir of Kuwait, Jaber Al-Ahmad Al-Jaber Al-Sabah, fled to Saudi Arabia, while his younger half brother, Shaikh Fahd Al-Ahmad Al-Jaber Al-Sabah, was shot and killed by the Iraqis.

News of the invasion of Kuwait ripped through the Arab world like a forest fire and vibrated strongly at our meeting room in Cairo. The Kuwaitis present at the OIC were naturally both afraid and frantic. In a matter of hours, their country had been brutally occupied, and their lives had been completely ruined. I recall some shouting madly, "Our money doesn't have any value anymore . . . our lives have lost their meaning. We don't have a country anymore!" I felt the bitterness of occupation—I had seen it all, once too often in my lifetime. The Palestinians had been living under illegal occupation since 1948, and my own countrymen in the Syrian Golan Heights had been subjected to a horrific Israeli occupation since 1967. Here were victims of occupation—again—left in oblivion, with nowhere to go; their passports, their money, and their entire nation now invalid. Amid all the craziness of that morning, one thought kept going through my head: sovereignty is an undeniable right—*nothing* in the world is as cruel as occupation. In the Arab world we had seen many occupations before, but all of them had been carried out by European powers during the first part of the twentieth century. This was the first time that an Arab country had invaded and occupied another Arab country.

Syria's Response to the Invasion of Kuwait

Our OIC meeting was temporarily adjourned, only to reconvene to issue a strongly worded letter to Saddam Hussein asking him to withdraw from Kuwait. That statement, along with many others, fell on deaf ears in Baghdad. From Cairo, Foreign Minister Shara immediately got on the phone with President Hafez al-Assad in Damascus. President Assad was clearly upset, having watched Saddam Hussein create nothing but havoc and disunity in the Arab world since he rose to power in 1979. Despite Syria's very tense relationship with Saddam (we had had no embassy in Baghdad since October 1980), our policy was to work with the Iraqi government to convince them of the ultimate and urgent need to withdraw from Kuwait. The long list of differences between us and Saddam seemed suddenly to no longer matter; what mattered was to liberate Kuwait and shelter Iraq from an upcoming catastrophe. That policy, outlined strongly by President Assad, was opposition to occupation, regardless of its form or circumstances.

President Assad famously sent Saddam Hussein an open letter, broadcast on Damascus Radio on January 12, 1991, saying, "Any harm that befalls Iraq also affects Syria and the entire Arab world."[2] Assad added that he would not go into detail as to whether it was right or wrong to invade Kuwait, noting: "this is neither the time nor place to discuss that. What is important at this stage is what we face regarding the very dangerous situation that is facing Iraq." He added, "Our concern for Iraq, its land, people, and army, is similar to our concern for ourselves because Iraq is a precious part of the Arab world." If an international war were launched on Iraq, he added, "The Arabs, whether united or divided, and in their forefront is Iraq, would be the losing party." Assad wrapped up his speech by saying that "some might say that Iraq would be targeted with an attack even if it withdraws from Kuwait. Here I would like to stress, in a brotherly oath: If that happens after you leave Kuwait, Syria will stand with all its capabilities, both financial and moral, next to Iraq in one trench, fighting along with it in all bravery, until victory is achieved."[3] Saddam's response, perhaps not surprisingly, was very negative. He was reportedly annoyed that President Assad had addressed him in an open letter rather than in secret correspondence, and as the world clearly remembers, he arrogantly turned down Syria's offer.

Meanwhile, the strong-minded US secretary of state James Baker had been conducting a regional tour, beginning in September 1990 aimed at singling out potential allies to join in a US-led coalition for the liberation of Kuwait. Baker, a Republican from Texas, was a seasoned US politician who had been President Ronald Reagan's chief of staff in the early 1980s. When President George H. W. Bush came to power in 1989, Baker became his trusted secretary of state, based on a personal friendship with the president that had lasted for twenty-five years. On his travel agenda was Syria, even though many voices in the Bush administration were opposed to such a visit, given that relations had been tense between Damascus and Washington because of the civil war in Lebanon. The United States disagreed with Damascus on a long list of issues but realized that if it wanted to succeed in building an Arab-backed coalition, it needed to have the Syrians onboard. In his memoir, *The Politics of Diplomacy*, Baker explained, "I felt that the symbolic importance of Syrian participation was far more crucial than their literal presence. With Syria represented, the credibility of our Arab coalition partners was immeasurably strengthened. But I had a more long-term purpose in mind. There was no way to move a comprehensive Mideast peace process forward without the active involvement of Syria."[4]

Baker's boss had reportedly wanted to engage Syria early in his presidential term but had been talked into changing course by George Shultz, the secretary of state during the Reagan years. Baker explains that Bush "always believed that Shultz made a serious mistake by cutting off contacts with Syria after the disastrous 1983 bombing of the US Marine barracks in Beirut. Vice President Bush had wanted to visit Damascus on his trip to the Middle East, but had been reluctantly dissuaded by aides fearful of the potential political fallout."[5] When Baker decided to visit the Middle East to prepare for the Gulf War in 1990, Bush told him, "I think you should consider going to Syria. I don't want to miss the boat again."[6]

Baker met President Assad in Damascus in September 1990. US secretaries of state had all been adequately briefed by their predecessor Henry Kissinger about his numerous encounters with the Syrian leader after the 1973 October War. In his memoirs, President Richard M. Nixon had written that Assad, whom he met in 1974, was a "tough negotiator [who has] a great deal of mystique, tremendous stamina, and a lot of charm. All in all, he is a man of substance, and at his age [then 44], he will be a leader to be reckoned with in this part of the world. This man really has elements of genius—without any question!"[7] When Jimmy Carter visited Syria, he wrote, "Little was known about his [Assad's] personal or family life, but former secretary of state Henry Kissinger and others who knew Assad had described him to me as very intelligent, eloquent and frank in discussing the most sensitive issues. I invited the Syrian leader to come and visit me in Washington, but he replied that he had no desire ever to visit the United States. Despite this firm but polite rebuff, I learned what I could about him and his nation before meeting him."[8] Carter then added, "During subsequent trips to Syria, I spent hours debating with Assad and listening to his analysis of events in the Middle East . . . he seemed to speak like a modern Saladin—as though it was his obligation to rid the region of foreign presence while preserving Damascus as the focal point of modern Arab unity."[9]

By the time Baker came to Damascus, Assad, in power since 1970, had already met two US presidents and fully understood the United States and its complex relationship with the Arab world. Baker recalled the first meeting, saying, "I told him I had heard he was a difficult bargainer but could be counted upon to keep his word once given."[10] "We have heard things about you, too," said the Syrian leader with a smile. "We have been watching reports of your opinions very carefully. We have come to the conclusion that you are strong and decisive, [and] you say what you mean, and this makes us believe that you are a straightforward man. Perhaps it would be better for us to say this behind your back, but this is an important trait. It is very important to be straightforward. It is important that a person be frank and direct, whether or not we agree. When these qualities are there, even when there is no agreement, there is trust. There should be no hidden issues between us."[11]

The magic word that Assad emphasized was "trust." He had mistakenly trusted Kissinger before realizing that he was encouraging Egyptian president Anwar Sadat to sign a separate peace with Israel. Many years later, when working with President Assad in the 1990s, I can safely say that he wanted to establish the same trust with Bill Clinton. In 1990, Baker made three things clear. First, from a US perspective, the invasion of Kuwait was the most dangerous world crisis in the final years of the Cold War, and throughout the post–Cold War era. Second, the United States was determined at any cost to prevent Saddam from success. Third, even in defeat, Saddam must not be seen as a hero, neither by the Arabs at large nor by his own people. Assad realized that the United States needed him, at that point, much more than he needed the Bush administration. A master politician, he paved the way for the upcoming ten years of Syrian-US relations, agreeing to send Syrian troops to the Gulf. "We will commit as many as required," he told Baker.[12]

Syria had every reason to want Saddam Hussein out of Kuwait. We must not forget that Saddam had started his era as a friend of the world powers—the same powers that turned against him in 1990 and eventually brought him down in 2003. He had made a state visit to France in 1976 and had close ties with French prime minister Jacques Chirac. The two first met in December 1974, when Chirac visited Baghdad to negotiate trade agreements, including the delivery of a nuclear reactor. When Saddam visited France the following year in September—his only visit to a Western country—Chirac said, "I welcome you as my personal friend. I assure you of my esteem, my consideration, and my affection."[13] He remained close to Chirac when Chirac became president of France in 1995 during the US embargo on Iraq. Throughout the 1980s, Iraq bought US$25 billion worth of arms from French concerns, including Mirage fighters, Super Etendard aircraft, and Exocet missiles.[14] The Iraqi government also picked French companies to build Saddam International Airport in 1982.[15]

The relationship between Chirac and Saddam went beyond the norm in Franco-Iraqi relations. When Chirac again became prime minister in 1986 after a decade out of power, the relationship once more blossomed. The following year, reports surfaced that Chirac had offered to rebuild the nuclear reactor destroyed by Israel in 1981.[16] In 1994, French oil companies Total and Elf won contracts worth billions to develop southern Iraqi oil fields.[17] The United Nation's oil-for-food program, inaugurated in 1996, allowed the Iraqi government to sell its oil in order to purchase food, medicine, and other humanitarian supplies. Saddam Hussein rewarded Chirac's government for its support; France quickly became Iraq's chief trade partner, a position it maintained until 2003. Saddam had also enjoyed an excellent relationship with the United States until 1990. Originally, the United States had feared him: five months after he came to power, the US State Department added Iraq to the list of states that sponsor terrorism. Iraq was removed from the list, however, when it went to war against Iran, the enemy of the United States, in September 1980. From 1983 to 1990, the US government sold Saddam around $200 million in arms for use in fighting the Iranians.[18] In 1983, President Ronald Reagan sent special envoy Donald Rumsfeld to Iraq to sell arms and give money to Saddam Hussein and to thank him for his war against Ayatollah Ruhollah Khomeini. Between 1983 and 1990, Iraq received $5 billion in credit from a corporation run by the US Department of Agriculture, beginning with $400 million in 1983 and increasing to over $1 billion per year by 1988.[19]

While the United States was generously supporting Saddam during the Iran-Iraq War, Syria held by its position, saying that it was the wrong war, with the wrong enemy, fought for completely wrong reasons. From day one, President Assad believed that Saddam was the aggressor, not the other way around. In reflecting on Saddam's turbulent history, the Syrian leader said, "He went into his war with Iran without any justification, and wanted to take all the Arabs with him to war. Of course, most of our Arab brothers—perhaps all of them—were enthusiastic toward that war. We in Syria refused this war, although when it first started, I did not know anybody yet from the Iranian leadership. I did not find any justification, however, for this war with Iran. Saddam has been in power for ten years and all of them have been filled with wars and their price had been heavily paid by the people of Iraq."[20] President Assad felt the same way about the occupation of Kuwait. As far as he was concerned, it was an illegal occupation, as brutal and wrong as the Israeli occupation of Palestine.

The Arab world, however, was divided on how to deal with the Iraqi occupation. Some leaders believed that the matter should be solved within the Arab family and not controlled by the United States. Another camp said that Iraq should be punished for its senseless adventure, through the US-led coalition that came to be known as Operation

Desert Storm. A tremendous amount of diplomacy was put forth by all parties to avoid the US operation in Iraq of January 1991. One effort was a conference in Geneva in January 1991, where Iraqi Foreign Minister Tariq Aziz met with James Baker. That meeting, which lasted for nearly seven hours, produced nothing: Saddam held to his position, refusing to withdraw from occupied Kuwait.

During all these monumental events, I was not in Syria, having gone to the United States to teach and conduct research at Duke University as a Fulbright scholar. Back then, the esteemed Palestinian scholar Hisham Sharabi was at Georgetown University, and he invited me to a conference on the occupation of Kuwait. I recall presenting a paper in which I outlined how this imminent war would be more damaging in a way than the one fought by the Arabs in 1967, which led to the occupation of the entire Sinai Peninsula, the West Bank, all of Jerusalem, and the Golan Heights. Being the first Arab-Arab war, this new war would divide the Arab world like never before, with repercussions that would last for decades to come. Twenty years down the road, as I look back at the Gulf War, I can safely say that Syria was absolutely right in its position toward Saddam. We did the right thing, all from a principled position vis-à-vis occupation in all its forms. How could we condemn the occupation of Palestine while turning a blind eye to the occupation of Kuwait?

Operation Desert Storm

With Saddam blocking all attempts at a peaceful solution to the crisis, the Gulf War started on January 16, 1991, launched by a UN-mandated coalition force of thirty-four nations led by the United States. The United Nations had passed Security Council Resolution 678, giving Iraq until mid-January to withdraw and empowering the coalition to use "all necessary means" to force Iraq out of Kuwait after the stated deadline. US president George H. W. Bush deployed US forces to Saudi Arabia, and an array of nations, Syria included, joined the coalition. This was the highest degree of coordination between Syria and the United States since bilateral relations were established in the 1940s. Saudi Arabia contributed approximately $36 billion of the $60 billion the war cost.[21] The other Arab states to join the coalition were Oman, Qatar, and the United Arab Emirates. Although they did not contribute any forces, Japan and Germany made financial contributions totaling $10 billion and $6.6 billion, respectively. US troops represented 73 percent of the coalition's 956,600 troops in Iraq. From the research that I conducted in later years, I understood that many Arab countries opposed Syria's joining the coalition, as did a number of Syrian intellectuals and writers, who circulated a petition to that effect. The war cost coalition forces 392 lives, and 20,000–35,000 Iraqis were killed, 3,000 of them civilians.[22] It took such a horrific death toll to get the Bush administration to embark on the long road to peace in the Middle East and start preparing for the Madrid Peace Conference. If it were not for the Gulf War, we might never have had Madrid.

Preparations for Madrid

At noon on February 6, 1991, the phone rang at the Presidential Palace in Damascus. President Bush was on the line, and he wanted to speak to President Assad. The war in Kuwait was coming to an end, and the two leaders discussed the situation in the Gulf, with Assad cautioning, "Beware not to strike at civilians, Mr. President. Only targets of utmost importance to the liberation of Kuwait must be hit."[23] Bush agreed, and he promised a serious effort to achieve peace in the Middle East once the liberation of Kuwait was complete. Exactly one month later, President Bush addressed Congress on March 6, 1991, in a speech that has often been cited as laying out a new US approach toward the Middle East. The centerpiece of his program was advancement of Arab-Israeli peace, as promised to President Assad, based on restoration of occupied land and fulfillment of Palestinian rights. Bush envisioned a multilateral track under the auspices of both the United States and Soviet Union, although early on, he had no clue what the conference would look like, where it would be held, and what it would achieve. What was clear to the US administration by mid-1991 was that the time was ripe to begin serious talks to try to resolve the Arab-Israeli conflict, picking up where earlier ones had failed. Between March and October 1991, Baker embarked on his famous "shuttle diplomacy" to the Middle East, trying to persuade Arab and Israeli leaders to talk peace collectively for the first time since 1948. In a memo to President Bush before his departure, Baker wrote, "I want to give you my thinking before we head off on this trip. I don't have high expectations but there are some new realities that make progress possible and we owe it to ourselves and to everyone else to make the effort."[24] Baker made his first postwar visit to Syria on March 13, 1991, during the holy month of Ramadan. He met with the Syrian president at 8:05 P.M., and four topics were on his agenda: security in the Gulf, weapons of mass destruction in the region, economic cooperation, and the Arab-Israeli conflict.[25] Assad responded that responsibility for security in the Gulf should be mainly shouldered by the Gulf countries themselves and expressed his full support for eliminating all "biological, chemical, and nuclear weapons" from the region. Assad, who trusted Baker from their several encounters prior to the war, made sure to remind his American guest of the unconditional shipment of arms Israel was getting periodically from the United States and Europe, noting that the Middle East will never be safe "so long as Israel is armed to the teeth." The two men then shifted to the topic that really mattered: the Arab-Israeli conflict. That, after all, was why Baker was in Damascus. President Assad told the secretary of state: "Based on what we read in the media regarding President Bush's positions, we believe he is ready to help to the best of his capacities [in achieving the] interests of the American people. In theory, the Americans want peace—just like any other people in the world. They have a great interest in bringing peace to this part of the world. This is what prompts the US president to take such a position. We believe that his position is correct and just, and it serves the overall interest of peace."[26]

President Assad took out the minutes of a recent meeting between his foreign minister and the Soviet chargé d'affaires in Syria. Although everybody knew that by now the Soviet Union was a superpower in decline, Assad believed that Baker must understand that this was still a bipolar world where Soviet views still mattered—or should matter—regarding the Arab-Israeli conflict. The Syrians and Russians had already agreed on resolving the conflict in a "just and comprehensive" manner, based on UN Security Council resolutions (UNSCRs) 242 and 338. Syria, he added, wanted "a full and unconditional Israeli withdrawal from all territories occupied in 1967; they should be restored to their rightful owners." Baker spoke of confidence-building measures, making reference to UN General Assembly Resolution 3379, passed in November 1975, which labeled Zionism "a form of racism and racial discrimination." The United States had voted against that resolution, which had been sponsored by twenty-five countries (Syria included). Baker tried to convince Assad of the need to reject such measures, but Assad replied, "If you want us to do that, the Arabs will lose an important factor that might convince the Israelis to go to the conference." That resolution, it must be noted, was eventually revoked by General Assembly Resolution 46/86 on December 16, 1991. In the entire history of the UN, Resolution 3379 is the only one that has ever been revoked. Sixteen years after its passing and nine months before it was revoked, it clearly still mattered to James Baker. The two men wrapped up their discussion without making any progress on the UN resolution, but they did exchange ideas on what the real definition of terrorism was; ten years prior to 9/11. They ended on the hopeful note that an international peace conference would be held "before too long."

Bladder Diplomacy

In April 1991, James Baker landed in Damascus again, this time carrying a letter from President Bush congratulating Assad on the Muslim Eid al-Fitr holiday. Bush wrote, "Syria's role today will be crucial. Based on our exchanges, I find myself confident that we can work together for regional peace."[27] He added, "During the past few months, we achieved great things together and I am sure that we can still achieve a whole lot more." Baker was in Damascus to lay out the many ways forward for Syria and the United States, and he had a full mandate to do so from the US president. The famous Assad-Baker meeting lasted for more than twelve hours, starting at 8:45 A.M. and lasting until 9:30 P.M.[28] It was held at the Presidential Palace in Damascus on April 23, 1991, attended by Foreign Minister Shara and US ambassador to Syria Edward Djerejian, an Armenian American of Syrian origin. Minutes of the marathon talks can be found in the archives of the Syrian presidency, precisely transcribed on 162 pages in meticulous detail by the Syrian leader's trusted aide, Iskandar Luka. These archives, to which I received access, were a historian's gold mine, an invaluable addition to all discourse about the Middle East peace process. The exchange below, although documented on several occasions from US and Israeli perspectives, has never been described from Syria's point of view. Syria's position did not change, whether speaking to the Americans behind closed doors or speaking to the Syrian public. Also, during the past twenty years, Syria has never altered its demand for a "just and comprehensive" peace, or a "peace of the brave," as President Assad once put it. It was and always has been complete return of the occupied Golan, based on the June 4, 1967, borders, UN Security Council resolutions, and the land-for-peace formula.

Baker began the talks by referring to a visit he had made to Kuwait the previous day, noting the devastating fires left behind by the Iraqi army when they set oil pipelines ablaze before withdrawing from Kuwait City. "I have never seen such destruction," he said, claiming that the fires—both metaphorically and physically—"can reach as far as

Iran and Turkey."[29] Smiling, Assad replied with his brilliant phraseology, "There are fires that we see and others that we don't. The invisible fires can sometimes be more dangerous than the actual ones." Baker then got down to business, briefing his Syrian hosts about talks held with the Palestinians in Jerusalem and similar meetings in Saudi Arabia and Egypt, and saying, "Everybody knows that without you [Assad] and Syria, a complete solution cannot be achieved [in the Middle East]. President Bush and I are ready to commit the full weight of the United States into solving all problems, including that of the Golan."[30] He quickly added that at this stage, he was not mandated to provide any guarantees but rather could only convey the US commitment to peace in the Middle East. The first obstacle to such a solution, added Baker, was the hard-line Israeli government of Yitzhak Shamir.

The Israeli prime minister, focused on a policy of increasing Israeli settlements in occupied Palestine, abhorred the idea of an international conference for peace. This was not strange for someone like Shamir who, as a young militant in the Stern Gang, had personally ordered the assassination of the UN's special envoy, Count Folke Bernadotte, during cease-fire talks for the first Arab-Israeli war in 1948.[31] First, Shamir was opposed to Soviet cosponsorship of the conference, believing that the Soviet Union was vehemently pro-Arab. Second, he did not wish to hold the conference under UN auspices, as Arab leaders had strongly insisted. "The United Nations had always been perceived, with justification, by Israel as a mortal enemy held at bay only by the American veto at the Security Council. The 1975 resolution equating Zionism with racism had cemented this view," wrote Baker in his memoirs.[32] The Syrians knew that only too well, which explains why they insisted on UN co-sponsorship, hoping that a UN mandate could force Israel to abide by peace resolutions. The last thing Shamir wanted was the UN breathing down his neck to implement deals with the Arabs. Third, he did not want the Palestinians to attend as a separate delegation, so that "the PLO's impact would be diminished." Fourth, according to Baker, "He was uncomfortable about the basis for the conference." To the Arabs (and most of the rest of the world) UN Resolution 242 envisioned exchanging territory for peace, which Shamir vowed he would never do.[33] Finally, Shamir was uncomfortable with European presence at the conference, "believing they were overwhelmingly Arabist."[34] In short, nothing about the conference was satisfactory to the Israelis. That is what James Baker seemed to be telling the Syrians. Shamir after all, had recently said, "Peace has nothing to do with land. This is the State of Israel and this is Israeli land. Nobody can change the borders of Israel."[35]

When asked by an Egyptian journalist whether he would ever withdraw from the Golan, Shamir had snapped, "Have you ever heard of anybody changing his country's own borders?" Assad made reference to these discouraging remarks, telling Baker, "I cannot but take these remarks very seriously. Indeed, the Israelis are not joking [when they say such things]."[36] He lamented, "If these discussions had taken place prior to the Gulf crisis, Shamir would have agreed to them, but he now believes that the Arabs are weaker than before and would do whatever is asked of them [by the United States]."[37] He smiled in a meaningful way and quickly added, "In my opinion, we will convince him of the contrary." Saddam Hussein, it must be remembered, had showered both Tel Aviv and Haifa with Scud missiles during the war, and the Bush White House had literally begged Israel not to launch a counterstrike. Shamir went along but expected the United States to pay him back, which seemingly came up when preparations for Madrid were under way.

Thanks to Baker's intense pressure, Shamir unwillingly agreed to attend the conference, provided that his demands were met regarding what kind of representation the Palestinians would get. He demanded that only Palestinians living in the Occupied Territories attend the conference, to make sure that the Tunis-based PLO, which had supported Saddam during the episode in Kuwait, be prevented from attending. As a result, Hanan Ashrawi and Haidar Abdul Shafi, who lived in the Occupied Territories but were members of the PLO, were invited as Palestinian citizens, whereas Yasser Arafat himself, who had embraced Saddam shortly before the war, was prevented from going to Madrid at Shamir's direct request. Shamir, however, had agreed to sign a document, according to Baker, saying that he would attend a conference "whose final outcomes would be based on UNSCR 242 and 338."[38]

"I knew that Assad would be the toughest Arab domino to topple," Baker wrote in his memoirs.[39] Assad made it clear that "only a madman would want to continue the state of war" while asserting that all options remained on the table for Syria, should peace talks fail with the Israelis. Syria objected to a statement made by the United States saying that the objective of the proposed conference was to "bring all sides to the negotiating table." Assad corrected him, saying, "The purpose, Mr. Baker, is to achieve peace, and not just to bring all sides to the table."[40] Baker asked the Syrian president to commit to the process, to refrain from criticizing the Palestinians willing to talk to Israel, and to "work with the PLO to keep their profile low." Assad, for his part, put forth four conditions. One was his insistence that the conference be branded an "international one" and not a "regional conference," as Shamir had demanded.

Such a term, he noted, would "belittle the significance of the conference; let us give it its due." He asked for assurances from the two co-sponsors of the conference on end results and said that it must be continuous to give impetus to the negotiations. The conference, he added, must have "international legitimacy" and "moral authority" and must be held under the umbrella of the United Nations.[41] "Is it an educational, economic, or cinema conference?" he asked Baker, adding, "It must have a name!" Egyptian foreign minister Esmat Abdul Majid had said, "A conference is a conference," so Assad suggested calling it a "peace conference" since its objective was to bring peace to the Middle East.[42]

Assad felt that by agreeing to the borders in place on June 4, 1967, the day before the Six-Day War began, Syria was already making a grand concession for the sake of peace, and he expected the Americans to reciprocate with goodwill. Baker in turn agreed to two of Assad's conditions, regarding the name of the conference and providing guarantees for its end result. "I can give 100% assurances on both," he told Assad. Apologetically, however, he said, "I cannot convince Israel to attend an international conference which is under UN sponsorship. It is just a fact of life that I cannot overcome. If you insist, I know I cannot make this work." Clearly irritated by the ostensible US helplessness, Assad asked, "If the UN umbrella was good enough for the Gulf War, why not here?"[43] Baker suggested inviting the UN as an observer to the conference, warning; "I am not sure that Israel will even agree to such a suggestion." He then told Assad, "I cannot stay permanently in this region [to find common ground between both parties]. What can you possibly lose by attending?" Firmly, Assad replied, "We will lose Arab domestic public opinion. This would not only be adventurism; it would be a form of suicide. It is one thing to adopt a suicidal policy if it brings benefits to the people, but it is truly foolhardy if there is no positive result. I don't want a UN monitor to sit there and just carry messages like a postman. The role of the UN should be very different."[44] Assad then asked for a clear and logical explanation as to why Israel was determined to restrict the role of both the UN and the Europeans. Baker suggested making the head of the European Commission (EC) a co-sponsor of the conference, should this please Syria. "We cannot bring in all twelve [members of the Commission]," he quickly added. Assad suggested the Troika (past, future, and current presidency of the European Commission), to which Baker wittily replied, "Between you and me, it wouldn't be correct for the US to be represented by one person, facing three people from Europe!"[45]

Trying to break the impasse, Assad made reference to his earlier encounters with US presidents, Richard Nixon in Damascus in 1974 and Jimmy Carter in Geneva in 1977. "Nixon used to sit here, right in your place," President Assad said to Baker, "and Dr. Kissinger used to sit where Gamal Helal [the interpreter] is seated. We would always have a great discussion. After much debate, we managed to convince Nixon, and he came out of the meeting totally in support of the Syrian position. He is someone who is honest with himself and who respects his convictions. After our meeting he issued a statement saying that his views were consistent with what the UN had said about the conflict. He then went back to the US and Watergate came along. Suddenly, Nixon disappeared. There was a speedy campaign against him, and we think this was related, in great extent, to his position toward peace in the region."[46] The same applied to President Carter, Assad added, saying that the latter "was and still is interested in peace" but could not deliver in his one term as president. "These are our experiences with the United States. In my opinion, we are at different times and in different circumstances. We will not allow the United States to remain monopolized by the Israelis forever."[47]

By that point in the April meeting, Baker had begun to wear out, muscled down by the heat, ultrasweet lemonade, and Assad's negotiating skills. Assad threw yet another bombshell at him: "I really can't think of a country in the world that will give billions of dollars to another country, along with plenty of arms, and then say it is unable to convince them to do anything. This is a very strange friendship indeed. There is no other such friendship in history!"[48] At the time, the US government was giving US$3 billion per year to Israel, and only two days prior to the Damascus meeting, the US Congress had raised the amount to $3.2 billion.[49] "Sometimes one can have a friend without having to pay him $3 billion dollars," the Syrian leader said, "especially when this payment is made at the expense of the average American citizen." Assad then made reference to Senator Bob Dole, who had been Gerald Ford's vice presidential running mate in the 1976 elections. Recently, Dole had infuriated the Israelis by saying, "What vital US interest is served by sending $1.2 billion a year in economic aid to a Likud-led regime whose behavior on the West Bank would trigger a US embargo if conducted by Mikhail Gorbachev to keep control of Lithuania?"[50]

Baker completely ignored President Assad's remark and went back to his earlier argument, stressing that UN sponsorship was very difficult, but in order to please the Syrians, he suggested that the current co-sponsors, both Washington and Moscow, give security guarantees to all parties attending, regarding the end results of what the conference would achieve. To further assure the Syrian president, he said his country was willing to make it obligatory for the UN to sign off on any treaty or agreement reached by the conference. This would give the UN a role that was "more than simply an observer yet less than co-sponsor."[51] Unimpressed, Assad replied, "This is routine. Any agreement between states, reached at such a conference, is ratified by the UN. You are actually offering me something that is nothing because it already exists!"[52]

Another difficult topic raised by Assad halfway through the conversation was continuation, or reconvening of the conference, should it get called off due to disagreements between attendees. Assad suggested that any party should be entitled to call the conference back into session, but Baker said that reconvening needed the approval of all the parties involved. Such a tedious process, Assad remarked, "would result in a never-ending situation."[53] Baker suggested using the 1975 Helsinki Declaration (a conference held on security and cooperation in Europe) as a template to follow for conference procedures.[54] That conference had been attended by thirty-five states, including the United States, Canada, and all of Europe except Albania and Andorra, a small country in southwestern Europe. Assad smiled, saying that the Europeans and Americans have very different standards for how they treat each other versus how they treat the Arabs. He agreed in principle to see what had been agreed at Helsinki, but Baker provided no document or argument to complement his original suggestion.

Baker finally threw in the towel, looking Assad straight in the eyes and saying, "Mr. President, I have spent [to date] 26 hours with you, and I always find myself saying *yes* to what you are saying." Assad cut him short, politely correcting, "But in fact, you are not saying *yes*, Mr. Baker . . . you are saying *no*! I asked you to say yes to UN sponsorship of the conference, but you said no."[55] Baker nodded, "I said no at that point because I simply could not say yes, knowing that the Israelis will never agree." Smiling, Assad asked, "Tell me then, what then is the yes that you gave me?" Baker countered, "Yes to the name of the conference, yes to the guarantees, and three-quarters of a yes to the reconvening process. This would take us up to 50 percent of what we want."[56] Assad, who despite his firm personality, always had a sense of humor, quickly nodded, "In order to reach 100 percent, we have to take our clothes off. We have a decision in Syria never to take our clothes off!"[57] He then wrapped up, saying: "Any guarantee that Israel doesn't want, we don't want. I say this because I believe we can substantiate the peace process and we're not afraid of the price. If they implement, we implement. If they don't, we don't. If they don't want guarantees, we don't want guarantees. If guarantees are not requested by Israel then they are not requested by Syria."[58]

Reading through the minutes of the Assad-Baker meeting, an excellent show of diplomatic ping-pong, one gets a clear image of how that long day went in Damascus. Here were two serious leaders, master negotiators in their respective countries, debating a very serious matter with the utmost precision, respect, and dedication of purpose. Both were fully aware that they would not be there forever, at least not in their political posts. "We have to do a job that never needs to be done again," Baker said to President Assad. The Syrian leader, aware of the place these talks would have in his country's history, made sure to tell Baker, "I need to talk to public opinion in Syria and to consult with the [Baath] Party and the National Progressive Front [a parliamentary coalition of leftist parties, under umbrella of the Baath, founded by Assad in the early 1970s]. Without their full support, nothing can be done in Syria." The Syrian leader added, "My discussions with them will be more difficult than my discussions with you." Baker suddenly stiffened, afraid that if these talks came out to the open, public pressure would prevent Assad from attending the conference. The Syrians, he well understood, were anti-Israeli to the bone. "Can you do this in confidentiality, with no press leaks?" he asked. Smiling, Assad replied, "I certainly can do it better than you can [in the United States]."[59]

In his memoirs, published a few years after he left office, in 1995, Baker commented, "Without any doubt, this was the most difficult and laborious negotiation I'd ever had." He then launched into his famous anecdote, "Six hours into the meeting, the call of nature captured Ambassador Ed Djerejian. Just as Assad launched a favorite monologue on the evils of the Sykes-Picot Treaty, the situation reached critical mass . . . Ed gestured the Syrian Foreign Minister that he needed to take an important telephone call. In his absence I revealed the true nature of Djerejian's mission. 'You have to wonder, Mr. President, why the Ambassador has gone to the men's room to make an important phone call.' Assad roared with laughter. An hour or so later, I pulled out a white handkerchief and waved it to Assad. 'I give up,' I confessed, 'I have to go to the bathroom.' Thus was coined the phrase which I will forever associate with my sixty-three hours of talks with Assad: bladder diplomacy."[60]

The Devil in the Details

Upon receiving Syria's acceptance letter in September, Baker had Ambassador Djerejian read it twice to make sure there was no Syrian loophole. Assad had firmly committed himself to peace, a just and comprehensive one, adding that peace was achievable within a year's time or even less, "two or three months," if the Israelis were ready to return occupied lands to their rightful owners.[61] Syria wanted the United States to abide by all promises made by the US secretary of state, noting that if there was any U-turn by the Americans, the entire peace process would collapse. Baker was busy hammering out details with his Soviet counterpart when he got the groundbreaking telephone call from Damascus. He then sent a note to President Bush, saying: "There is no ambiguity. They have accepted what we have proposed. We have a yes and we are going to try and build on that!" On July 18, Baker returned, yet again, to Syria, for a two-and-a half-hour meeting with President Assad. Such a "short" meeting, he wrote, "was barely a light workout" for President Assad. "I cannot overstate the dramatic and profound effect your letter had around the world. You are now seen to have chosen peace. Your acceptance has galvanized the G7 summit in Europe! The Brits, the French, the Italians, the Germans, the Canadians—even the Japanese—are talking about your positive response."[62] He added, "No matter what I say, I cannot express what the US and the entire world feels about your acceptance—you have now put the ball in Israel's court." Assad's response was delivered to the G7 conference just as Soviet leader Mikhail Gorbachev was making a grand entrance. "You stole the lights from Gorbachev," said Baker in excitement, to which Assad humorously replied, "We actually did that on purpose to create some problems for Gorbachev."[63] Writing about the meeting, Baker noted that Assad had ceased to insist on having an observer from the UN attend the conference: "It was quickly apparent that while this was his preference, it wasn't a condition for his participation." This July meeting in Damascus was intended, apparently, to express US gratitude to the Syrian president, with Baker telling him, "I am coming to Syria only to say 'thank you.' Without your position, a peace conference would have been impossible."[64]

The Syrian response ripped through Israel like a forest fire. It left them confused, embarrassed, and very angry that they had been outsmarted by Hafez al-Assad. The first public response to Assad's acceptance of the US invitation to a peace conference came from the Israeli defense minister, the Likud member of the Knesset, Moshe Arens. He noted, "If Syria has truly approved the American proposals, they have to come and negotiate with us."[65] Assad was clearly not amused. Since 1977, the year of Sadat's ill-fated visit to Israel, its leaders had proposed that Assad make a similar visit, but with no luck. Baker, however, found Israel's response "encouraging," claiming that 68 percent of Israelis now accept the "land-for-peace" formula. "Before we began our talks," he said, "it had been no more than 48 percent."[66]

On September 20, Assad and Baker met again, this time to speak of details. The US secretary of state was accompanied by the new US ambassador to Syria, Christopher W. S. Ross (who had just replaced Edward Djerejian), Dennis Ross, and Margaret Tutwiler, spokeswoman for the Department of State. Earlier in July Assad had received Congressman Wayne Owens and American philanthropist Daniel Abraham at his summer residence in the port city of Latakia.[67] With them he stressed arguments made later to Baker about the need to apply adequate pressure on Israel if the peace conference was ever going to take place. On August 28, he met Congresswoman Mary Rose Oaker, who was of Lebanese origin, for the same purpose. She spoke to him about the Jewish lobby in Washington, saying that a similar lobby should be created by the Arabs to impose their will on US decisionmakers. Assad knew that although such a lobby was needed, it would be unlikely to succeed, given the blind favoritism toward Israel that prevailed in the upper echelons of power in the United States.

In his next meeting with Baker in mid-October, Assad held a copy of the US invitation to the conference, objecting to the words "direct, face-to-face" talks between Syrians and Israelis. "They are direct. Isn't that enough?" asked the Syrian president. He was clearly having second thoughts about the fact that his team would have to sit "face-to-face" with enemies he had fought so vigorously against in 1967, 1973, and 1982. Baker—ever the diplomat—tried to convince him with the comment, "Face-to-face is better than back-to-back [that is, speaking to their respective delegates instead of each other]." Assad was annoyed: "All that is missing is [for you to say] 'and smiling!'"[68] Also, the Syrian president did not want multilateral committees to discuss regional issues, as the Americans had proposed, while the Israelis still occupied an inch of Arab land. What was the use of talking about water rights, refugees, or economic cooperation, Assad asked, when fundamentals like South Lebanon and the Syrian Golan were still not liberated? Multilateral talks, he stressed, should only take place after bilateral ones "were successfully completed." Assad logically explained, "I don't want to enter such a minefield, one in which minesweepers would not work. We in Syria cannot agree to something like this unless we have something tangible to bring our people. We cannot move even one step in this direction. I cannot even move in words. If I did, I would be responsible before my people."[69] That meeting, not surprisingly, ended with no results, forcing Baker to leave Damascus emptyhanded—except for a long list of fourteen points that Assad wanted to change in the US letter of assurances. Baker was frantic; the conference was scheduled for October, and time was running out.

A sixth and seventh round took place at the Presidential Palace in Damascus on October 15–16. The Syrians produced a handful of other revisions to the original US letter of assurances. One of them, articulated by Foreign Minister Shara, was that Jerusalem had to be considered part of the Occupied Territories. The Americans, he added, must never acknowledge the 1967 annexation of Jerusalem, making reference to UNSCR 242. This should be done in writing, said the Syrian president, adding, "You must say, at the end of the first paragraph, that the conference aims at "securing the legitimate rights of the Palestinians, including their political rights."[70] Assad was unhappy with Palestinian representation at the conference, under chairmanship of a Jordanian delegation because there was no Palestinian state to represent them. "Regardless of how any delegation is composed, this must not be reason for any preset judgment [regarding the status of Jerusalem]. Preventing any Palestinian delegate from East Jerusalem effectively kills the Palestinian right to demand the return of occupied Jerusalem."[71] He stood firmly behind rights of the Jerusalemites, saying that they must be given a say on whatever form of government the conference would produce for them in the Occupied Territories. Assad, it must be stressed, never felt, not for a moment, that he was speaking on behalf of the Syrians only. As an Arab leader who had grown up admiring Egyptian president Gamal Abdul Nasser in the 1950s, he was firmly committed to Arabism in its widest form and felt that he had to stand up for the rights of all Arabs, not just Syrians, and particularly those of the Palestinians. He had spent his entire career combating the hated Sykes-Picot Agreement that carved up the Arab world into its present form during World War I and was not going to soften his positions for the sake of a successful conference so as to please the US government. Baker was infuriated by the Jerusalem remark, which was strange for the Syrians, who thought they had made this demand clear to him from day one. He angrily replied, "You are asking me more than the Palestinians asked. I don't think that's appropriate. We will discuss it in the negotiations, and we do not acknowledge its annexation, but you are pushing us too far. Maybe you don't want a process. I don't want to give Israel any reason not to come. Maybe you do!"[72]

Assad calmly took out an old letter from President Carter and read it out loud. It was dated March 27, 1978. Carter had said, "Withdrawing from the Occupied Territories applies to all parties and there must be a joint resolution to all elements of the Palestinian Problem, including the right of self-determination."[73] He then looked firmly at Baker and took out another letter, this time from President Ronald Reagan, addressed to Assad personally and dated July 28, 1988. Assad read that Reagan's policy had been to "improve the chances of Arab-Israeli peace on all fronts. This is still a top priority for the US in order to reach implementation of UNSCR 242 and 338, including the "land-for-peace" formula, which is the essence of 242. Second it is to ensure the legitimate national rights of the Palestinian people."[74] Waving both letters at Baker, Assad asserted, "This, Mr. Baker, is the policy of the United States! What American presidents say *is* the American policy."[75] At this point, Baker, at his wits' end, snapped, "It's a good letter! If you don't like what we are doing and you think you can get the Golan back [without sitting down with the Israelis], then go ahead and get it back."[76] Assad was completely unshaken by his guest's outburst—in fact, he was surprised that such a senior diplomat would lose his nerve so quickly. "Why is he angry?" the Syrian president asked his aides. "We're negotiating."[77] He then calmly told Baker, "You are not doing this for us in the first instance. You also have interests." Fearing that if pushed too far, the US secretary of state would no longer be able to deliver, President Assad finally gave him what he wanted: acceptance of the US letter of assurances, with no mention of multilateral talks—for now. Dennis Ross, then a member of the State Department's Policy Planning staff, scribbled a note to Baker, "Take the money and run! Let's get out of here."[78]

The final question on everybody's mind was where to hold the peace conference. Eleven delegations had confirmed attendance, with 700 delegates, and anywhere between 6,000 to 7,000 reporters. The site needed to be big, it needed to be equipped, and it needed to be neutral. The obvious first choice was Washington, D.C., a venue favored by the Israelis but not so much by the Russians, who preferred Prague.[79] A compromise city would be Cairo, said the Russians. Shamir objected to holding a peace conference in an Arab capital, although the Egyptian-Israeli peace treaty of 1978 was then entering its twelfth year.[80] Switzerland wanted the role, but the strong UN presence in Geneva was frowned upon by the Israelis. Members of the US team suggested The Hague, home of the International Court of Justice, hoping, in Baker's own words, that that location would be attractive to the president of Syria.[81] They came to him with photographs, maps, and floor plans, but "[their] efforts failed to sway him."[82] Hafez al-Assad flatly rejected the idea, given that the Netherlands had recently voted to impose economic sanctions on Syria and there was no Syrian embassy at The Hague. "A neutral country is better for us all," he told Baker. The Americans suggested Brussels and Copenhagen, but Assad ruled them out as well, also because of no embassy, and Prague, because "it is not suitable." A drained Baker helplessly asked President Assad, "What country would be acceptable?"[83] Assad replied, "Rome, Bonn, Paris, Geneva, London, Lausanne, Vienna—any Italian city is acceptable." Baker smiled. "Monte Carlo?" Assad appreciated the joke: "The negotiations will indeed be gambling!" "How about Madrid or Lisbon?" Baker asked. The Syrian leader considered it briefly and answered, "Madrid is better."[84]

The Soviet Factor

When reading through the preparations for Madrid, one cannot ignore the important role of the Soviet Union, which Assad stressed to Baker in their meeting on May 13. Most historians covering the pre-Madrid era often overlook the Soviet factor, given that by 1991 the Soviet Union was a power in decline. Looking back twenty years later, I can safely say that had it not been for the Russians, Madrid would probably not have happened. Five days prior to the May 13 Assad-Baker meeting, Aleksandr Bessmertnykh came to Syria during his brief tenure as Soviet minister of foreign affairs. A newcomer to the complex world of the Arab-Israeli conflict, Bessmertnykh had just replaced Eduard Shevardnadze at the job but realized, thanks to clear instructions from the Kremlin, that peace in the Middle East was impossible without the Syrians. Right from the start, the Russians stressed that the conference should be named a "peace conference" rather than a regional one, as Shamir had suggested to the Bush White House.[85] They also insisted that it should be convened based on UN Security Council resolutions and that Moscow and Washington should provide any required written guarantees regarding outcomes and the reconvening process. Israel, Assad told Bessmertnykh, "wanted a ceremonial conference" and seemed more interested in a peace process than in a peace treaty with the Arabs. If it fails, he warned, "Israel will tell the world that the Arabs shoulder responsibility for its failure and that the Arabs are to blame. The world will believe Israel's story because of its strong access to international media—and its side of the story will prevail."[86] Assad, it must be noted, was keen that his country should never miss an opportunity to remind the world of the occupation of the Golan, regardless of whether it would lead to any concrete results. As far as he was concerned, it was Syria's duty to try.

Bessmertnykh took plenty of notes during his meetings in Damascus and then headed to Israel for talks with Prime Minister Shamir. The latter had, very unwillingly, agreed to Soviet co-sponsorship of the conference but refused to commit to a date for resuming diplomatic relations between his country and Tel Aviv until after the conference took place. The Soviet minister returned to Syria on May 14, where before heading to Egypt for talks with President Husni Mubarak, he met with Baker, who had just wrapped up his third trip to Damascus in 1991. Assad smiled and said, "It is interesting indeed, for the Soviet foreign minister to be coming from Israel and the US secretary of state to be coming from Syria."[87] Appreciating the witty remark, Bessmertnykh replied, "It seems to be the beginning of a phase of historical contradictions."[88] Prior to the May 13 meeting, Assad briefed his Soviet guest about all the previous sessions with the Americans, making it clear that any party that refuses UN sponsorship of the conference is guilty of being a deliberate obstacle to peace in the Middle East. "How can the US pressure Israel to withdraw from occupied Arab land," Assad complained to Bessmertnykh, "if it cannot apply enough pressure on Israel to accept UN sponsorship of the conference? Who said I have to accept what Israel refuses?" He then added, "I will nevertheless try my best [to make it happen], but if Israel were to decide on the conference's format, this certainly will not be a road that leads to peace."[89] Assad reminded Bessmertnykh how the late Egyptian president Anwar al-Sadat had visited him in Damascus before making his trip to Jerusalem in 1977—which the Syrians strongly condemned and still do, more than thirty years down the road. It gave the Israelis far too much, he believed, and in return, the Egyptians got very little. In his meeting with Assad at Damascus International Airport, Sadat had famously pledged to try to restore both the Sinai Peninsula and the Golan. "I felt, right there and then, that Sadat and I were going to part for a very long period of time despite the fact that we had gone to war together [in 1973] and once had a joint political and military command. I could not agree with him at the time because he was in a hurry to go to Jerusalem."[90] Haste never produces wise decisions, he noted, adding, "If the road to Paradise runs through humiliation, we refuse to tread it! If we were forced to choose between succumbing to Israeli conditions and continuing to have occupied land, we choose the latter—that is easier than giving in to Israeli dictates!" Assad then firmly added, "If I were an ordinary citizen, I would say that Syria without the Golan—but with dignity—is better than Syria with the Golan, deprived of its dignity. There is not a single family in Syria that did not offer a martyr in our conflict with the Israelis."[91]

On the Margins of the Pre-Madrid Era

When reading through the official Syrian records regarding the negotiations that led up to Madrid, two very important realities emerge that need to be highlighted. One was Syria's absolute refusal, despite Baker's unspoken blessing, of any Syrian role in Iraqi domestic politics after the Gulf War. Syria's role would come to an end, Assad would always say, the minute Kuwait was liberated from Iraqi occupation. Baker twice made mention to the Kurdish and Shiite rebellions in Iraq, hinting that Syria might be interested in using the turmoil to weaken Saddam, a traditional enemy. Assad would hear nothing of it: "We refuse to interfere, whatsoever, in the internal affairs of Iraq. That is up to the Iraqi people to decide, and we will never meddle with the domestic issues of a sovereign Arab country, regardless of whether we agree with its government or not. We have never done it in the past and will never involve ourselves in such activity—that is not how Syria operates, Mr. Baker."[92] That position has often been overlooked by Middle East analysts, who tried to draw parallels between the war of 2003 and that of 1991. As far as the Syrians were concerned, those were two very different wars, fought for very different reasons, although against the same player, Saddam. The Gulf War in 1991 was a war fought to liberate an Arab country, whereas the Iraq War in 2003 led to the occupation of an Arab country. Big difference! During the years 2003–2008, many in the administration of George W. Bush accused Syria of intervening in the domestic affairs of Iraq and fanning the so-called "Sunni insurgency." Why would the Syrians do that in 2003 when they refused to do it in 1991? Syria curtly refused such action even when covert activity was protected, and in fact encouraged, by the United States. Seeing Saddam removed from power would have been a dream come true, especially given that those who would have toppled Saddam in 1991 were the Iraqi people themselves, and not the invading US army. Assad believed, however, that this was strictly for the Iraqi people to decide, not for the Syrians or Iranians—and certainly not the Americans.

The second observation reached from reading Syrian archives relates to Lebanon. In all the meetings between Assad and Baker, Lebanon was mentioned only once, on July 18, 1991. The subject was raised when discussing the positions of Israeli defense minister Arens vis-à-vis the situation in Beirut. Baker felt Arens's remarks were encouraging, but Assad said, "All of them are bad, especially in regard to Lebanon."[93] He added, "What they are trying to do is destroy things in Lebanon. The Israelis do not want [the civil war] to come to an end in

Lebanon." Baker replied, "We differ with them and with their assessment regarding the situations in Lebanon. As you know, we support the Taif Accords [reached in Saudi Arabia to put an end to internal fighting in Lebanon]. We support disarming the militias, all militias, and we oppose obstructing the Taif Accords."[94] Baker added, "The Lebanese government [headed at the time by President Elias Hrawi] is now in a good position to function; it needs your support. There are still some militias that should be disarmed. We do not differentiate between different militias. All of them have to stop—including Hizbullah and Lahad [a Lebanese one created by the Israeli Defense Forces, or IDF, to administer—and terrorize—the residents of occupied South Lebanon]."[95] Not only did Assad refuse to cooperate with the Americans on Lebanon in 1991, but he said, "According to our information, the heavy and medium-sized armaments of all militias have been confiscated by the Lebanese state. Hizbullah doesn't have heavy arms." Foreign Minister Shara interjected, "Not even medium ones." Assad smiled. "Probably Samir Gagea [the Maronite warlord and chief of the Lebanese Forces] does, however, and he gave some of them to Lahad!"[96] After refusing the parallel between Hizbullah and Lahad, Assad sternly noted, "The Lebanese army is the only party capable of doing such a job."[97]

Hizbullah, it must be noted, was back then not half as powerful as it became after the liberation of South Lebanon in 2000 or after the war of 2006. Assad believed in its resistance from day one, accepting its mandate to liberate all of South Lebanon from Israeli occupation. Baker remarked, "We know that without Syrian support, the Lebanese government would not have been able to function so well [since Hrawi's 1989 election]. That is why we will talk to the Israelis about the disarming of Lahad. We will continue in our policy which aims at expelling all foreign parties from Lebanon, and disarming all militias." President Assad corrected, "According to Taif . . . but bear in mind that Hizbullah is a resistance movement, not a militia."[98]

The brief exchange over Lebanon effectively debunks a snowballing conspiracy theory that claims Syria was given a green light to stay in Lebanon during the Assad-Baker talks of 1991. No such deal was ever brought up, and such an idea never even crossed the Syrian president's mind. What did was the sustainability of the Lebanese resistance, which continued to be Syria's main concern even after its withdrawal from Lebanon in April 2005. The argument that Lebanon was given to the Syrians by the United States in exchange for Madrid is sheer fantasy, imagined by Israeli and Lebanese journalists and politicians who tried in vain to prove it. The minutes of the Assad-Baker meetings are recorded in extreme detail, and after digging through more than 500 pages of documents, I could not find a single mention of such a deal. Assad went to Madrid because he wanted peace—not war, and not Lebanon.

Conclusion

Wrapping up, Assad said, "We are satisfied with the discussion. There is no substitute for such one-on-one encounters. Hopefully this will enable us to accomplish more in the future. It is in the interest of all our countries and peace in the Middle East. I want peace in a real way."[99] Some say that Assad wanted to go to Madrid because of his conviction that the Soviet Union was about to collapse and he needed to open a channel with the United States. Others claim that Assad did it to jumpstart a serious peace process, saying that it was his requirement for joining the Americans in Operation Desert Storm. Many claim that by 1990–1991, President Assad realized that war alone would not succeed in restoring occupied territory, based on the realities of the wars of 1967 and 1973. I disagree with all these theories; I believe that I knew President Assad quite well. Even on the eve of the October War of 1973, he had said, "Our hobby is not killing and destruction. All what we want is to defend ourselves against war that is launched against us. We were never aggressors and never will be aggressors."[100] Being a decorated air force officer who, as defense minister, had commanded the Syrian army in 1967, President Assad never believed in wars; he knew what wars cost. More than many others in the Middle East, he fully understood the consequences of war for his country and the region as a whole. He strove to meet Baker halfway because of his conviction that what can be achieved through negotiations was certainly less costly, and perhaps more effective, than what comes from war. At the end of the day, Syria had one clear objective: restoration of the occupied Golan, in full, based on UN Security Council resolutions. Years later, Assad would tell President Clinton, "I was always keen to meet with every American president."[101] Even at the height of the Syrian relationship with the Soviet Union, he always appreciated and wanted a relationship with the United States. When talking to a US delegation, he said to them, "We are not asking you to have a relationship with us against your own interests. We are asking you to take into account your interests—pure American interests—and not the interests of others [in reference to Israel]."[102] It must be noted, however, that he never really believed Israel wanted peace but would always say, "This is their problem; on my side, I am going to try."[103] He never wanted to miss an opportunity to place the Golan Heights as a high priority on the international agenda.

On a personal note, I returned to Syria in June 1991, shortly before the Madrid Peace Conference, which started on October 30 and lasted for three days. Back then, some people were asking, "If we are going to peace negotiations, why not ask for the removal of Syria's name from the US list of state sponsors of terrorism?" Syrian officials sincerely believed that if we showed goodwill by going to Madrid and eventually signing a peace agreement, then the United States would automatically and naturally remove Syria's name from the State Department's list. This, I believe, was a fundamental cultural difference between us and the Americans. In the US mindset, you lay out your conditions immediately—you trade for what you want. As Arabs, however, we feel that once we do something and prove our goodwill, our interlocutors will return the favor by doing things that would please us without making us ask for them. We deal with sensitive issues from our own moral standard, but in the political world, business is business. That is why the Americans say, "Soft on persons, hard on issues." The Americans are not shy about what they want. I am just stating a fact without making judgments, but I do believe that had we asked the United States to remove our name from that list, then Bush and Baker would have immediately agreed. They wanted Madrid to succeed so badly. Many have said that had it not been for Saddam Hussein, we would never have had the Gulf War. True, but had it not been for Hafez al-Assad, we would never have had Madrid.

Notes

1. Clark, *War Crimes: A Report on United States War Crimes Against Iraq*, 66. Ambassador Glaspie reportedly said to him, "We have no opinion on Arab-Arab conflicts."
2. See the full speech in Damascus Radio Archives, January 12, 1991.
3. Ibid.
4. Baker, *The Politics of Diplomacy*, 295.
5. Ibid., 296.
6. Ibid.
7. Nixon, *The Memoirs of Richard Nixon*, 1013.
8. Carter, *Palestine: Peace, Not Apartheid*, 72.
9. Ibid.
10. Baker, *The Politics of Diplomacy*, 297.
11. *The Unpublished Assad-Baker Minutes,* September 13, 1991.

12. Ibid.
13. Kenneth Timmerman, "They Met in Paris, Fell in Political Love and Built a Death Machine," *Los Angeles Times*, December 22, 1991.
14. *International Herald Tribune*, March 7, 2003.
15. Guitta, "The Chirac Doctrine," *Middle East Quarterly* (Fall 2005), 43–53.
16. *L'Express*, February 13, 2003.
17. Guitta, "The Chirac Doctrine."
18. *The Unpublished Assad-Baker Minutes,* September 13, 1991.
19. Ibid.
20. Personal conversation with President Hafez al-Assad, June 1992.
21. RAND Corporation, "Out of Area or Out of Reach: European Military Support for Operations in Southwest Asia," Santa Monica, CA, 1995.
22. *World Almanac and Book of Facts*, p. 176.
23. *Unpublished Minutes of the Assad-Bush Talks,* February 6, 1991.
24. Baker, *Politics of Diplomacy*, 297.
25. *Unpublished Minutes of the Assad-Baker Meetings,* February 6, 1991.
26. Ibid.
27. *Unpublished Minutes of the Assad-Baker Meetings,* April 23, 1991.
28. Ibid.
29. Ibid.
30. Ibid.
31. Ilan, *Bernadotte in Palestine*, 194.
32. Baker, *The Politics of Diplomacy*, 448.
33. Ibid.
34. *Unpublished Minutes of the Assad-Baker Meeting*, April 23, 1991.
35. Ibid.
36. Ibid.
37. Ibid.
38. Ibid.
39. Baker, *The Politics of Diplomacy*, 447.
40. *Unpublished Minutes of the Assad-Baker Meeting*, April 23, 1991.
41. Ibid.
42. Ibid.
43. Personal conversation with President Assad, June 1992.
44. *Unpublished Minutes of the Assad-Baker Meeting*, April 23, 1991.
45. Ibid.
46. Ibid.
47. Ibid.
48. Ibid.
49. Ibid.
50. *Washington Report on Middle East Affairs*, "Words to Remember," March 1990.
51. *Unpublished Minutes of the Assad-Baker Meeting*, April 23, 1991.
52. Ibid.
53. Ibid.
54. Ibid.
55. Ibid.

56. Ibid.
57. Ibid.
58. Ibid.
59. Ibid.
60. Baker, *The Politics of Diplomacy*, 454–458.
61. Ibid.
62. *Unpublished Minutes of the Assad-Baker Meeting*, July 18, 1991.
63. Ibid.
64. Ibid.
65. *Al-Baath*, July 20, 1991.
66. *Unpublished Minutes of the Assad-Baker Meeting*, July 18, 1991.
67. *Unpublished talks of President Assad with visiting American guests in Latakia*, July 1991.
68. *Unpublished Minutes of the Assad-Baker Meeting*, September 20, 1991.
69. Ibid.
70. *Unpublished Minutes of the Assad-Baker Meeting*, October 16, 1991.
71. Ibid.
72. Ibid.
73. *The Unpublished Assad-Carter Letters*, March 27, 1978.
74. *The Unpublished Assad-Reagan Letters*, July 28, 1988.
75. *Unpublished Minutes of the Assad-Baker Meeting*, October 16, 1991.
76. Ibid.
77. Ibid.
78. Baker, *The Politics of Diplomacy*, 507.
79. *Unpublished Minutes of the Assad-Baker Meeting*, September 20, 1991.
80. Personal conversation with President Assad, June 1992.
81. Ibid.
82. Baker, *The Politics of Diplomacy*, 511.
83. Ibid.
84. Ibid.
85. *Unpublished Assad-Bessmertnykh Talks*, May 8, 1991.
86. Ibid.
87. *Unpublished Assad-Bessmertnykh Talks*, May 14, 1991.
88. Ibid.
89. *Unpublished Assad-Bessmertnykh Talks*, May 8, 1991.
90. Ibid.
91. Ibid.
92. *Unpublished Minutes of the Assad-Baker Meeting*, September 20, 1991.
93. *Unpublished Minutes of the Assad-Baker Meeting*, July 18, 1991.
94. Ibid.
95. *Unpublished Minutes of the Assad-Baker Meeting*, July 18, 1991. Assad was making reference to General Antoine Lahad, leader of the South Lebanon Army (SLA) from 1984 to 2000, when Israel withdrew from South Lebanon and the SLA was dissolved. Lahad then took refuge in Israel, where he still resides, and has been sentenced to death in absentia by the Lebanese government.
96. Ibid.
97. Ibid.
98. Ibid.

99. *Unpublished Minutes of the Assad-Baker Meeting*, October 16, 1991.
100. President Assad's October War Speech, Damascus Radio Archives, October 6, 1973.
101. Personal conversation with President Assad, March 2000.
102. Ibid.
103. Personal conversation with President Assad, June 1992.

2

Blessed Are the Peacemakers

I SHALL NEVER FORGET THE DAYS THAT PRECEDED OUR TRAVEL to Madrid. They were filled with anxiety and fear, yet we were certain that we were on the right track. It was a very unusual and very difficult time for me on a personal level. My daughters were young: Nahid was nine and Nazek was only five years old. A mother would not want to leave her two children for an unspecified period of time and distance herself from a university career at its finest hour, unless it was for a worthy cause. We were told that it might be a long trip; our embassy in Spain was already arranging to rent or buy apartments and cars for the delegation. Throughout the negotiations prior to Madrid, we were deeply fearful that things might not be as easy or productive as we would have wished them to be, but we knew that Syria was willing to act in good faith with the Bush administration for the sake of peace in the Middle East.

When it was clear that we would be traveling in late October, I approached my mother and father, husband, and two children saying: "I am going with a delegation to participate in negotiations with the Israelis." Emotionally and socially, it was not easy to utter those words. I was firmly convinced, however, that sometimes one has to rise above personal feelings for the sake of a worthwhile objective. I personally had confidence in the unwavering leadership of President Assad. Clearly, he was not thrilled about talking peace—this was the same man who had ardently fought the Israelis in 1967, 1973, and 1982. Politics, however, is the art of the possible. As Arabs, we had all realized by 1991 that wars lead to nothing but more wars and plenty of destruction. Perhaps it was about time, we reckoned, to give negotiations a chance, especially in light of the determination expressed by the Bush administration. Had Anwar Sadat not divided the Arabs with a separate peace in 1978, and had the Arab world not been damaged beyond repair by Saddam's senseless wars against Iran and Kuwait, then perhaps the Arab reality would have been somewhat different. What we knew quite well was that we had a window of opportunity in front of us, opened by the logic and good faith of the Bush administration. We were willing to take our chances to restore Palestine to the Palestinians and the Golan Heights to Syria. If Hafez al-Assad was willing to take his chances, then certainly so would we as Syrians.

My daughters were too young to understand the magnitude of what was happening in the Middle East that October, but my parents were worried, as any caring mother and father would be. Both of them had witnessed the brutal occupation of Palestine in 1948 and raised us as sincere Arab patriots, overwhelmingly committed to the Palestinian cause. They were worried about my personal safety, the objective of our mission, and our reputation as negotiators. If things were to collapse at Madrid, how would people look at their daughter, who had sat face-to-face with a traditional enemy? Ordinary Syrians, however, who were weary from decades of conflict, were surprisingly optimistic. I remember meeting people on the street who would smile, pat me on the back, and encouragingly say: "*Inshallah*, you will succeed. *Inshallah*, one day, we will see peace in our part of the world." In Arabic, *inshallah* means "If God wills." These people had suffered too much from war—and, as President Assad had told Baker, each and every Syrian family had lost a member during the forty-three-year-old conflict. They were fed up, and rightly so, and wanted to live a normal life. In looking back, I can safely say that as far as President Assad was concerned, he was trying to make peace for their sake. He wanted to give them and their children a better life, free of conflict, war, and destruction.

In total, the Syrian delegation that went to Madrid comprised twenty-two people, headed by Foreign Minister Farouk al-Shara. It included, in addition to myself, the seasoned diplomat Muwafak al-Allaf; our ambassador to London, Mohammad Khodor; our ambassador to Washington, Walid al-Mouallem; his predecessor, Rafiq Juwayjati; and Ambassadors Majid Abu Saleh, Zakariya Ismail, Raslan Allush, Abdul Wadod Atasi, and Mohammad al-Jazzar. Additionally, Clovis Khury from the Foreign Ministry was onboard, and so were Adnan Tayara and Fawzi al-Khatib from the Armistice Committee. Other delegates included Farouk al-Tabba, Elias Rizq, Riad Daoudi, and Ahmad Arnous, the bureau chief (chief-of-staff) for Foreign Minister Shara. They were among the finest men in the Syrian Foreign Service, dedicated career-diplomats with talent and character who had been part of the Arab-Israeli conflict for years. It was agreed beforehand that Shara would attend only the opening session, while all bilateral talks would be handled by Allaf and the Israeli negotiator, Yossi Ben Aharon, bureau chief to Yitzhak Shamir. Foreign ministers did not enter into direct talks, it must be noted, until 2000, when they first met at Shepherdstown during the Clinton presidency. Shamir attended the Madrid Peace Conference because he held the portfolio of foreign affairs in addition to the premiership in Israel.

On the day of our departure, we headed first to Latakia on the Syrian coast to receive instructions from President Assad on what to do and say in Madrid. I recall that while driving to the airport, billboards all along the road were covered with the president's words about "Syria's choice for a just and comprehensive peace." Public opinion was being prepared for the upcoming peace talks, and Assad had previously told us that the process—if orchestrated correctly by the United States—could take anywhere from two to three months to one year.

President Assad was in a calm and sober mood. This was the sixth time I had met him. The first was at the Military Academy in Homs in 1971. The second was the next day at the Presidential Palace. The third was a "thank-you" visit with other students, also in 1971. The fourth was a cordial visit after receiving my MA, during one of my brief visits from Britain to Syria in 1977. The fifth was when I was taken by the foreign minister to translate for him, in 1990. The sixth was this time, in Latakia, right before we traveled to Madrid. He fully understood the challenges awaiting us in Spain and gave us detailed instructions, "We will be flexible, but not on the principle of land for peace." The bottom line, he added, was that every inch of Syrian territory had to be returned to its rightful owners, based on UN Security Council resolutions. If anything short of that was put on the table, we were fully mandated to pack up and return home. Baker had mentioned that the ultimate objective of Madrid, if peace were achieved, would be "normalized relations" with Israel. Assad had changed the wording to "normal relations." A separate Syrian-Israeli peace was out of the question, President Assad added, stressing that Palestinian rights and statehood must be achieved, and so should liberation of South Lebanon, which had been under Israeli occupation since 1978. It must be a comprehensive deal, not just a Syrian one. We were not going to Madrid to speak only for Syria; Assad wanted us to speak on behalf of the Arab world and to coordinate our efforts, in as much as possible, with other Arab delegations. The Israelis, he added, might want to shake hands or take a photograph and then transform any such gesture into a big story, given their firm control of Western media. This might be one of their objectives, warned Assad, asking us to be careful not to fall into such a trap.

The original plan was to present a unified Arab delegation to Madrid: one nation, one cause, one delegation to the conference. When that fell through because of major Arab disagreement, we began to put together the Syrian team, which was headed by the foreign minister. We boarded a Syrian Arab Airways plane and headed to Spain, where we stayed at the luxurious Ritz Hotel on the Plaza de la Lealtad in the heart of Madrid. A baroque palace landmark in the heart of the city's Golden Triangle, the hotel dated to 1910, when it was built at the command of King Alfonso XIII. Its architects probably never imagined that it would one day witness one of the most vital conferences in the history of the twentieth century. On day of our arrival, I recall that when heading down to the lobby, I was confronted by a stranger at the lift. He extended his right arm and said, "Hello, I am from Israel!" I was taken completely aback by his gesture; never before had I been put in such an awkward situation, asked to shake hands with a traditional enemy. I immediately turned away and took the lift down to the lobby. This was nothing, however, compared to what I was about to witness during the long, tedious peace process that started that day in Madrid and lasted until President Assad's untimely death, less than nine years later, on June 10, 2000.

Assad gave two back-to-back interviews to CNN and *Newsweek*, one shortly before the conference's start, on October 29, and the other during the proceedings.[1] *Newsweek* had the president's photograph on the front cover, with the title, "His Peace Plan: A Talk with Syria's Assad." The interview started with a fairly straightforward question: "Are you willing to accept a Jewish state in the Middle East?" Assad replied, "What I can say is that Syria stands by all UN Resolutions." The interviewer tried yet again, stressing that Israel's existence was now "a stable fact in [Middle Eastern] politics." Assad dodged the question, saying, "This needs to be discussed at the [Madrid] Conference." The interviewer then asked him whether anything had changed inside Syria for its top leadership to accept going into direct talks with the Israelis. "We did not change," said the Syrian leader firmly. "Whatever happened for us to change? We have always demanded a just and comprehensive peace, and we are still saying precisely that." He then elaborated, "The United States is a great power and shoulders particular responsibility toward world peace. If, after all the political and military support the United States gives Israel in a systematic manner, it cannot even pressure Israel [into concession], then this would be incomprehensible to the human mind."[2] When asked about Syria's procurement of arms from North Korea, Assad said that although that had occurred in the 1970s, it was no longer the case in 1991. "We purchase defensive arms, while Israel buys arms for aggression from the United States." Syria's military spending was 20 percent lower than that of Israel, he added. He then noted, in what was seen as a message to the Israelis and an additional instruction to us, "Confidence-building measures are not the way to solve the Arab-Israeli conflict." There are UN resolutions, he added, that address the conflict, and "need to be implemented, 242 and 338."[3]

Despite his caution, the president was clearly optimistic, thanks to all the guarantees given since January by both President Bush and Secretary of State Baker. He showed a certain appreciation for both men: they meant what they said and were seemingly committed to peace. "Whatever you say, or whatever you do," Assad reminded us, "keep in mind that our people have to know about it. There is nothing secret about Madrid. We have nothing to hide." Assad disliked secret deals and repeatedly refused any "under-the-table" agreements with either the Americans or the Israelis. Before seeing us off with his warm "Good luck," the president smiled and said, "I am wondering why we did not do this thirty years ago?"

Having said that, it must be noted that there was a great difference between what the Arabs did at Madrid in 1991 and Anwar al-Sadat's separate peace deal in 1978. Madrid was a detailed and collective effort, planned in a meticulous manner, with very clear terms of reference that were approved by President Assad, King Fahd of Saudi Arabia, King Hussein of Jordan, President Hrawi of Lebanon, and both the United States and the Soviet Union. Camp David however, was a highly dramatic unilateral event, and so was the Egyptian president's 1977 visit to Jerusalem. It was more of a public relations stunt than a substantive act aimed at advancing the interests of Egypt. The Egyptian street was never in favor of Camp David, but the Arab street in 1991 was psychologically and politically ready for peace.

From Latakia, we flew directly to Madrid.

The Conference

The Syrian delegation arrived in Spain on October 30, but the first round of direct talks did not start until November 3. Upon his arrival,

Shara immediately met with President Bush and Secretary of State Baker. This was Bush's second meeting with a Syrian diplomat, the first being Ambassador Mouallem back in the United States. "This is a historic moment," the US president said, "and the United States will do everything it can to make peace happen."[4] He reviewed what had earlier been confirmed in writing, that the terms of reference for Madrid were UNSCRs 242 and 338. It was the first time I personally came face-to-face with a US president. I was later to meet President Jimmy Carter several times in Damascus and President Bill Clinton as well, when he developed a good working relationship with President Assad in the 1990s. President Bush struck me as a genuine person. He was a humble, very nice elderly man who respected those around him and "noticed people." Many people, after all, do not notice the interpreter, especially if he or she is standing next to someone like Hafez al-Assad. President Bush, however, was not like that. After meeting with Bush, we realized that there were plenty of details that still needed to be sorted out before we could begin the conference in Madrid. The Israelis, for example, did not want a multilateral meeting, preferring to talk to each Arab delegation separately. They did not even want the Arab delegations to stay at the same hotel. They wanted to have only one meeting in Madrid and to hold a second round in Cairo—very different from what we had been brought to believe by Baker during his numerous visits to Damascus. We thought all of that had already been settled, but we were in for a big surprise as very intense negotiations took place in the forty-eight hours prior to the opening session. We were constantly on the phone with Damascus speaking to President Assad because every single issue was a problem.

The conference was held at Madrid's Royal Palace, a splendid venue for a peace conference. Eight stunning chandeliers hung from the ceiling above us in the Hall of Columns, as representatives from Syria, Lebanon, Palestine, Saudi Arabia, and Jordan sat around a T-shaped table, presided over by President Bush, Mikhail Gorbachev, and King Juan Carlos of Spain, with observers from both the European Commission and United Nations. Baker recalled the event a few years later… "Delegates appraised one another furtively, shunning direct eye contact and taking pains to avoid even a perfunctory handshake."[5] We agreed to refrain from placing any national flag on the table because Israel objected to the presence of the Palestinian flag. Shamir also objected when Palestinian negotiator Saeb Erekat walked in wearing the famous black-and-white-checked Palestinian *kufiyya*, which had become symbolic of the Palestinian stone throwers in the Occupied Territories.

The excitement from our arrival in Madrid was somewhat damped down when President Bush opened the conference with a historic speech that failed, nevertheless, to mention the land-for-peace formula. We were completely surprised. Shara spoke to reporters immediately after the first session, finding a sensible excuse for the US president: "Not making reference to land-for-peace does not mean an American retreat from its earlier position, given that there is a letter of assurance provided by the Americans to Syria, based on both resolutions 242 and 338."[6] We had another shock when Shamir delivered his country's speech, which was very negative and accused Syria of sponsoring terrorism, in reference to its unwavering commitment to the Palestinians. In looking back today, more than twenty years later, I don't think we should have been surprised by Shamir's speech. "Once a terrorist, always a terrorist," I said to myself. "Shamir never wanted to go to Madrid." Shamir, who died on June 30, 2012, twenty-one years after Madrid, will go down in the region's history books as an outspoken opponent of peace with the Arabs and remembered most for what he failed to achieve in Madrid, rather than for any breakthroughs.

Shara began his speech very calmly: "Our desire is sincere toward achieving peace. There is no alternative to total withdrawal from every inch of occupied land and guaranteeing the rights of the Palestinians."[7] He then added, "The Syrian Arab delegation came to this conference, despite Syria reservations, to try to reach a just and honorable peace for all aspects and fronts of the Arab-Israeli conflict. Our delegation came with an unlimited reserve of good faith and sincere desire to achieve peace." Israel, he reminded everyone, "has an expired ideology of expansion based on the building of settlements [in Occupied Palestine and the Golan]. Half a million Syrian citizens have been uprooted from the Golan and to date they have not been able to return to their homes."[8] He added, "Public opinion realizes today, more so than ever after the Gulf War, that double standards are no longer acceptable."

By then, Shamir had already walked out on the conference and returned to Israel, clearly uninterested in hearing Syria's position, which spoke volumes about how serious he actually was. Shara then broke into his historic improvisation: "I wanted to read from a written text, but the president of the Israeli delegation has left early . . . he is not interested in peace!"[9] The Syrian foreign minister then took out a newspaper clipping from 1948, with a picture of Shamir and the words "WANTED" written above it in bold letters. Shara addressed the conference with a booming voice, explaining, "I will just show you, if I may, an old photograph of Mr. Shamir. Why was this picture distributed? Because he was wanted! He helped, as I recall, in the assassination of Count Bernadotte, the UN mediator in Palestine in 1948. He kills peace mediators!" The Arab delegates were thrilled by Shara's historic remark. The Israelis were furious, we the Syrians were extremely proud, and the Americans looked the other way. They couldn't challenge what Shara had said—they knew it was 100 percent true—and they realized that Yitzhak Shamir deserved it because thanks to his hard-line attitude, Madrid nearly collapsed before it even took off. Farouk al-Shara was the star of Madrid, and we all warmly applauded him as he returned to his seat. Syria had made its point, loud and clear: we were the peacemakers and seekers, not the Israelis.

When the opening session ended, with all its high drama and spectacle, I went back into my hotel room for some rest and slumped into a couch to watch what television channels were saying about Madrid. Every channel across the planet—even those that did not agree with Syria's position—had our foreign minister on its evening news broadcast. Spanish television was particularly proud of the event its government had put together, with only eleven-days notice from the Americans and Russians. I later found out that Syrian television gave prime coverage to the entire ordeal at 8:30 P.M. Damascus time, and one could see our television anchors smiling as they read the news.

Futile Diplomacy

The next day, we went into direct talks with the Israelis at 10:30 A.M. this time, without Foreign Minister Shara or the Americans. For the first time in forty-three years, we were there in the same room with the Israelis, face-to-face around a conference table. Our former UN ambassador Muwafak al-Allaf took charge of the Syrian team. A very able diplomat, Allaf had served as Undersecretary-General of the UN in Geneva and he knew Syria's position inside and out. A graduate of Damascus University who understood the Western mindset, he spoke fluent English and had been decorated with the highest award of the Austrian Republic by Chancellor Kurt Waldheim in 1987. Allaf was a very serious, very sharp, and very cautious person. He was someone who wanted results but who, after the first session, became totally convinced that the Israelis were not in Madrid to do business. They were in Spain for two reasons: to get the US government to stop breathing down their necks and to attract media attention that might—they hoped—distract attention from the atrocities they were committing in the Occupied Territories. They were clearly more interested in a peace process than a peace treaty. If Shamir's speech made us wonder, Ben Aharon's handling of the direct talks convinced us that we did not have a serious peace partner at Madrid.

The first thing the Israelis did was to emphasize that they were negotiating from the Shamir Plan, which had been made by their prime minister back in April 1989. That proposal had been devised by Shamir, Moshe Arens, and Yitzhak Rabin shortly before outbreak of the first intifada. The four-point plan called for the establishment of the 1978 Camp David Accords as the foundation for the peace process, an "end to Arab hostility and belligerency to Israel, multinational efforts to solve the Arab refugee problem, and the election of Palestinian delegates to negotiate an interim period of self-governing administration." All that was completely unacceptable to the Syrians, including Shamir's insistence on using Hebrew names for Arab territories when he spoke of "free elections in Judea and Samaria." Allaf firmly said no to the Shamir Plan: "We are here on the basis of the Bush and Baker initiative and that of the USSR—and nothing else. That is what we agreed upon originally and that is why we are here!"[10] That meeting lasted for five long hours and produced practically nothing. If historians were to analyze its minutes, they would conclude from the tone of the Israelis that the meeting was going nowhere. It was, in every sense of the word, a dialogue of the deaf. The chief negotiators were the only ones speaking—rarely did anybody else say anything. Ben Aharon started the negotiations this way: "We are here to talk; do you acknowledge the right of the State of Israel to exist?" Allaf, taken aback by the dramatic violation of the agenda, calmly replied: "We came here in order to discuss 242 and 338!" Ben Aharon turned a deaf ear, completely ignoring Allaf: "We are happy to be here and to start negotiations with Syria. It's always good to have direct discussions. The best way to solve problems among neighbors is to sit with each other and to talk about problems. We are here on the basis of the Israeli Peace Initiative of 1986." Allaf, starting to lose patience, repeated firmly: "We are here for 242 and 338!" Ben Aharon looked up at him and said: "We implemented 242 when we returned the Sinai Peninsula to Egypt."[11]

"This is not the implementation of 242," the Syrian diplomat reminded him. "[UNSCR] 242 was about the return of all Arab land occupied in 1967 and not just Sinai." I remember fidgeting in my seat and telling myself, "Calm down, Bouthaina. One has to be very patient." During every single one of the 300 minutes wasted at that meeting, I was dying to walk out of the room—and so was the entire Syrian delegation.

Ben Aharon looked at us and remarked: "Before we start negotiations, could you tell me whether you acknowledge me as an independent state? If you won't, why then are you negotiating with Israel? When you sit and talk with me, you are offering de facto recognition of my existence!" Allaf, sensing the uneasiness in the room, decided to play by the Israeli game: "If you truly want me to acknowledge you, you have to tell me first, what are your borders, Mr. Aharon?"[12] Ben Aharon refused to answer, skipping directly to his second provocative statement: "So, do we set a date for a second meeting? I suggest that we establish channels of contact between us. What about naming an ambassador or anybody from your side, to exchange phone numbers with somebody in our delegation? This would be so that we don't have to go through the Americans every time we want to talk to Syria. We can talk directly."[13] Allaf, infuriated, replied: "I am hearing things that have nothing to do with the ethics and basics of negotiations! I am not here to listen to such arguments." Allaf had a very sharp sense of humor—very cynical in a sense. He quickly added: "Do you have any other irrelevant issues you would like to bring to the table?"[14] The first round of talks took us down a long road that eventually led to nowhere. The Americans considered it a breakthrough, but in Syria, we realized that by virtue of achieving nothing, Madrid had actually failed. The architect of Madrid, James Baker, thought otherwise, however, writing in his memoirs: "By every reasonable barometer, Madrid was a resounding triumph. Its enduring legacy was that it happened at all."[15] Baker told reporters on October 30, "We have to crawl before we walk, and we have to walk before we run. And today, I think we all began to crawl."[16] Crawling—I believe—is a very demeaning human act, done by people when they are under occupation, afraid, hiding, or under attack. Although I do appreciate Baker's analogy, I don't think anybody needed to crawl to Madrid. Speaking for myself and my colleagues, I can firmly say that Syria went to the Madrid Peace Conference neither crawling nor walking but marching, with head held high, because we knew where we stood and knew what we wanted to achieve. We had UN resolutions in our pockets, which should have guaranteed a legal, just, and honorable solution to the Arab-Israeli conflict. We had occupied land that the international community agreed needed to be returned to Syria. We had a wise president who had lived through war, hated war, and wanted peace, seeing it as a noble mission that he owed his countrymen and -women. We had the Bush administration, which was willing to walk that extra mile for the sake of peace. Unfortunately, however, we also had an Israeli government that was simply uninterested and seems to have come to Madrid only to put on a "show of peace" for the world media to consume while doing everything contradictory to back peace in the Middle East.

The Shara-Ross Meeting

With the conference and all its flaws behind them, the Syrian peacemakers returned to Damascus in early November, very disappointed that nothing tangible had been achieved at Madrid. The Americans have since labeled it a milestone in the history of the Middle East, but as far as we were concerned, the Madrid Peace Conference produced zero results for Syria. As this section will prove, neither did the Washington talks that took place in December 1991. The symbolism of Madrid, which meant a lot to both Baker and Bush, was of little significance to us as Syrians. Frankly, what mattered to us were the terms of reference agreed to at Madrid, that is, land-for-peace and the international community's commitment to UNSCR 242 and 338. Shortly after we returned from Madrid, however, the Knesset decided to formally annex the occupied Golan Heights to Israel, throwing dirt in the face of the peacemakers. Israel was saying it in so many different ways: "We were muscled into going to Madrid by President Bush. The peace process started by the Bush White House does not concern us simply because we are uninterested!" That message was heard, loud and clear, in the upper echelons of power in Damascus, but despite the very negative Israeli response, we continued to keep our fingers crossed and put our faith in President Assad.

On November 9, 1991, Foreign Minister Shara met with the new US ambassador to Syria, Christopher Ross. Like Ed Djerejian, Ross knew the Arab world well, having served as his country's ambassador to Algeria in the 1980s and as presidential envoy to Lebanon, and speaking fluent Arabic. At the meeting, the US diplomat relayed his country's assessment of Madrid, and, for his part, the Foreign Minister expressed Syria's anger at the recent Israeli annexation. President Assad and the people of Syria, added Shara, were satisfied with how our delegation had performed at Madrid.[17] There was grave disappointment, however, with both the Israelis and President Bush's opening speech.[18] As mentioned earlier, despite earlier assurances from the secretary of state, Bush made no reference to land-for-peace or to UNSCRs 242 and 338. "As an expression of goodwill toward the United States," Shara noted, ". . . we did not say anything to the media to that effect."[19]

Ross, however, was looking at the glass as half full, praising

Madrid as a diplomatic breakthrough while stressing the desire to pick up from where Madrid had ended. Shara read the penultimate paragraph of the first page of the US assessment of the Madrid Peace Conference, which stated: "We strongly believe that we are crossing to a decisive beginning and a new phase in the Middle East if bilateral negotiations were to be launched." Immediately, the foreign minister objected; bilateral talks had already started at Madrid. What more did the Israelis and Americans want? President Assad had made it clear on several occasions that one-to-one discussions on issues related to water, borders, and security would not start unless fundamental principles had been agreed upon with the Israelis. He then told Ross what Ben Aharon said to us in the first round of talks on November 3—he expressed a desire to talk directly to Syria, completely bypassing the United States. Ross initially dismissed the claim, noting that it was an informal chat and not a formal request. If the Israelis really wanted peace, added Shara, "why is Israel striking in South Lebanon and continuing to build settlements in Palestine?" Shara then raised the Israeli decision to use the Madrid talks only as an occasion to discuss another venue for talks, with Cairo being a prime suggestion. "What is that supposed to mean? Changing the venue after one session is not what we agreed upon, Mr. Ambassador. Please convey this strongly to Mr. Baker!"[20]

By occupying all parties with venue rather than substance, the Israelis were clearly trying to waste time to avoid any serious talks with the Arabs. "We went to Madrid along with other Arab delegations on the basis of President Bush's initiative. Israel, however, has made no reference to the 'land-for-peace' formula that was outlined by your president," Shara said, adding, "Instead, they talked about the Shamir Plan! The rest of the conference should be held in one country, one city, and in the same building. We are prepared to go to a country that has no animosity toward either Syria or Israel."[21]

Round I

It was eventually decided that all parties would head to the United States for a new set of discussions in Washington, D.C. In looking back, I think that Madrid was a prototype for what was awaiting us in Washington: big talk, big hopes, long hours of travel, jet lag, and exhausting logistics, not to mention the parting with families and friends. Our delegation, headed by Muwafak al-Allaf, arrived in Washington in December, and we began our first session with Israelis at the State Department at 10:00 A.M. on Tuesday, December 10. Elsewhere in the same building, Jordanian and Palestinian delegations were also present, discussing their own tracks with the Israelis. The Americans, it must be noted, were absent from all these meetings at the direct request of the Israelis.

The Syrians picked up where they had ended in Madrid one month earlier: UN Resolutions 242 and 338. Israeli representative Ben Aharon did the same, referring to a statement made by Allaf about "other irrelevant topics that you [the Israelis] would like to raise?"[22] The Israeli official said, "If you are going to decide, on my behalf, what is relevant and what is not, I can also decide for the Syrians what is relevant and what isn't!" Smiling, Allaf did not lose his calm: "That is up to you to decide; it does not concern us. I am only saying that we are ready to discuss only what is relevant to the peace process on the basis of UNSCRs 242 and 338." Ben Aharon then broke into an elaborate explanation as to why he preferred replacing Madrid with either Cairo or occupied Jerusalem, expressing his "unease at the Arab position." He was clearly disturbed at Syria's insistence on a "comprehensive peace agreement," noting that "land-for-peace, as a principle, is an interpretation that is not binding given that it is not mentioned verbatim in UNSCRs 242 and 338." Finally, he addressed our delegation chief, expressing unrest at an interview recently conducted with Allaf in our daily newspaper, *Tishreen*, on November 8. Allaf, according to Ben Aharon, had misquoted Yitzhak Shamir all throughout the interview and referred to him in an insulting manner. That interview, he added, "left a big question mark in the minds of the Israelis—if you want a media war, this is exactly what you will be getting, Mr. Allaf." Such rhetoric, he told us, was no different from the Syria-backed UN resolution that equates Zionism with racism. "If you want peace with Israel, for starters, you can call on the UN to consider this resolution null and void." Such anti-Israeli legislation, he added, was counterproductive and, as far as Tel Aviv was concerned, "should be thrown in the Hudson River!"[23]

The long list of Israeli dictates did not end there. Ben Aharon went on to mention George Habash, the Palestinian resistance leader whose Popular Front for the Liberation of Palestine (PFLP) was based in Damascus. We considered him a freedom fighter, but as far as Ben Aharon was concerned, he was a terrorist. "Why don't you expel him—as a minimum—from your land? If it were up to me, I would have put him under my soil!"[24] I remember sitting there with eyes wide with shock, taken completely aback by Ben Aharon's rudeness. This couldn't be true, I kept saying to myself. This man was here to talk about killing rather than to negotiate. That meeting, like all those that preceded and succeeded it, obviously led nowhere. It was another fifty-five minutes of a wasted dialogue of the deaf. Ben Aharon was provocative and lacked the minimum degree of courtesy or manners for negotiations. When it was his turn to speak, Allaf snapped at his Israeli interlocutor, reminding him of massacres committed by the State of Israel against Palestinians and Arabs of different nationalities, in Syria, Lebanon, and Jordan. "But let us not go back too far in history, Mr. Aharon. While we were meeting in Madrid, your army was engaged in brutal state terrorism, shelling villages and entire cities in South Lebanon. You killed innocent men, women, and children. Isn't it rather ironic, that while you headed your country's delegation to an international peace conference, the IDF was engaged in state terrorism?"[25] During the first Syrian-Israeli meeting in Madrid, Allaf continued, "your government announced the building of new settlements in the occupied Golan. Since the convening of Madrid less than two months ago, your "brave" soldiers killed dozens of Palestinians. And here you are, after all this bloodshed, criticizing me for an interview given in my country, distorting what I had said in that interview!" Allaf then angrily concluded, "If we were to take your earlier statements, and those of your Prime Minister, at face value, we would not be here today!"[26]

Deep in my heart, while watching the exchange unfold before me, I was thinking about how futile an exercise this was turning out to be. "We probably should not be here; they are clearly uninterested and only want to shelter themselves from blame for the collapse of the peace conference." Although too much tension was already in the air, Ben Aharon requested another meeting later that same afternoon. Allaf said no. "We think it is better to sit back and reflect on what has been said—and not achieved." If this was going to be the negotiating strategy of the Israelis, it would be better to call off the talks altogether, he added. It was obvious that Allaf was boiling with rage but did not want the Israelis to say, "The Syrians walked out first. They are to blame for not achieving peace in the Middle East."

The Palestinian Track

While we were busy debating nonsense with Ben Aharon, the Jordanians and Israelis were reaching similar dead ends. They had already met twice, and a third meeting was scheduled for December 11. Would it be wise, they asked, to sit for another round while the Syrian-Israeli and Lebanese-Israeli tracks were going nowhere? The talks with the

Lebanese, it must be noted, were also difficult. The Israelis wanted bilateral meetings with Lebanese officials to discuss security and were eager to jump directly into an ill-planned Lebanese-Israeli peace treaty, similar to the one signed by former president Amin Gemayel in 1983. The Lebanese, however, under strict orders from President Hrawi, insisting on implementing UN Security Council Resolution 425, which was issued after the 1978 Israeli invasion of South Lebanon, calling for a complete withdrawal from all occupied Lebanese lands.

A debate ensued among Arab delegates at the residence of the Palestinian delegation on whether to collectively suspend talks with Israel or continue talking on the Palestinian front—even though all the talks were going nowhere—to avoid being blamed by the Americans and the international community. The second question was, if the Palestinian or Jordanian tracks collapse, should the Syrians and Lebanese continue in their talks with Israel? Some Palestinian delegates wanted us to express our concerns to the State Department. Others wanted to seek the assistance of Saudi Arabia and Egypt, arguing that with no backing from Arab heavyweights, the Americans would never apply real pressure on the Israelis. Haidar Abdul Shafi, the seasoned Palestinian statesman, was in favor of continuation, claiming that the letter of invitation to the Washington talks spoke of an Arab-Israeli track and of a separate Palestinian-Israeli one, regardless of the Jordanian umbrella given to them at Madrid. His colleague Hanan Ashrawi, a prominent Palestinian academic and politician, added that she had spoken to Ed Djerejian many times and he kept saying to her: "Don't close all the doors, and don't lose your patience! Just keep going." Saeb Erekat, the top Palestinian negotiator, looked at Allaf and asked for more detail about the latest Syrian-Israeli meeting. "From what the media has been saying, it went well," he added. Allaf explained, "Not at all, Saeb . . . nothing of the sort is true." He had been on the telephone with Damascus all afternoon, seeking instructions from President Assad. Abdussalam al-Majali, the future Jordanian prime minister who headed his country's delegation to Madrid, added, "We reminded the Israelis what was agreed upon at Madrid. The idea of two tracks, rather than a united Arab one, was originally an Israeli proposal. The Jordanians, we told them, simply cannot speak on behalf of the Palestinians." By insisting on one delegation, the Israelis had actually wanted to drown the Palestinian national identity—and indeed, make the Americans look weak and silly. Proving what Majali told us, when two rooms were prepared for talks, one for the Jordanians and one for the Palestinians, Israel insisted that it meet both delegations jointly. Just as it refused to have a

Palestinian flag on the conference table at Madrid, it refused to acknowledge an independent Palestinian delegation in Washington. Ahsrawi told us, "At the beginning, the Americans were indeed dealing with us independently of Jordan. When Baker spoke to us directly and when invitations were sent out, we got ones that were independent from the Jordanians. In light of Israeli insistence, however, the Americans suddenly took a step back, and left us to confront the Israelis on our own!"

Round II: Along the Road to Nowhere

On December 11, as planned, we held our second meeting with the Israelis at the Department of State. As expected, it too led to nowhere, being an exact replica of what took place on December 10. Ben Aharon repeated the same logic, asking why normal relations cannot be achieved between Syria and Israel "like the ones between Belgium and Germany?"[27] This time Allaf said, "You said it all, didn't you? But you failed to mention one crucial point: whether or not you are ready to withdraw to the June 4, 1967, borders of Israel? That and only that will make Syrian-Israeli peace possible." Allaf then met with Djerejian to complain about Israel's attitude toward both Syria and the Palestinians. The former ambassador to Syria knew us—perhaps too well—and realized that we had walked that extra mile to make Madrid—and now Washington—a success. "Patience, my dear Muwafak," he cautioned, "please be patient regarding tactical issues. We are ready to use our influence as far as core issues are concerned, but would prefer patience when it comes to details. What has been achieved over the past two days is indeed important."[28]

Israel seemed to be aware of the fact that the United States was desperate for a success story in the Middle East and under no circumstances did it want the Washington talks to collapse. That would have killed all the momentum achieved at Madrid and embarrassed both the US president and his secretary of state. Fully aware of this Achilles' heel, Israel used and abused the Bush administration during those cold December days in Washington. I always wondered, how could people who are looked upon by the entire world as history makers be wasting their time in such a vain fashion? To be fair, the Syrians were trying their best to gear negotiations toward tangible results, but the Israelis never lacked topics to digress upon, and they made sure that they never answered one question or tackled a real issue. To be frank for the sake of history, during the Washington talks we completely lost hope of achieving any peace with the Shamir government. Instead, I kept worrying about my two daughters left behind in Damascus. Their mother, supposedly helping change the face of the Middle East, was wasting her time in the United States—doing nothing—while there was nobody to put them to bed, make them dinner, or send them to school every morning.

Meeting III

The third meeting took place at 10:00 A.M. on December 12. This time Rafiq Juwayjati, a veteran diplomat who had served as our ambassador to the United States under Reagan, took charge explaining the importance of UNSCR 242. He explained the principle of "non-acquiescence of land by force, and the prohibition of resorting to force in international relations." Juwayjati also cited the paragraph that frankly refers to the "withdrawal from occupied territories," noting that "there is no right to any claimed right of occupation even under the pretext of self-defense."[29] A just and comprehensive peace is conditional on 242, he added. Ben Aharon once again objected to the term "comprehensive," claiming that no peace can be comprehensive if it is not achieved with Libya, Tunisia, Iran, or Saudi Arabia. Allaf responded, "Let us make peace between Syria and Israel, which will be one component of comprehensive peace, especially as Israel is conducting negotiations with other parties whose lands are occupied. The hope is that all parties will reach a just and comprehensive peace." He then firmly added, "Let us not leave this room without having reached something tangible to tell our peoples, and the world."[30]

Ben Aharon retreated once again, giving a very biased, flawed account of history, claiming that it was the Israelis who were acting in self-defense, not the Arabs. He spoke of the Jewish exodus from Europe, their persecution in Arab lands, and the wars of 1948, 1967, and 1973. "I cannot accept 242," he finally said, "while ignoring all that history that needs to be addressed." Allaf looked at his watch. "We have only half an hour left, and until now, not a single useful sentence has been said between us. Meetings are going to be adjourned until Monday and I would like to reach an idea—one single constructive idea—that would signal progress."[31] That of course, did not happen.

While driving back to the Hilton Hotel where the Syrian delegation was staying, I kept remembering an old Arab proverb repeated often by

Mother: "You can tell what a letter contains from its address!" That address, as far as we were concerned as peacemakers, was obviously unproductive. That evening, my colleagues and I went over the recordings of our three meetings with the Israelis. They seemed to be endless—very long exercises in failed statesmanship. Once again, I thought of my two daughters, Nahid and Nazek, sitting back home with big dreams and high expectations for their mother. The poor girls were probably thinking that I was making history in the United States. Little did they know that I was stuck at a Washington hotel, waiting for the weekend to pass while listening to rubbish given to us by the Israelis. What made things worse was the realization that putting an end to this nonsense was very difficult and would be very embarrassing for Syria. We seemed to have walked into a trap, and there was no telling how and when it would end. After a very tedious weekend, Monday morning finally came, when we were scheduled to hold our fourth meeting with the Israelis.

Ben Aharon suggested summing up all points raised previously and trying to find some common ground or points of agreement. I couldn't help but grin at his statement. "There are none, you fool," I said to myself. Allaf hinted that progress was so distant because neither the Americans nor Russians were allowed to sit at the negotiating table. Ben Aharon sidestepped that statement, noting that "today" the UN resolution on Zionism was going to be debated at the General Assembly. "Will Syria maintain the position it expressed in 1975 about Zionism?" Allaf was furious, purely enraged. "You are only misleading us by saying that you want to name points of agreement! Instead, all you are doing is repeating things you have said one million times since the start of the peace process!"[32] It was his turn to give Ben Aharon a good history lesson, reminding him of Israeli atrocities in the Occupied Territories, starting with 1948 and continuing through the Palestinian intifada of 1987, when then–defense minister Yitzhak Rabin had called on the IDF to "break the bones" of Palestinian children. I was thrilled. Allaf had seemingly crawled into my mind and read my thoughts, speaking so strongly about this terrible waste of time. Ben Aharon asked for a break, inviting Allaf for tea, but the Syrian negotiator said no, storming out of the room in rage.

Next morning, December 17, it was business as usual for all of us. We had breakfast and then headed to the State Department at 10:00 A.M. for our fifth round of talks with the Israelis. Allaf began by saying: "Yesterday I asked three specific questions that I request an answer to this morning. The first question is whether Israel is ready to implement

Security Council Resolution 242 in good faith and in a way that guarantees the full Israeli withdrawal from all Syrian territories occupied in 1967. The second question is whether Israel is ready, as a sign of good faith, to stop building settlements in Palestinian lands. The third question is whether your delegation is ready to stop wasting our time by endless digressions and stick to the crucial issues that matter for Arab-Israeli peace. Ben Aharon seemed calm: "We do have serious differences about what is relevant and what is not and what you consider a waste of time." Allaf responded, "It seems to me that all what you want from these meetings is to say to the Americans: We are sitting and negotiating with the Syrians! Are you prepared to withdraw from territories you occupied in 1967? Are you prepared to accept the land-for-peace formula?"

Ben Aharon did not reply. Instead, he suggested postponing the talks until January 1992. Allaf said that Christmas was in eight days and the Syrians were willing to stay in Washington until then to achieve any breakthrough. The two sides met one last time on December 18, and unsurprisingly, nothing was achieved. At 1:00 P.M., the Americans met with the heads of all delegations for a quick briefing about what had been achieved over the past week. This time Ben Aharon was much clearer and got straight to the point: "We shall not leave the Golan," he told us, "until you recognize the legitimacy of Israel and allow the last Jew to leave Syria. Also we shall not negotiate implementation of 242 until you agree to put an end to violence." The meetings we had in Washington were depressing, to say the least. Before wrapping up, Ben Aharon—very rudely—asked whether we could issue a joint communiqué about the Washington talks. Allaf barked, "About what? You want us to tell the world that something was achieved when in fact we have not advanced one inch toward peace!" And thus 1991 came to a close without a single achievement on the Syrian-Israeli track. The other tracks were not any better as the Palestinians could not get separate meetings with the Israelis; no real progress was achieved on any track.

In the afternoon I went shopping, buying clothes for my two girls, cheered up by the fact that I was finally returning to Damascus. All I wanted to do was to buy more presents for my daughters, Nahid and Nazek, and fly to spend Christmas in Syria. At one point, I asked myself: "Do I really understand politics? What was the use of this entire adventure in Madrid and Washington?" The Americans kept telling us to keep the faith, insisting that all breakthroughs at Washington were good and would ultimately serve Middle East peace. Today, twenty years later, I look back at my feelings of impatience and sense of waste and say: "I was correct!" What a waste of time indeed. We returned home empty-handed. When packing and all throughout our flight, which reached Damascus via Paris, I kept asking myself: "Was it worth it, Bouthaina?" How could people at this level waste so much time and energy knowing that they are getting nowhere? I had no reason to be optimistic but every reason to be happy that I was going back home, away from these depressing, futile exchanges. I was proud—all of us were—that we managed to uphold Syria's position at every single juncture, living up to the faith President Assad had placed in all of us.

Notes

1. *Tishreen*, November 1, 1991.
2. *Newsweek*, October 29, 1991.
3. Ibid.
4. Archives of the Syrian Ministry of Foreign Affairs, Dispatches from the Syrian Delegation to the Madrid Peace Conference to Damascus, October–November 1991.
5. Baker, *The Politics of Diplomacy*, 512.
6. Syrian Arab News Agency (SANA), November 3, 1991.
7. *Tishreen*, October 31, 1991.
8. Ibid.
9. Ibid.
10. Archives of the Syrian Ministry of Foreign Affairs, Minutes of the 1991 Madrid Peace Conference.
11. Ibid.
12. Archives of the Syrian Ministry of Foreign Affairs, Minutes of the 1991 Madrid Peace Conference.
13. Ibid.
14. Ibid.
15. Baker, *The Politics of Diplomacy*, 512.
16. Ibid.
17. Archives of the Syrian Ministry of Foreign Affairs, Minutes of the Shara-Ross Meeting, November 9, 1991.
18. Ibid.
19. Ibid.
20. Ibid.
21. Ibid.
22. Archives of the Syrian Ministry of Foreign Affairs, Minutes of Meeting I at the State Department, December 10, 1991.
23. Ibid.
24. Ibid.
25. Ibid.
26. Ibid.

27. Archives of the Syrian Ministry of Foreign Affairs, Minutes of Meeting II at the State Department, December 11, 1991.
28. Ibid.
29. Archives of the Syrian Ministry of Foreign Affairs, Minutes of Meeting III at the State Department, December 12, 1991.
30. Ibid.
31. Ibid.
32. Archives of the Syrian Ministry of Foreign Affairs, Minutes of Meeting IV at the State Department, December 16, 1991.

3

The Rise of Bill Clinton

AS WE PREPARED TO RETURN TO WASHINGTON, D.C., THE United States was in a frenzy, busy with the 1992 presidential election. There were three major candidates competing for the White House: the incumbent, President Bush; the Democrat from Arkansas, Governor Bill Clinton; and the independent Texas businessman, Ross Perot. After his successful performance in the Gulf War, Bush's approval ratings stood at 89 percent, and many considered his reelection very likely. As far as the Middle East was concerned, we watched with great interest, not knowing what to expect from Clinton or Perot but at first certain that if reelected, Bush would push hard for peace, eager to crown his Madrid initiative with success. Clinton, positioning himself as a centrist, or "New Democrat," as they called him in the United States, was still unknown in the Arab world and to us in Syria. His first breakthrough was winning the primary in Georgia, after which he swept all the Super Tuesday primaries in March 1992, making him a solid front-runner. Clinton won the Michigan and Illinois primaries and then scored a thundering victory in New York and a close one in Wisconsin. By that spring, the young forty-six-year-old presidential candidate had secured the Democratic Party nomination. Suddenly he began to matter to the Arabs because he ran a high chance of becoming the next US president. At that point his name began to appear on the front page of Syrian dailies, which closely monitored the US elections.

From where things stood in January 1992, however, Clinton was still just a presidential hopeful, and if we wanted to achieve anything concrete in terms of Middle East peace, we had to deal with the Bush White House.

My personal thoughts about the second round of Washington talks were very negative—to say the least—and what made it worse was the thought of yet again leaving my children back home in Damascus. Once they heard I was about to travel, they fell silent and looked at me with long faces, which spoke volumes about what they really thought about the Middle East peace process. As far as they were concerned, it might as well go to hell because all it did was to "take Mommy away from them." Khalil, my husband, kept telling them: "You should support your mother because she has an important job and an important mission." At eight and ten years old, they were very polite girls who never argued with their father, but the look on their faces clearly showed how unimpressed the two of them were with the Washington talks. No wonder, I said to myself, because so was their mother and the rest of the Syrian delegation who were heading to Washington, D.C.

I tried to put on a brave face, echoing what my husband was telling them and promising to bring them back all the Barbie accessories they wanted, along with plenty of lovely winter clothes and a variety of drawing and coloring pens. But they wanted none of that; what they wanted was to stay close to their mother. It is a big illusion to think that children can be compensated for the loving care of a mother with toys and material objects—and a big lie. The Washington talks taught me that my two girls did not need colorful crayons or Barbie dolls—all I was trying to do was to give them psychological compensation. The reason I mention my daughters repeatedly is that there were plenty of other parents leaving their families behind and boarding planes heading for Washington, D.C., from Amman, Beirut, Ramallah, and Damascus. Some of them, like myself, are now proud parents of very successful children, while others, I am sure, are proud grandparents by now, twenty years down the road. As we advance in age and knowledge, we weigh out our life experiences and tend to think back and ask: "Did we do the right thing? Where did we go wrong?" Looking back, I don't think the peace process was worth it—simply because it produced absolutely nothing. I don't know whether any of my Arab colleagues experienced the same sinking feeling I did when driving toward the airport, with their hearts racing back home and with a hunch that traveling to the United States was illogical, undesired, and very unproductive. In any event, that was my state of mind as I left with the Syrian delegation for Washington, D.C., on January 9, 1992.

We arrived in the United States on a cold evening in January 1992 and were scheduled to begin the second round of talks with the Israelis on January 13. Needless to say, because of our December experience, I was not the slightest bit optimistic that we would achieve anything tangible in Washington. The Israelis were clearly not ready for peace, and Shamir was totally uninterested. Period! As for the Americans, although they were still committed to the principles of Madrid—at least in words—they were also very busy with the presidential race and seemed to have little time left for the complex web of Middle East politics. The momentum for peace, which had intensified with Baker's shuttle diplomacy in March–October 1991, seemed to have evaporated into thin air.

The Last Round Under President Bush

Immediately after we arrived in the United States, Muwafak al-Allaf went into talks with US personnel to prepare for the first session. Very much like the rest of the Syrian delegation, he too was expecting the worst from Ben Aharon and insisted on talking about nothing other than UNSCRs 242 and 338. His first meeting was with Ambassador Djerejian and David Aaron Miller, an influential adviser to the secretary of state. Attending the meeting was Walid al-Mouallem, our ambassador in Washington. It should be noted that throughout the month of December, the Palestinians had been in the corridors of the State Department, refusing to hold joint meetings with the Jordanians, while the Israelis were refusing to recognize the Palestinians as an independent delegation representing the people of Palestine. That, among other things, made the situation tense from day one. Allaf tried talking Ambassador Djerejian into using his heavyweight influence to persuade the Israelis to change their tactics and to secure a line from them that was different from the one we had heard in December. But the US ambassador's response was not encouraging. "We only interfere with major issues, while the parties involved have to solve pending issues on their own."[1] Instead, both he and Miller were more interested in persuading Allaf to have tea or coffee with the Israelis in order to "build confidence" and "break the ice" on the Syrian-Israeli track. "Isn't it enough that we are actually negotiating directly with the Israelis without the Americans in the room?" asked the Syrian diplomat.[2] "Instead of asking us for such gestures, it would be better if you talked the Israelis into showing some seriousness rather than raising irrelevant issues like changing the venue!"[3] Then Allaf attended a meeting with heads of all the Arab delegations, and it was decided that none of them would accept changing the venue, which was what Ben Aharon had persistently demanded since December. In a remarkable show of solidarity, all agreed that they would wait for the outcome of a 10 A.M. meeting the following morning between the Palestinians and Israelis, to see whether or not the Israelis would agree to deal with the Palestinians as an independent delegation. All the heads of the Arab delegations had their doubts about the seriousness of the Israelis and the ability of the Americans to press the Israelis into being truly committed and productive.

We held three sessions with the Israelis January 13–15, and no progress was achieved in any of them. We could not even agree on what number to give this new round of talks in Washington. As far as we were concerned, Madrid was Round I, while Washington, in December–January, was Round II. Ben Aharon, however, argued otherwise, claiming that "Madrid was not a round but rather an opening session for talks," and saying that Washington was actually Round I.[4] Although we considered the February talks to be the fourth round of talks with Israel, the Israelis considered them to be the third round. Instead of discussing UN resolutions, the Israelis were busy with what was happening back in Tel Aviv, fearing that the narrow right-wing Shamir coalition was about to collapse. Radicals were threatening to walk out on the aging Israeli premiere if his representatives in Washington were going to discuss self-determination and nationhood with the Palestinians. The Israeli politicians put their words into action and actually called for early elections, bringing down Shamir later that year when he was replaced by Yitzhak Rabin's Labor Party. As far as we Syrians were concerned, Labor or Likud did not really matter—what we cared for were commitments and principle. The Shamir interlude was used and abused by Ben Aharon in order to refuse to commit to anything, and it became a pattern in the peace process that lasted until 2000, when Ehud Barak claimed that he could not sign a peace agreement with Syria because of elections in Israel.

With the Shamir government on the verge of collapse, we entered into yet another round of nonsense with Ben Aharon. The same issues were raised over and over again: Would the Syrians recognize Israel's right to exist? Would they cease their media attacks against Israel? Would they allow Syrian Jews to migrate to Israel? All this was being said without a single word of commitment on the part of the Israelis regarding Resolutions 242 or 338, or anything about the Madrid terms of reference. The Palestinians were calling on Shamir to cease building settlements in the Occupied Territories, but their calls were falling on deaf ears in Washington, D.C., and Tel Aviv. Not only that, but the Israelis were trying to play one Arab delegation against the other, pretending to have reached breakthroughs with the Palestinians, ostensibly to infuriate the Syrians, and vice versa. For example, they tried telling the media that they were very close to reaching a deal with Jordan, so as to corner the Palestinians into agreeing to their conditions, and did the same with the Jordanian delegation.

What made things worse was the diminishing role of US politicians, whether due to the presidential elections or to the strong Zionist lobby in Washington that was opposed to any deal with the Arabs. At one point, so colorless were the Americans—after the Democratic Party was getting the upper hand in the election campaign—that we seriously contemplated freezing the talks to wait to see who would replace Bush at the White House.

On February 11, President Assad received a letter from Secretary of State Baker, carried by Ambassador Christopher Ross, explaining why no progress was being made in Washington.[5] The Syrian leader was very disappointed with Bush and Baker, arguing that "no progress has been made and we seriously expected something different from the Americans, given all of what we had heard in the pre-Madrid talks."[6] If this was all Bush could deliver, then one could only wonder about what would happen to the peace process if newcomers like Perot or Clinton made it to the White House. "Only the Israelis are benefiting from these lengthy and futile negotiations, considering them a media and PR gain before world public opinion," Assad stressed in his response to Baker via Ambassador Ross.[7] Instead of properly analyzing why the Arabs were getting nowhere in the United States, Baker tried talking Assad into entering into multilateral talks with the Israelis. He seemed desperate for a success story in peace that could be used in the upcoming presidential elections in November.

Assad, however, was crystal clear: "We are not going into any multilateral talks without having progressed one inch on bilateral ones, Mr. Ambassador," he told Ross.[8] "We don't have a single indication that Israel is interested in peace . . . not a single one."[9] Assad commented further: "They [the Israelis] are trying to normalize relations with certain Arab countries without returning occupied land or acknowledging the legitimate rights of the Palestinians. Doors are being opened to Israel throughout the international community where it is marketing itself as a peacemaker, arguing that for one year now it has been talking peace, not war, with the Arabs."[10] Some countries that previously had no relations with Israel might now start asking: "Why should we be more Arab than the Arabs themselves?"[11] Ross told President Assad that Bush would take a "strong position" on a $10-billion loan the United States was planning to give to Israel. Washington was going to freeze the loan, he added, if settlement building did not cease in the Palestinian territories. Ross added that according to a recent opinion poll, 41 percent of Americans believed that Israel, rather than the Arabs, was the main obstacle to Middle East peace.[12] That was not enough, Assad replied. What mattered was how the international community was starting to treat Israel as a peacemaker, even though it had ceased none of its war rhetoric, mentality, or behavior. False messages were being sent to the world, Assad warned, and he claimed that the Bush administration was responsible.

Clinton and the Arab World

While Baker and Bush were trying to salvage the peace process, Bill Clinton and his running mate, Al Gore, were taking over the United States. Clinton and Gore were taking bus tours across the country, while Bush and his running mate, Dan Quayle, were in clear panic mode. They tried to slander Clinton's character with accusations that varied from infidelity to draft dodging. Clinton was inexperienced in international politics, they added, while Bush banked on a long career, in the CIA, as vice president under Reagan, and as US president. But none of this worked, and Clinton won the 1992 election with 43 percent of the vote, while Bush received 37.4 percent. Perot, who stood a slim chance of winning to start with, came in as the runner-up, with only 18.9 percent. It was the US economy, however, rather than the Middle East peace process, that made Clinton the forty-second president of the United States, sending Bush into retirement at the age of sixty-eight. Clinton's victory, seen as a breath of fresh air by the Arabs, ended twelve years of Republican rule in the White House. For the first time since Jimmy Carter, the Democrats were now in full control of the US Congress, and undoubtedly this would have a positive impact on the peace process. In Syria, we were optimistic and positive about the new president, who was billed as the youngest ever in US history.

When taking his oath of office in January 1993, President Clinton came out and said: "Our founders saw themselves in the light of posterity. We can do no less. Anyone who has ever watched a child's eyes wander into sleep knows what posterity is. Posterity is the world to come, the world for whom we hold our ideals, from whom we have borrowed our planet, and to whom we bear sacred responsibilities." He added, "We must do what America does best, offer more opportunity to all and demand responsibility from all. It is time to break the bad habit of expecting something for nothing: from our government, or from each other. Let us all take more responsibility, not only for ourselves and our families but for our communities and our country."[13] That is exactly what he did during his years at the White House: offer more opportunity for peace and dialogue in the Middle East. In looking back at our experience with Clinton, on which I will elaborate in the chapters ahead, I can safely say that our relationship with him was mature, serious, and positive, and it achieved major breakthroughs in Syrian-US relations. He developed an excellent working relationship with President Assad, built on trust and respect, stronger perhaps than that of any of his predecessors, and this lasted until the Syrian president's death in 2000. We actually came very close to achieving peace under Clinton. It did not happen in the end, not because of the US president, but because of other hidden factors that I shall try to elucidate as we progress in our analysis of the peace process.

During his early hours in office on January 20, 1993, however, the peace process was not on his mind, and neither the Arabs nor Israelis were mentioned in his inaugural address.

On February 21, 1993, Clinton's new secretary of state, Warren Christopher, made his first visit to Syria for a meeting with President Assad. A seasoned and principled US politician from North Dakota, Christopher had served as deputy attorney general under President Lyndon B. Johnson and deputy secretary of state under President Carter. He knew the Middle East well, and as our experience with him was to prove, he also knew what it takes to achieve results in the Arab-Israeli peace process. Christopher told Assad that peace in the Arab world was a top priority for the new US president. Assad smiled: he had heard that line all too often under Presidents Nixon, Carter, and Bush. "The previous administration was also serious," he reminded Christopher, "but when elections started, everything related to peace came to a grinding standstill."[14] This time things were different, insisted the US secretary of state. He stressed Clinton's commitment to peace, promising to put his country's full weight behind the process that had started at Madrid. "We are committed to the terms of reference and letter of guarantees provided by Secretary Baker," Christopher told Assad.[15] He then handed President Assad a written letter from Clinton, stressing full American partnership in the peace process. "The President is willing to work closely with Syria to bring positive change in the bilateral relationship between Syria and the United States."[16] Assad was willing to give Christopher the benefit of the doubt, just as he had done with Baker one year earlier. "Everyone will work for the achievement of peace," he said. "The entire world needs peace and perhaps Israel, which has obstructed peace since Madrid, is the party that needs peace the most."[17]

The Oslo Accords

Five weeks after entering the White House, President Clinton convened his first National Security Council (NSC) meeting on March 3, 1993. Until then, only Bosnia, Somalia, and Haiti were on the new US president's foreign policy "to-do" list. Warren Christopher's Middle East trip was bound to change that, given that he had just wrapped up a successful tour of the Arab world, including a brief stopover in Damascus. The new secretary of state reported on the Syria visit, which was to be the first of nineteen to the Syrian capital, saying that President Assad had promised "full peace with Israel" if there was "total Israeli withdrawal from the Golan Heights." By 1993, Yitzhak Shamir had been ejected from office and replaced by Yitzhak Rabin, the seventy-one-year-old Labor Party heavyweight who had held the job in the 1970s. During the Israeli elections in June 1992, Rabin had declared that he would "never come down from the Golan" but would rather "solve problems" in the West Bank and Gaza within his first nine months of office, granting the Palestinians limited autonomy in the Occupied Territories. With such an attitude, we had very low expectations from the new Israeli leader. He actually added nothing new to the Washington talks that resumed between us and the Israelis in April, except that he replaced Ben Aharon with another Israeli hard-liner, Itamar Rabinovich, who was to become his country's future ambassador to the United States.

The United States viewed Rabin as "a general who had seen too many wars and now intended to end them."[18] They admired him and viewed him as a Washington insider, given that for years he had served as Israel's ambassador to the United States. When Christopher visited him in Tel Aviv in early 1993, Rabin showed interest in what President Assad had recently said to the Americans, a striking contrast to all his rhetoric during the Israeli elections. According to President Clinton's Middle East adviser, Martin Indyk, "Rabin concluded that Israel should focus on the Syrian track. He explained to Christopher that Assad was a leader who could make decisions and that peace with Syria would be a strategic achievement for Israel."[19] Rabin would not define the extent of Israeli withdrawal, however, until Assad accepted that a Syrian-Israeli agreement would "stand on its own feet."[20] In other words, he wanted a deal with Assad that was independent of the Palestinian, Jordanian, and

Lebanese tracks. The Syrian president, however, was uninterested in a separate deal. The world now hails Rabin as a "visionary peacemaker," remembering the retired general for the Nobel Peace Prize he received after signing the Oslo Accords in 1993. But as far as we in Syria were concerned, the Rabin of 1992–1993 was nothing but a hard-line former defense minister who had ordered the "breaking of the bones of Palestinian children" during the popular intifada of 1987.[21] Whether it was Rabin or Shamir, it did not really matter to us as peacemakers. We in Syria concentrated on deeds, commitment, and action rather than on words or personalities. If Rabin wanted a separate deal with Damascus, then he did not yet fully understand Hafez al-Assad.

What convinced us that Rabin was not ready for peace were the questions he put to President Clinton when they first met in Washington, D.C., in March 1993. The Israeli prime minister asked, "Would Israel have to make a full withdrawal from the Golan? If so, what would the United States be prepared to do? Would the [US] President be prepared to put American troops in the Golan to replace the Israeli army there?"[22] Colin Powell, then chairman of the Joint Chiefs of Staff, was asked whether Israel would ever really give up the Golan. "No military officer would want to give this up," he said to Clinton.[23] His professional advice was that the United States needed to insert a brigade of US troops (around 4,000 soldiers) on the Golan to make sure that a Syrian-Israeli deal held.[24] This was much larger than the one battalion of US troops (up to 1,000 soldiers) deployed in the Sinai Peninsula after Camp David—and it added to our conviction that neither Powell, Clinton, nor Rabin had fully grasped the statesmanship needed for a "just and comprehensive peace" in the Middle East. President Assad would have flatly rejected such a proposal, given that he would never accept replacing Israeli troops in the Golan with US military forces. Clinton asked Rabin, "Do you believe that it will be possible to achieve a peace agreement with Syria without full Israeli withdrawal from the Golan Heights?"[25] Rabin gave a straightforward answer: "No!"[26] The US president then added, "If you have adequate security agreements as you have in the Sinai—backed up by American forces—if you have a genuine Syrian offer of peace, and if the agreement stands alone, would Israel be prepared to withdraw from the Golan?" Rabin replied, "I don't exclude the possibility."[27]

Remarking on that meeting in his 2009 memoirs, *Innocent Abroad*, Martin Indyk said, "When it came to respecting their treaty obligations, the Syrians were puritans. Assad had scrupulously observed the Golan Heights Separation of Forces Agreement, which Kissinger negotiated in

1974; there had been only one minor violent incident in almost twenty years."[28] Clinton, however, realized that good intentions were not enough for peace with Syria. A peace agreement required adequate US pressure on Rabin to discuss water rights, effective early warning systems, demilitarized zones, and full withdrawal from the Golan. This explains why Clinton advocated a "Syria First" agreement in the Arab-Israeli conflict and worked hard at achieving it during his second term, which ended in 2001. The reality back in 1993, however, was very different from what Clinton wanted.

Prior to the signing of the Oslo Accords, which will be discussed in detail later in this chapter, the Syrian team held three rounds of negotiations with the Israelis in Washington, D.C., all of which—as mentioned earlier—were as futile as those that took place during the final months of the Bush administration. The ninth round took place on April 26 and lasted until May 13. The tenth started on June 14 and lasted until July 1, and the eleventh took place on August 31 and lasted until September 9, 1993. They all comprised nothing but sophisticated (yet useless) jargon: for example, concentrating on a press interview somebody had given back in the 1950s or a position taken by a particular Arab country ten years previously. They dealt with none of the core issues raised by Clinton during his Cabinet Room meeting at the White House in March.

When we arrived in the United States in August 1993, we heard rumors that a separate deal was being negotiated between Yasser Arafat and the Israelis somewhere in Europe. At first we did not take them seriously, until one day, to our very great surprise, we heard the news on CNN. I remember sitting in the living room suite of Muwafak al-Allaf at the Hilton Hotel, watching television with our Palestinian colleague, Haidar Abdul Shafi. Words in red beamed across the screen on CNN: "Breaking News: The PLO reaches a peace deal with the Israelis in Oslo!" We immediately discovered that President Assad knew nothing about this, and neither did Foreign Minister Shara, Muwafak al-Allaf, nor Haidar Abdul Shafi. Arafat had managed to keep the talks that took place in Norway under lock and key, hiding the news even from his most trusted aides and top negotiators. Abdul Shafi, a highly dignified and principled character, was furious and bitterly remarked, "At least I deserve a phone call. I should have been informed!" Saeb Erekat was also taken completely aback, saying that he too had heard the rumors while in Vienna, just like the rest of us, but did not think they were substantial. In a matter of seconds, everything started to make sense to the Arabs assembled in Washington, D.C., that summer. Pieces of the puzzle that had so perplexed them began falling into place, as they began to realize why nothing of substance had been achieved in the seventy-seven rounds of talks that had taken place between the Arabs and Israelis during almost two years since Madrid. The Israelis had given us absolutely nothing, fully aware that their government was already engaged in another, more solid, track that promised to give them what the Washington talks would never have given them. We had been left in the dark—all of us, Palestinians included—while Arafat had been busily hammering out the details of the Oslo Accords, thus creating a permanent rift in the Arab community. Abdul Shafi told us that day, "If he [Arafat] truly wanted to preserve the interests of the Palestinians, then this is not the way to do it. What was agreed upon in Oslo clearly runs against our interests. The withdrawal that was decided should have been from all Arab territories, not just the West Bank."

Most of the world hailed Oslo as a "milestone" in the Arab-Israeli conflict. We, however, saw it as a shameful, separate peace that undermined the frame and mechanism of Madrid and ruined everything achieved since October 1991, no matter how symbolic. The talks were completed on August 20, 1993. On September 13, Mahmud Abbas, on behalf of the PLO, and Israeli foreign minister Shimon Peres signed the accords on the White House lawn. Secretary of State Warren Christopher witnessed the ceremony on behalf of the United States, along with his Russian counterpart, Andrei Kozyrev. Although invited, the Syrian delegation did not attend the signing ceremony, but our ambassador to Washington, Walid al-Mouallem, showed up along with other Arab diplomats already in the US capital. To show just how angry we were with Arafat, we did not even report the event on the 8:30 P.M. news bulletin on Syrian television. The accords provided for the creation of the Palestinian National Authority (PNA), which would administer territories under its control. The Israeli Defense Forces were required to withdraw from parts of the occupied Gaza Strip and West Bank. This arrangement would ostensibly last for a five-year interim period, after which a permanent agreement would be signed no later than May 1996. What was shocking for us as Syrians was that the issues that really mattered—Jerusalem, the right of return of Palestinian refugees, settlements, and borders—were all left to be decided at a later stage. Interim Palestinian self-government was to be granted by the Israelis to Arafat "in phases." The US media immediately began making reference to a speech by former president Bush, dated September 11, 1990, when he spoke of a "rare opportunity" to move toward "a new world order" in which "nations of the world, east and west, north and south, can prosper and live in harmony." Bush signed off, saying, "Today, the new world is struggling to be born."[29] Had we known that this was how this "new world" was going to look, we probably would never have gone to Madrid. For decades Syria had worked hard at uniting Arab positions toward Israel. In the blink of an eye, Arafat had destroyed that work, with complete disregard for the terms of reference agreed to at Madrid, which the Palestinians had approved from their PLO headquarters in Tunis.

Many attribute Arafat's decision to go to Madrid to the fallout he suffered on account of his position vis-à-vis the Gulf War, when he sided with Saddam Hussein after the invasion of Kuwait. Others argue that he was desperate to please the United States, given that with the collapse of the Soviet Union he had lost his most powerful international ally. Exiled to Tunisia after the Palestinian exodus from Lebanon in 1982, Arafat realized that his career had suffered a dramatic blow on account of the fact that he was geographically distant from Palestine and therefore unable to lead a military resistance against Israel. The 1987 intifada had made him all the more irrelevant with regard to what was happening within the Occupied Territories, as a new generation of local leaders—such as Haidar Abdul Shafi and Faisal al-Husseini—took command of the Palestinian street. By the late 1980s, it was the young stone throwers in Palestine who represented the Palestinians, not Arafat or his aged and ailing PLO. The fact that he had not been invited to Madrid added to the PLO chairman's worries; he felt that he needed to act fast to preserve his status as leader of the Palestinians. He was equally desperate for a new relationship with the United States, and when arriving at Andrews Air Force Base in September, he excitedly told the Saudi ambassador, Bandar Bin Sultan, "Andrews, Bandar! We're at Andrews!"

We were later to discover that Oslo was not born in August 1993. The handwriting had been on the wall for eight months, since December 1992, when Norwegian diplomat Terje Rød-Larsen had set up an appointment between PLO leader Ahmad Qurai and the Israeli history professor Yair Hirschfeld. The two men met fourteen times in Oslo, with the full backing of both Arafat and the Israeli government, for creative, unconventional Track II talks, away from the media. Track II of course is, when resorted to, when official diplomacy, being Track I, fails. In Track II, independents are mandated to carry out talks, with implicit backing of their governments. If they succeed, governments take over the glory, as Arafat did, whereas if they fail, they distance themselves from them, saying that they were never authorized by the state. Usually Track II diplomacy is done through academics, businessmen, and, in some cases, influential cultural figures or artists. The situation in Norway was very different from that in Washington, D.C., where Palestinian negotiators were kept in the dark and lurked in corridors because no Israelis would meet with them independently of the Jordanians. Qurai (known as Abu Alaa) was lodged at the same residence as the Israelis, where they had breakfast, lunch, and dinner at the same table. The Norwegian government covered their expenses, provided security, and kept the meetings away from the public eye, using the research institute Fafo as a front.

We were told that the Clinton White House did not know about Oslo beforehand and that Clinton's special envoy to the Middle East, Dennis Ross, had been taken completely by surprise by the news, but we never believed that—not for a minute. After signing the agreement, Arafat and Clinton sat down for a one-on-one meeting in the Map Room in the White House. Clinton told him, "Rabin cannot make further concessions until he can prove to his people that the agreement he just made with you can work. So the more quickly we can move on your track, the more quickly we will be able to move on the Syrian track."[30] Indyk remarked, "We had made no effort to conceal our intentions to pursue a deal with Syria first, and the amount of attention that Clinton and Christopher paid to Assad since coming into office may inadvertently have helped convince Arafat to do his own deal with the Israelis ahead of Syria."[31] The Americans never hesitated to play one party against the other, sending Arafat messages that a deal with Syria was around the corner in order to pressure him into making more concessions on the Palestinian track. In August 1993, Israeli foreign minister Shimon Peres wrote a letter to his Norwegian counterpart, Jørgen Holst, warning of a near-deal with Syria. The letter was intended only to move Arafat into panic mode—no such deal was in fact on the horizon with Damascus. Peres did this yet again in a conversation with Terje Rød Larsen, saying, "Israel might go for a quick deal with Syria instead of concluding an accord with the PLO." It is either Syria or the PLO, said Peres. The truth is, however, that Rabin was uninterested in peace, and when meeting Clinton in Israel on July 8, he bluntly said: "I don't think I can move on two fronts at once—that will reinforce my opposition."[32] He then added, "Assad doesn't look like he is in a hurry. Peace with Israel is not a burning issue for him."[33]

At Oslo, Arafat agreed to recognize the State of Israel and pledged to reject violence. In turn, the Israelis said they would recognize the PLO as the official representative of the Palestinian people and allow Arafat to return to the West Bank. In theory, the accords called for the withdrawal of Israeli forces from parts of the Gaza Strip and West Bank and affirmed a Palestinian right of self-government within those areas through the creation of the PNA. The jurisdiction of the Palestinian Parliament would cover the West Bank and Gaza Strip, except for issues that would be finalized in the permanent status negotiations. The two sides viewed the West Bank and Gaza as a single territorial unit. The five-year transitional period would commence with Israeli withdrawal from the Gaza Strip and Jericho. Furthermore, the two sides agreed in the 1995 Interim Agreement (signed and witnessed by the United States, the European Union, Egypt, Jordan, Russia, and Norway) on a division of their respective jurisdiction in the West Bank into areas A and B (Palestinian jurisdiction) and C (Israeli jurisdiction). This of course was an annex to the 1993 Oslo agreement. They defined the respective powers and responsibilities of each side in the areas they controlled. Israel's powers and responsibilities in Area C included all aspects regarding its settlements—all this pending the outcome of the permanent status negotiations. This division was accepted by Arafat.

The Israeli Knesset voted in favor of Oslo on September 23, 61–50, while eight members abstained. Palestinian reaction was divided. Haidar Abdul Shafi, as mentioned earlier, was furious because he considered Oslo to be a permanent break from the unified Arab negotiating strategy that had prevailed in Washington. Saeb Erekat immediately jumped onto the accords bandwagon so as to please Arafat, trying to market them as one of the finest achievements in Palestinian diplomacy. "Plenty of money is going to come into Palestinian coffers," he told us in Washington, D.C., but Abdul Shafi snapped, "The only ones [who are] going to get that [US] money are the Israelis, not us!" Other Palestinian groups, such as Hamas, Islamic Jihad, and the Popular Front for the Liberation of Palestine, immediately rejected the accords and accused Arafat of treason.

In Syria, we felt that Oslo was a catastrophe for the Arab world. It was immediately clear that nothing concrete was going to come of it—it was more of a memorandum of understanding than a peace treaty. Shortly after it was signed, Arafat visited President Assad in Latakia on September 20 to brief him in person regarding the accords. Indyk was incorrect when he said of that meeting that Assad told Arafat, "You have taken care of your interests and now we are free to take care of ours."[34] That is not true—and there is not a shred of evidence proving that President Assad uttered such words, since he regarded Oslo as a dramatic setback rather than a blessing in disguise, as Ambassador Indyk implies. I was not there; because both leaders spoke Arabic, they did not need a translator. However, President Assad later told me that he had said to

Arafat, "I will never support Oslo; that is for sure. But also I will not work against the agreement. We do believe that what you have signed is wrong because it falls short of achieving Palestinian rights and statehood. Abu Ammar [Arafat], each item in this agreement requires a separate agreement of its own!" He reportedly asked Arafat whether this interim agreement would lead to a permanent status agreement. Arafat explained that Oslo provided for permanent status negotiations to begin within three years. Assad then firmly asked, "Is Jerusalem assured?" Arafat dodged the question, saying that Israel had agreed to put Jerusalem on the agenda for the permanent status talks. In the official statement released by the Presidential Palace after the talks, Syria said that it "agrees and supports" everything decided upon by the Palestinian people.

President Assad, it must be remembered, always had his doubts about Arafat. The two men had known each other since the 1960s, and the Syrian leader considered him to be a maverick and a conniving politician who was rarely true to his word and who cared more for his personal interests than those of the Palestinians. Assad had come to his aid during a 1970 showdown in Amman between the PLO and King Hussein but fought him during the Lebanese civil war in 1976, arguing that Arafat was trying to hijack the fragile and divided Lebanese state. Explaining the lack of chemistry between the two of them to me many years later, Assad said, "I saved Arafat from three assassination attempts. In looking back, I don't know if what I did was right!" Very telling in that regard were the facts and figures coming out of Israel vis-à-vis the construction of settlements in the Palestinian Territories. The Oslo Accords stated that the settlements should come to a halt, but nevertheless Rabin continued to construct them left and right, although not as aggressively as Shamir. In 1991–1992, there were 14,320 settlements in the Palestinian Territories, but after Oslo 3,850 emerged, followed by another 3,570 in 1996–1997, both during the Rabin era. The settler population in the West Bank continued to grow by around 10,000 per year, and Arafat was unable to halt this.

In a 2001 video, Israeli prime minister Benjamin Netanyahu, apparently unaware that he was being recorded, said, "They asked me before the election if I'd honor [the Oslo Accords] . . . I said I would, but I'm going to interpret the Accords in such a way that would allow me to put an end to this galloping forward to the '67 borders. How did we do it? Nobody said what defined military zones were. Defined military zones are security zones; as far as I'm concerned, the entire Jordan Valley is a defined military zone. Go argue!"[35] Netanyahu then explained how he conditioned his signing of the 1997 Hebron agreement on US consent that there be no withdrawals from "specified military locations" and insisted he be allowed to specify which areas constituted a "military location"—such as the whole of the Jordan Valley. "Why is that important? Because from that moment on I stopped the Oslo Accords," Netanyahu affirmed.[36]

Oslo proved to us what we had been saying for years, that the Israelis were playing one party off against the other, trying to gain worldwide media attention, and were firmly uninterested in real peace with the Arabs—and certainly not with the Palestinians. They were furious with Syria's insistence that the Arabs should be represented as one delegation, both in Madrid and Washington, D.C.; with one set of demands; one objective; and one legal basis—UNSCRs 242 and 338. When James Baker came to us in September 1990, we clearly said to him that as far as Syria was concerned, the Palestinian issue remained at the core of any peace effort. What Syria wanted was frankness, coordination, and cooperation between the Arab countries. We wanted the Arabs to stand as one unified force, not as weak, divided, and helpless countries eager to grab at whatever the Israelis and Americans gave them. Our objective was comprehensive peace, and we were very keen on knowing what others were thinking, doing, and saying. Arafat, however, was uninterested in any of the above.

On September 9, Clinton got on the phone with President Assad to stress again his commitment to the Syrian track. Assad said that he was still interested but warned, "If there is no comprehensive peace, this agreement [Oslo] will not stand."[37] Clinton then gave an interview to Thomas Friedman of the *New York Times* on September 11, 1993, emphasizing that it was vital to reach peace with Syria.

In late September, Foreign Minister Shara headed to New York to attend the UN General Assembly, accompanied by Ambassador Mouallem. It was there, on October 7, 1993, that we had our first encounter with President Clinton, who had previously spoken over the phone with President Assad but had never come face-to-face with a Syrian official. Clinton's future national security adviser, Sandy Berger, was there, and so was Ambassador Indyk. The US president was clearly very proud of the Oslo Accords, whose signing he had hosted at the White House. Clinton wanted to assure Shara that Oslo would not affect the Syrian-Israeli track, reaffirming the US commitment to restore the Golan to the Syrians. At that point, we found this hard to believe. For nearly two years, the Americans had been telling us that collective peace was possible but had suddenly made a U-turn, arguing that Oslo was needed because Israel had to tackle one track at a time and could not juggle all tracks simultaneously.

Conclusion

In looking back at Oslo, twenty years after the signing of the accords and seven years after the death of Arafat, I think that both the Israelis and Americans outwitted the Palestinian leader. I don't think Arafat knew what Oslo meant for the Palestinians, or where it was going to lead them, or him. True, it restored something called "Palestinian Territories" to the world map, but the West Bank and Gaza combined are not Palestine—not even half of it. After Oslo, Arafat returned to the West Bank, where he was elected president of the PNA with an overwhelming majority. For a few years he was greeted with red carpets wherever he traveled, with Palestinian flags fluttering in the breeze. Did that really matter? His people were still denied entry into most countries around the world and were still held up at Israeli checkpoints, given that the PNA was sealed off completely by the IDF. When the second intifada broke out in September 2000, the Israelis built the Separation Barrier, in complete disregard of Oslo, massacred Palestinians in Rafah, and then arrested Arafat at his office in Ramallah for three years—ignoring the fact that he was an elected head of state. I often wondered how the world could roar for the fate of Gilad Shalit, a young Israeli corporal held hostage by Hamas, but do nothing when Arafat, an elected leader, was confined to his compound in poor health, with no water, no electricity, and no access to foreign visitors.[38] This was the fate of the man who signed Oslo, the man who stuck his neck out for the Israelis and Americans in 1993, against the will of other Arabs.

Notes

1. Archives of the Syrian Ministry of Foreign Affairs, Dispatches from the Syrian Delegation to the Washington Talks, January 13–15, 1992 (Allaf meeting with Djerejian, Ross, and Miller).
2. Ibid.
3. Ibid.
4. Ibid.
5. Archives of the Syrian Presidential Palace, Assad-Baker Correspondence, letter dated February 11, 1992, Arabic translation.
6. Ibid.
7. Ibid.

8. Unpublished Minutes of the Assad-Ross Meeting, February 12, 1992.
9. Ibid.
10. Ibid.
11. Ibid.
12. Ibid.
13. Warshaw, *The Clinton Years,* 369.
14. Unpublished Minutes of the First Assad-Christopher Meeting, February 21, 1993.
15. Ibid.
16. Archives of the Syrian Presidential Palace, Assad-Clinton Correspondence, February 1993, Arabic translation.
17. Unpublished Minutes of the First Assad-Christopher Meeting, February 21, 1993.
18. Indyk, *Innocent Abroad,* 15.
19. Ibid., 18.
20. Ibid.
21. Tucker, Spencer, *The Encyclopedia of the Arab-Israeli Conflict,* 473.
22. Indyk, *Innocent Abroad,* 18.
23. Ibid.
24. Ibid.
25. Ibid., 28.
26. Ibid.
27. Ibid., 29.
28. Indyk, *Innocent Abroad,* 21.
29. *Al-Hayat,* September 12, 1990.
30. Indyk, *Innocent Abroad,* 76.
31. Ibid.
32. Ibid., 85.
33. Ibid.
34. Indyk, 93.
35. Curtis Wong, "Netanyahu in 2001: 'America Is a Thing You Can Move Very Easily,'" *Huffington Post,* July 16, 2010.
36. Gideon Levy, "Tricky Bibi," *Haaretz,* July 15, 2010.
37. Archives of the Syrian Presidential Palace, Unpublished Assad-Clinton Correspondence, September 1993.
38. Gilad Shalit was eventually released in October 2011, having been held captive by Hamas since June 2006. In exchange for his release, Israel promised to set 1,027 Palestinian prisoners free.

4

Syria's Honeymoon with Clinton's America

DURING THE COURSE OF 1993–1994, THE PRESIDENTS OF SYRIA and the United States exchanged many letters regarding peace in the Middle East and spoke extensively over the phone. It was a period of unmatched diplomatic craftsmanship and confidence building between Damascus and Washington. As a firsthand observer, I can safely say that no such good faith ever preceded this, and nothing since has come close to matching the Assad-Clinton honeymoon. President Assad received five letters from Clinton, dated April 8, May 27, July 4, September 4, and December 2, 1993 (see Appendixes 2–5). Two historic summits ensued between the two leaders, one in Geneva in January 1994 and the other in Damascus later that year in October. Additionally, Secretary of State Warren Christopher made a total of ten visits to Syria in 1994, the first being on April 30 and the last on December 6. Dennis Ross, the chief coordinator of Clinton's Middle East policy, came to Syria twice in just under six months, on March 23 and September 20. Meanwhile, the US ambassador to Syria, Christopher Ross, became a familiar face in Damascene society. He met many businesspeople, artists, and intellectuals in the gardens of his vast mansion in the residential Rawda neighborhood, as he was eager to learn more about a country that was suddenly on everybody's radar in Washington. The Syrian elite, who expressed their fervent hope that the Clinton administration would deliver real and sustainable peace in the Arab world, courted Ross and entertained him lavishly. It should be noted that Clinton reminded Syrians of John F. Kennedy, a US president who was charismatic, young, and remembered for an even-handed policy when it came to the Middle East. Everywhere he went, Ambassador Ross heard the same fervent plea:

"Syria is fed up with war and is now eager to reach a just and comprehensive peace in the Middle East." Simply put, the country wanted the Golan Heights back, in full, to end the state of war that had dominated and haunted their lives since 1948. Ambassador Ross, like Ed Djerejian before him, blended in perfectly in Syrian society. Residents of Damascus remember his evening jogs throughout the Syrian capital, often with limited or no security, and recall how he spoke flawless Arabic, which over time acquired a Syrian accent. Locals would walk up to him and say that Damascus was safer than downtown Manhattan—a fact that he had to acknowledge. These people-to-people contacts, the long hours of talks in the upper echelons of power in Damascus, the warm and genuine correspondence that ensued, and the seriousness of all players involved created a completely new mood in Syrian-US relations. It was stronger than that which had prevailed under Presidents Nixon, Carter, and Bush, thanks to the commanding influence of President Clinton, who came across as a sincere US president who really wanted to turn over a new leaf with regard to Syria. For the first time in very many years, Syrian and US officials began to understand each other better and in some cases to sympathize with each other's concerns. The Americans who came to Syria throughout 1994 were there neither to lecture nor to dictate; they came to Damascus to listen and debate.

Mid-Morning at the Intercontinental Hotel

Shortly after the New Year, we began preparing for President Assad's high-profile visit to Switzerland. A Syrian-US summit meeting had been contemplated for almost a year now. Clinton and Assad both wanted to meet, which was very clear to all those who worked with the two presidents. It was the fourth summit between a Syrian and US president since bilateral relations had been established back in the 1940s during World War II.[1] It was also President Assad's third visit to Geneva, where he had previously met Presidents Carter and Bush. Assad often told me that he had no desire whatsoever to visit the United States as other Arab leaders had done, so long as Israel continued to occupy Arab land. Clinton respected that wish and immediately agreed to a meeting in neutral Switzerland. The meeting took place at 10:00 A.M. on January 16 at the Intercontinental Hotel on the Chemin du Petit-Saconnex Boulevard in Geneva, attended by National Security Adviser Abdel Raouf al-Kassem (a former Syrian prime minister), Foreign Minister Shara, the trusted notetaker Iskandar Luka, and myself as private interpreter to President Assad. The US delegation included Secretary of State Warren Christopher, National Security Adviser Anthony Lake, Dennis Ross, Martin Indyk, and my counterpart Gamal Helal, President Clinton's long-serving Egyptian-American interpreter.

The Syrian leader was at the apex of his career. He had survived the turbulent 1980s, including the Muslim Brotherhood conspiracy of 1982, as well as the collapse of his old ally, the Soviet Union. The Americans, who for so long had differed with his vision for the Middle East, were now knocking on his door, seeking his support for a new era in Syrian-US relations. All this implied US recognition of a paramount role for Syria in the Middle East, which had been denied by previous US presidents. Assad, then age sixty-four, had seen the rise and demise of five US administrations since coming to power in 1970. He immediately noted that President Clinton was different from any president who had preceded him—he was certainly much sharper, more charismatic, and more capable of hammering out sustainable solutions to the complex problems of Middle East politics. The two men got along brilliantly from day one. In his memoirs, *My Life*, Clinton spoke of the Geneva Summit, saying, "On our visit, I was impressed by his [Assad's] intelligence and his almost total recall of detailed events going back more than twenty years. Assad was famous for long meetings—he could go on for six or seven hours without taking a break. I, on the other hand, was tired and needed to drink coffee, tea, or water to stay awake."[2] He then adds, "Our discussion produced two things I wanted: Assad's first explicit statement that he was willing to make peace and establish normal relations with Israel, and his commitment to withdraw all Syrian forces from Lebanon and respect its independence once a comprehensive Middle East peace was reached."[3] Clinton makes note of the "personal chemistry" between him and Assad, describing Assad as "brilliant."[4] Years later, he would tell White House visitors and various players in the peace process, "This is a man who delivers and respects his word. This is a man with whom I can do business."[5]

As we walked into the meeting room, President Assad handed me a big file filled with papers and notes about the peace process, previous talks with the Americans, Lebanon, and other topics on the agenda. "Keep it with you. I might need it," he whispered. President Clinton, however, had flashcard with him, presented by his aides to help him when he was groping for ideas.

Clinton began the meeting by recounting a trip he had recently made to Europe, which included a high-profile stop in Moscow for talks with President Boris Yeltsin. "The people of Russia trust President

Yeltsin but are uncertain as to the future of Russia, especially in the upcoming century," he said. He was clearly worried about the ongoing war in Bosnia and felt responsible, as head of the world's only remaining superpower, for bringing an end to the bloodbath in the Balkans.

President Assad listened carefully to what the US president had to say and then picked up on the Balkan note. "Just look at the 500,000 Lebanese [out of 600,000] that came to Syria during the Lebanese Civil War. Just look at the Syrian sacrifices during the Lebanon War—at a time when others did not present anything to Lebanon. The fighting in Lebanon, Mr. Clinton, was more difficult and barbaric than what is happening today in Bosnia."[6] Lebanon, recently relieved of a bloody sixteen-year civil war, was a perfect introduction to the Middle East, setting the tone for the meeting of the two presidents. I took a deep breath—a brilliant show of statesmanship was just about to start.

Clinton remarked, "Mr. President, you just mentioned Lebanon. I want to stress that we support the Taif Accords [that were signed under the co-sponsorship of Syria and Saudi Arabia in 1989]. We also support a sovereign Lebanon that is free from all outside intervention." He then added, "[Yitzhak] Rabin believes that both you and the King of Jordan truly want peace. He also believes that should you so wish [given Syria's influence in Lebanon] then peace is also achievable with Lebanon. Perhaps Prime Minister Rafiq al-Hariri [who had come to power with Syria's blessing in 1992] will be strong enough to achieve that peace if he is bolstered and given adequate backing by Syria."[7]

Assad embarked on a subject about which he was continuously asked for the remainder of the 1990s: Lebanon and the dynamics of Syrian-Lebanese relations. "I have previously told Mr. Christopher that decisionmaking in Lebanon is not monopolized by any one person. The officials in Beirut, President Hrawi, the Speaker of Parliament Nabih Berri, and Prime Minister Hariri all realize, inasmuch as we do, that if Syria and Lebanon do not move together, hand-in-hand and shoulder-to-shoulder, then the Lebanese track cannot progress on its own. The issue of war and peace is a grassroots one in Lebanon that is not solely in the hands of the government. Our grassroots considerations also prevent us from moving ahead of Lebanon [on the topic of Middle East peace]." Assad then added, "As Arabs, we do not have land that is cheap and land that is precious. I cannot consider that Palestinian land is precious, or that Syrian, Jordanian, or Lebanese land is cheap."[8] Assad explained further that this was not a cliché but rather a reality based on mutual history, culture, heritage, and blood relations binding the people of the region. He noted that when the Israelis signed the Oslo Accords, "They considered that peace had been achieved in the Middle East. In reality, however, peace as we see it remains a distant reality."[9]

Clinton reaffirmed his commitment to a comprehensive peace process on all tracks. "I believe, and always have believed, in peace. Peace between Syria and Israel remains the key to achieving a just and comprehensive peace in the region." He added, "I have decided to dedicate this year to achieving a real breakthrough in the Middle East. I am going to commit my personal efforts, and those of my country, toward achieving that."[10] He noted that there should be maximum coordination of overt and covert talks on all fronts, building upon the "grand achievement" of Christopher and the Syrians since January 1993. "Rabin has reaffirmed to me [his] commitment toward complete withdrawal from the Golan."[11] The Israeli prime minister, however, could not specify the terms of his withdrawal from occupied land before knowing the depth of Syria's commitment to peace.

Several Western authors of books on Syria have written detailed accounts of Assad's extensive knowledge of history, claiming that he began all his meetings with lengthy lectures on the Crusades and Saladin before critiquing the Sykes-Picot Agreement of 1916. Although the first part of their accounts is indeed correct, the second is flawed. President Assad was indeed very well versed in history, but he only ever raised issues that were pertinent to the subject being discussed. In this meeting with Clinton, for example, he referred to the 1973 Arab-Israeli War and the disengagement agreement orchestrated by Henry Kissinger. "From everything we have experienced since then, we don't trust the Israelis. All of their alibis have collapsed, including the one that we heard for many years, being that Arabs in general and Syrians in particular are not interested in peace. Dennis Ross visited us in Damascus after the signing of Oslo and presented a variety of scenarios regarding a Syrian-Israeli track, all aimed at buying time for the Israelis while waiting for a better moment to arise for the Israeli public to digest the Gaza-Jericho agreement, a 1994 follow-up agreement to the Oslo Accords.

Ross said that the United States needed four months after signing the Palestinian track to commence on the Syrian one, and today those four months are over."[12] At this point Warren Christopher intervened, reminding everyone present at the meeting that Rabin had asked for four years to withdraw completely from the Golan "in phases." Phase I, he proposed, would see the establishment of embassies in Damascus and Tel Aviv, whereas evacuation of settlements would occur during Phase III. Assad looked up and smiled, saying, "When we agreed on disengagement in 1974, the Israelis withdrew from territory far greater than the Golan within fifteen days only!"[13] British author Patrick Seale, remembered in the West for his biography of the Syrian president, wrote at the time that Assad's strategy was to "shrink Israel's influence to more modest and less aggressive proportions."[14]

Clinton then spoke of security arrangements in the Golan, saying that should Syria and Israel agree, then the United States was willing to get involved by deploying troops on the Syrian-Israeli border.[15] He added, "Peace must be comprehensive, but each track needs to move along at the pace that it sees as suitable. There needs to be progress on both the Syrian and Lebanese fronts." Clinton also remarked, "I agree with what you have proposed, Mr. President, regarding security arrangements. They need to be satisfactory and equal to both parties. With regard to timing, Israel is a complex country where no single perspective [on peace] prevails. There is 100 percent consensus among the Israeli public vis-à-vis peace either with Syria, Jordan, Lebanon, or the Palestinians. I don't agree, however, with what you said regarding buying time for Israel in order to digest the Palestinian-Israeli agreement. I have said to Rabin that I do not wish to get involved unless a comprehensive and sustainable peace is achievable between Israel on one front, and Syria, Lebanon, Jordan, and the PLO on another. Rabin accepted what I told him and said that he actually expected peace to be signed first with Syria, despite the fact that both of you are fierce enemies of one another. Rabin told me, however, that when Hafez al-Assad gives his word, we in Israel can count on it. He honors his commitments."[16] He then revealed that Rabin "does not trust Arafat but he trusts you, Mr. President. He believes there will be no final peace in the region if Syria is not part of it or if it is not signed off by Damascus. Simply, peace will not succeed with Jordan or Lebanon if it does not succeed first with Syria. He doesn't want history to label him as an Israeli prime minister who tried and failed."[17]

Clinton then suggested, "Let us reach an agreement over initial principles on the bilateral track, and let the United States be the party with whom these principles are deposited. This agreement, which will be dated and agreed upon by both you and Rabin, will remain secret until both Syria and Israel agree the time is right to make it public. There should be no ambiguity in such a track, as [was] the case in Norway. The Palestinians and Israelis are still paying a high price for the ambiguity of Oslo. We don't want to commit the same mistakes made by the previous [Bush] administration. Should you agree, what would be your strategy?"[18] Clinton was clearly saying that he had Rabin's pledge to withdraw from the Golan in one pocket and wanted to fill the other with a Syrian pledge on normalization and security arrangements. He then asked Assad for a "public and bold declaration," aimed at greasing the wheels of the peace process, and also inquired how he envisioned the final outcome of a Syrian-Israeli peace agreement. "You don't have to commit yourself to anything; it would be only a vision, not an agreement. If you mention something that is new, it would open windows of opportunity for the peace process. That way I will be able to say more and give more than what other Americans have said or done; that way I can be more supportive and more just."[19] Clinton, of course, was clearly referring to what has since been famously dubbed the "Rabin Deposit," in which he pledged to withdraw from the Golan, in full, up to the borders of June 4, 1967.

Getting carried away by his own suggestions, Clinton even proposed that President Assad should meet with Rabin—fully aware, perhaps, that the Syrian leader was going to refuse. "If such a meeting does indeed take place," said Assad, "there would no longer be a peace process. No Syrian would be able to understand or accept their president meeting with Rabin at a time when Israel continues to occupy Syrian land. We have half a million Syrians in Damascus alone who were displaced from the Golan. They are waiting for the day when they can return to their towns and villages, Mr. Clinton. A head of state, after all, no matter how powerful, cannot sign peace on his own without the consent of his people."[20] The sparkle in Assad's eyes seemed to connote certain sympathy for Clinton, a sympathy that seemed to suggest that he was aware that Clinton was asking for the impossible. "Poor Clinton. He actually thinks I will meet Yitzhak Rabin before any peace is achieved between us and Israel!"

Clinton concluded the meeting on a positive note, deciding to build upon what was achieved rather than what wasn't, with his Syrian counterpart. There was optimism in the air, and both he and Assad could feel it. The peace process was indeed about to move forward, and so were bilateral Syrian-US relations. The US president then raised a number of last-minute issues, apparently less crucial to him at the time than peace in the Middle East: drug trafficking in the Bekaa Valley, terrorism, human rights, the long-held Arab boycott of Israel, and the travel ban on the community of 1,500 Syrian Jews who wanted to travel abroad. A handful of them had been allowed to leave Syria after the first Gulf War, and now Clinton was asking Assad to allow those who remained in Syria to leave.

Assad promised to act immediately regarding the last topic, instructing the Interior Ministry to grant travel permits to any Syrian Jew wishing to leave the country. They would be required to give only a few days notice to the ministry rather than seven months, as had previously been requested by Syrian authorities.[21] President Assad then suggested that Secretary of State Warren Christopher and Foreign Minister Shara create follow-up committees to deal with all the other bilateral issues. He reminded Clinton that Muslims frown upon the cultivation, sale, and use of drugs in all their forms "because they are prohibited by our society and religion, both spiritually and morally."[22]

As the meeting ended, both delegations began preparing to break for recess. President Assad looked at the big file sitting on the table, which he had given me three hours previously. Smiling, he said, "Oh, gosh, we forgot to consult the papers!"

Mother Diplomacy

The two presidents then went into a closed session, where I served as interpreter, before holding a joint press conference in the ballroom of the Intercontinental Hotel, where the world's press was tightly packed. In private, President Assad paid his condolences to President Clinton for the death of his mother, Virginia Cassidy Kelley, who had died at the age of seventy ten days earlier on January 6. Assad's own mother had also recently passed away, and the two men found plenty to talk about when it came to their mothers. Clinton, who famously was very close to his mother (referring to her with a capital "M" as Mother in his memoirs), replied, "The death of one's mother is a great reminder of one's own mortality." Assad agreed, almost tearfully remembering his own mother, Mrs. Nuessi, and how she had traveled with her sons from the village of Qardaha to the port city of Latakia in the 1930s, where they attended school. "She used to rent a room in Latakia in order to take care of us, making sure that all of us studied well, did our homework, got to sleep early, and woke up on time for school. She was a formidable and remarkable woman indeed!" Assad's mother had lived to witness his own successful career, first as an air force officer, then as defense minister, and finally as president of the Republic. She died of old age in the early 1990s, shortly after the first Gulf War, and Assad had named a grand mosque after her in Qardaha. Both presidents were apparently very grateful to their mothers and so fond of them that they forgot about peace and started to speak about the role of mothers in particular and women in general. Assad then looked at me, perhaps suddenly remembering that I too was a proud mother of two children. He thoughtfully noted,

"Bouthaina is also a writer. She has written a book in English." He was referring to my book *Both Right and Left Handed: Arab Women Talk About Their Lives*, which I had published in the UK in 1988 and in the United States in 1991. I had already presented President Assad with an autographed copy, and President Clinton remarked, "I too would love to have a copy, Bouthaina." I nodded, very proud of the conversation taking place about me and the fact that the presidents of both Syria and the United States were interested in my book. "Please send him a copy, Bouthaina," said President Assad. (Upon returning to Damascus, I did just that, and shortly thereafter received a thank-you letter from the White House, signed by President Clinton.) While all this "mother" talk was taking place, I could not help but think that all the journalists beyond the closed doors must be wondering what on earth the two presidents were discussing in this room. Nobody would believe that it had nothing to do with peace, security, and borders, but rather with motherhood and the morality of strong leaders. I had to remember that even the most powerful of men were human and had a soft heart.

Assad and Clinton finally walked out into the ballroom, both looking very satisfied, and were perceived as such even by Clinton's own peace team, who were watching from a distance, wreathed in big smiles. The US delegation had spent the night preparing for the press conference and had been cautious about how many Israeli journalists would be allowed to attend, in order to be careful not to offend President Assad. The US team sat in the front row with the Syrian delegation, while I rushed into the translation cabin to continue with my job. In his memoirs, *Innocent Abroad*, Martin Indyk captured the Kodak moment, saying, "We, too, thought we had reason to be satisfied. Our Israeli friends had told us on the Summit's eve that the one thing they would be listening for, as a sign of Assad's intentions, was whether he would speak about normalizing relations with Israel."[23] When it was his turn to speak, President Assad cleared his throat and with a loud, booming voice, said in Arabic: "Syria seeks a just and comprehensive peace with Israel as a strategic choice. We want the peace of the brave, a genuine peace which can survive and last. If the leaders of Israel have sufficient courage to respond to this kind of peace, a new era of security and stability with normal peaceful relations for all shall dawn anew."[24]

It was then time for questions from the media. Barry Schweid of the *Associated Press* spoke first, addressing his question to President Clinton. He asked whether Assad's words meant open borders, free trade, and diplomatic relations with Israel. Clinton responded firmly, saying, "Yes, I believe President Assad has made a clear, forthright, and very important statement on normal relations."[25] CNN's Wolf Blitzer repeated the same question. Assad smiled, saying that he and Clinton had "completely agreed" on the requirements of peace. "We will respond to these requirements," he added.[26] The Clinton team then met separately with the US journalists to make sure they understood how significant Assad's words had been and what they meant for Middle East peacemaking.

Clinton immediately dispatched Martin Indyk and Dennis Ross to Israel to brief Yitzhak Rabin on his meeting with Assad. Unlike the United States, the Israelis were furious about the breakthrough in Syrian-US relations. The Israeli newspaper *Haaretz* headlined that Prime Minister Rabin "wiped the smiles off their faces."[27] Indyk recalled the cold shoulder he received in Israel, saying: "If the President [Clinton] embraced something Assad had offered, Israelis immediately felt pressured rather than reassured. Since Assad had made a concession, they now expected they would have to do the same and so immediately devalued what we brought from Geneva."[28] Both Rabin and the Israeli press aggressively tried to downplay the Syrian-US summit, arguing that by insisting on a comprehensive track, Assad was throwing dust in the eyes of the peacemakers. "I cannot buy anything if it's linked to Jordan," Rabin told the Americans.[29] "I prefer [signing peace with] Jordan—it complements the Palestinians."[30] Desperate for an exit strategy from making peace with Syria, he began pushing for a Jordanian-Israeli peace, given that King Hussein was about to travel to Washington, D.C., to meet with Clinton.

Secret talks between Jordan and Israel had already commenced in London during the second week of December 1993, but they were more focused on bilateral issues, ranging from sharing water and returning territory to displaced Palestinians living in Jordan. King Hussein had actually visited Damascus in November 1993 and had assured President Assad that Jordan would "never" go ahead and sign a separate deal with the Israelis without taking into account Syrian concerns in the peace process. But the assurance, of course, was never validated. Rabin noted: "I would prefer the President ask the King: are you ready to sign with Israel or not? If there is any option to go with Jordan, then *forget* about Syria."[31] He was also unhappy with Clinton pressuring him to fully withdraw from the Golan: "You committed us to full withdrawal but it doesn't stand on its own. If I lose this bargaining chip, I am crippled. This is the problem when you are working with a mediator. I put it in a context, but when you convey it, the context gets lost and you undermine my bargaining power."[32] He then told the United States bluntly,

"You look at it from your point of view, and I look it at from my point of view." Rabin's chief of general staff Ehud Barak, however, who had always lobbied for a deal with Syria prior to a deal with the Palestinians, claiming that he could never trust Yasser Arafat, did not share this negativity. He thought that Clinton and Assad had made "an important and impressive" breakthrough in Geneva and tried to build upon it when he eventually came to power in July 1999.[33]

Back in Geneva, the moment we finished the press conference, I gathered my papers and rushed out of the translation cabin and up to my room to pack my belongings. I had been told that we were immediately heading back to Damascus. As I approached the lift, President Assad was already inside, together with the commander of the Syrian Republican Guard, Adnan Makhlouf. "We are ready to leave, Mr. President," said the latter, totally disregarding the fact that I was exhausted and still very unready for travel. I had spent the last five hours undertaking the translation at the conference, while the logistics team in the Syrian delegation had been sitting around sipping coffee and tea. I had not slept for almost forty-eight hours. So I looked up at Makhlouf and said: "But I am not ready!"

Always the gentleman, President Assad chuckled and patted me on the shoulder, saying, "Don't worry, Bouthaina, we would never leave Switzerland without you!"

The Fallen Knight of Damascus

One week after we returned from Geneva, tragedy struck in Damascus. On Friday, January 21, 1994, President Assad's oldest son, Republican Guard officer and horseback-riding champion Basel al-Assad, died in a car crash on the foggy road to Damascus International Airport. The Damascus University–trained engineer was only thirty-four. Basel was very popular in Syria, having championed computer literacy through the Syrian Computer Society and having become an iconic figure for young Syrians with his reformist policies and athletic record, both as a parachutist and horseback champion. Although it was a weekend, the president was scheduled to receive a US congressional delegation early that morning. I got up early to prepare myself for the meeting but received a phone call from the palace saying that it had been postponed. There were no more details. Strange, I thought to myself, because it was very unlike President Assad to postpone or cancel a scheduled meeting with such short notice. I got dressed and waited for a second call, which came shortly afterward. It was not the Presidential Palace on the other end of the line but Higher Education Minister Salha Sankar. She asked me to visit her at the ministry, but I apologized, saying that I had a meeting with the president. "There is not going to be a meeting with the president, Bouthaina," she said calmly. Upon hearing her words I was horrified, thinking that something dreadful must have happened to President Assad. I immediately rushed to the ministry in Mezzeh with a million thoughts racing through my head. All of them were bad, and I expected the worst, but I did not for a moment imagine that something had happened to any of the president's children. Sankar welcomed me with a frozen expression on her face and then said, "Basel al-Assad has just died in a car crash." As she slowly muttered those words, a nearby mosque made the announcement public, and it echoed through the empty streets of Damascus because it was a Friday. It vibrated strongly through my head. I couldn't believe what I was hearing. He was such a fine young man, well mannered, intelligent, and with a very high profile. He had died so suddenly, seemingly for a most irrelevant reason. He wasn't sick; he suffered from no terminal illness; he hadn't died in battle or because he'd suffered some terrible sports injury. His death was because of heavy fog on the airport highway; it was such an ugly way for a person to die. All I could think of at that moment were his poor mother and father. They must have been devastated beyond belief. From Salha Sankar's office I headed to the Assad residence to pay my respects to the president.

 I had met Basel only occasionally, but his older sister Bushra, a pharmacologist, was a very dear friend of mine. In fact, I considered her a sister, notwithstanding my working relationship with her father. It was my duty to be by her side during that fateful morning. Apart from the misery and sobbing of weeping women, what I recall most vividly is the image of President Assad walking up the stairs into the family home, supporting his grief-stricken wife, Mrs. Anissa Makhlouf. He seemed to have aged ten years since the last time I saw him, only a few days earlier. Only one week previously, Hafez al-Assad had been a proud president in Geneva, courting Bill Clinton while skillfully playing the delicate game of power politics that he had mastered in the Middle East. He was powerful, strong, patient, and immutable when it came to Syria's rights within the international community. Now the "Lion of Damascus," as the Western world often labeled him, had suddenly been transformed into a bereaved father who had lost his favorite son. It is very hard indeed to understand how difficult it is to lose a son during the golden years of his life. Usually children bury their parents; it is highly unusual for parents to bury their children. I stood in the corner with Bushra, not entirely sure of what to say or do in the circumstances. I then walked up to the president and his wife and expressed my condolences. President Assad shook my hand but did not say a word. I kissed the first lady, and she looked up at me from behind her tears and muttered words that reflected her inner thoughts, "No, not Basel. I love all of my children, but Basel is different . . ." She was speaking to herself, not to me, Bushra, or the president.

We spent the day at the president's residence, shouldering the tragedy with his family, and then headed to Qardaha, their home village, the following morning to attend the massive funeral. In addition to the hundreds of thousands of mourners in Damascus and Latakia, the funeral was attended by Arab leaders such as President Elias Hrawi, Prime Minister Rafiq al-Hariri, Speaker of Parliament Nabih Berri, the Jordanian crown prince Hasan Ibn Talal, and Egyptian president Husni Mubarak. Many would recall how, when ascending the steps of the airplane that was to transfer Basel's coffin to Qardaha, President Assad walked up to the cockpit and waved to the masses from the tiny window. "Be brave," he seemed to be saying, "be strong and keep the faith, because this is the desire of God Almighty." This man had just lost his son yet still had the good sense to act as leader of his people.

For the next seven days, we observed a mourning period in Qardaha, as is the custom in Islamic countries. President Assad spent many hours receiving condolences from state dignitaries and would then sit by himself alone. It was not easy, I would often say to myself, being constantly reminded of Basel with photographs, songs, programs on television, and giant posters plastered on the walls of every city throughout Syria. At one point a group of athletes who had trained with Basel marched by the Assad residence on horseback in silence, paying their respects to the fallen knight. Assad stood watching the parade, where every horse had its jockey except for Basel's Arabian horses, which had been draped in black. I was horrified by how inconsiderate and inappropriate the entire ordeal seemed to be; hadn't this man and his wife had enough misery and anguish? Why remind them over and over again of the tragedy that had just hit their family?

One day Bushra came to me and said: "Please go to the sitting room where my father is as he is going to receive a phone call from President Clinton." I was shocked to see the small, simple room that looked so much like my sitting room in my humble apartment. I said, "Is this where you sit all day, Mr. President?" He looked up at me quietly with a sad yet firm expression, as if to say, "Where should I sit? What is wrong with this room?" Then he gently answered my question, saying, "Bouthaina, in this world, one can concentrate on one of two things: either houses and money, or work. I chose to concentrate on my work." I never forgot this statement. A few years later I voiced an opinion that he seemed to like, and he said to me, "You seem to have concentrated on your work," and then winked at me as a reminder of what he had said to me on that sad day. That was a supreme compliment gifted to me by President Hafez al-Assad, and I always bear in mind the choice I made of concentrating on my work rather than on houses or material things.

Clinton briefly mentioned this episode in his memoirs. "When I called to express my condolences, Assad was obviously heartbroken, a reminder that the worst thing that can happen in life is losing a child."[34]

Notes

1. During the short-lived United Arab Republic (1958–1961), Gamal Abdul Nasser had traveled to the United States in his capacity as president of both Syria and Egypt and met President Dwight D. Eisenhower. Before that, the US government had canceled a scheduled meeting between former Syrian president Shukri al-Quwatli and Franklin D. Roosevelt in 1945.
2. Clinton, *My Life*, 574–575.
3. Ibid.
4. Ibid., 574.
5. Personal conversation with President Assad, September 1994.
6. Archives of the Syrian Presidential Palace, Unpublished Minutes of the Assad-Clinton Meeting, January 15–16, 1994.
7. Ibid.
8. Ibid.
9. Ibid.
10. Ibid.
11. Ibid.
12. Ibid.
13. Ibid.
14. Seale, "Assad's Regional Strategy and the Challenge from Netanyahu," *Journal of Palestinian Studies* 26, no. 1 (Fall 1997): 36. See also Rabinovich, *The Brink of Peace*, 244–245.
15. Archives of the Syrian Presidential Palace, Unpublished Minutes of the Assad-Clinton Meeting, January 15–16, 1994.
16. Ibid.
17. Ibid.
18. Ibid.
19. Ibid.
20. Ibid.
21. Personal conversation with President Assad, September 1994.

22. Archives of the Syrian Presidential Palace, Unpublished Minutes of the Assad-Clinton Meeting, January 15–16, 1994.
23. Indyk, *Innocent Abroad*, 104.
24. *Tishreen*, January 17, 1994.
25. Indyk, *Innocent Abroad*, 105.
26. Ibid.
27. *Haaretz*, June 18, 1994.
28. Indyk, *Innocent Abroad*, 107.
29. Ibid.
30. Ibid.
31. Ibid.
32. Indyk, 108.
33. Personal conversation with President Assad, September 1994.
34. Clinton, *My Life*, 575.

5

The Deposit That Never Was

WITHIN DAYS AFTER BASEL'S FUNERAL HAD TAKEN PLACE AND condolences had poured in, President Assad was back at work, both mentally and physically. Every morning he was behind his office desk at 8:00 A.M., conducting back-to-back meetings that lasted as long as it took to get the business done, sometimes well into the late hours of the night. He would often spend hours on end without a single interruption, even forgetting to take a lunch break, with his wife having to call him to remind him to eat.

On February 10, 1994, less than one month after the horrific accident, he received a delegation of US Congressmen at the Presidential Palace in Damascus. I remember how, when one guest clasped his hand to pay his respects, the president's face froze, almost as though he were in a trance. It was as if he had suddenly been reminded of the agony of what had happened in his personal life, which he had tried to bury beneath piles of paperwork, to no avail. Every day, in one way or another, reality would creep back to remind him that he had just lost a son, and life was never the same for him without Basel. The president gently said to his guest, "This is God's will and there is nothing we can do. Life and death are not in our hands. In my life I have often helped save the lives of people's children, but when it came to my own child, I was able to do nothing!" He looked very uncomfortable saying this and wanted to change the subject immediately.

I think that had it not been for numerous Arab and foreign guests flying in and out of Damascus during those early months of 1994, it would have been even more difficult for him to get over the devastating trauma of losing Basel. But, just as he said, life does indeed go on, ei-

Bouthaina Shaaban (left) with President Hafez al-Assad and Foreign Minister Farouk al-Shara, welcoming foreign ambassadors to Damascus in the mid-1990s.

ther with or without our loved ones, and there was urgent business to take care of: a peace process that needed attending to and occupied land waiting to be retrieved.

Dennis Ross returned to Syria in February with a photograph of the presidents of Syria and the United States in Geneva, dated January 16, 1994. A bulky signature graced the photograph: "With my warm and best regards, Bill Clinton." President Assad took the thoughtful souvenir from Ross with a smile and then handed it to me. Ross said, "Mr. President, you don't know how forthcoming President Clinton is toward you." The president smiled yet again—he had recently spoken with Clinton over the phone. "He never stays on the phone with anybody as long as he does with you," Ross added almost warmly (I say "almost" because, in fact, it was difficult to see Ross warming to any issue).

According to the US envoy, Clinton had recently told his aides, "This is a man I can and want to work with!" When discussing Syria that February, Rabin had said something similar to Clinton: "What I like about Assad is that he honors his word and delivers." Ross conveyed Rabin's attitude toward the Syrian leader to the president, saying, "He respects leaders who are tough and straightforward. Even before we began the negotiations, he had a great deal of respect for you, Mr. President, saying that you are tough but true to your word." When writing about Rabin's view of Assad a few years later, Ross added, "Rabin believed that reaching any agreement with Assad would be extraordinarily difficult, but if reached, Assad would live up to it, just as he had with the 1974 [disengagement] agreement."[1]

After initial pleasantries, followed by some updates about the Gaza-Jericho agreement, Dennis Ross got down to business, saying: "Rabin is ready to withdraw from the Golan."[2] Ross often tried to come across as more knowledgeable than his colleagues, privy to information from Tel Aviv that nobody else enjoyed—not even President Clinton himself. Although we regarded Clinton as a genuine friend and honest broker, we always felt that Ross considered himself "Israel's man" and therefore found it difficult to take a fair stance toward us.

Seeing that President Assad was completely unmoved by his comment, Ross went on: "Full withdrawal, Mr. President. Full withdrawal in exchange for full peace! This is new; we have never heard Rabin say this before."[3] President Assad stared at Ross with a stony expression on his face, waiting to hear something more substantial from the US diplomat. After all, he had heard all this before—only too often.

Ross took a deep breath and said, "Rabin is going to formulate a suggestion within the next two weeks and leave it with us. His proposal is going to be *very* important!"[4]

Assad looked up at him and, after a pause, finally said, "Very good. When it is ready, we are ready to listen to what Rabin has to offer."[5] Assad was not trying to belittle the offer—far from it. He appreciated what was being said but wasn't going to commit himself to anything until he understood precisely what Rabin's offer was going to be. Ross tried to get the president to reciprocate with a similar statement of goodwill, but the Syrian president refused to say another word until the Americans conveyed in detail what was on Yitzhak Rabin's mind.

The Hebron Massacre

The momentum for peace in the Middle East suffered a heavy blow—almost ruining the entire Geneva Summit—on Friday, February 25, 1994. An Israeli settler named Baruch Goldstein, dressed in the military reserve uniform of the IDF, took a machine gun, went into a mosque in Hebron, and opened fire on unarmed Palestinians during morning prayers. Twenty-nine of them were shot dead in cold blood before Goldstein himself was killed by angry worshipers. It was no surprise that the peace process once again came to a grinding halt. There was outrage in Arab capitals, from Ramallah and Beirut to Cairo and Damascus. Now nobody in their right mind could take the Israelis—or the Americans—seriously. To continue to talk peace after the Hebron massacre would have been political suicide for any Arab leader. President Assad condemned the killings and declared that peace talks should be suspended until further notice. Clinton immediately dispatched his peace team, Aaron David Miller, Martin Indyk, Daniel Kurtzer, and Dennis Ross, to meet with Arafat in Tunisia. A furious Arafat outlined a long list of demands: an international presence in Hebron to protect the Palestinians, the deployment of Palestinian police, and the evacuation of forty-five Jewish settlers from Tel Rumeida in the heart of Hebron. He then asked for a UN Security Council Resolution condemning the massacre—fully aware of how sensitive the United States was about the disapproval of Israel's actions at the UN. "We are not asking for the moon," Arafat angrily snarled at the Americans. Indyk wrote, "The Clinton Administration had a severe allergy to dealing with the Palestinian issue at the Security Council. There, in the spotlight of international public opinion, the Palestinians as the underdog would always enjoy a majority, and the United States would always stand in the dock alongside Israel."[6] Washington, however, called up Arafat shortly after the meeting in Tunis, telling him "in no uncertain terms" that the United States would veto any resolution against Israel at the United Nations.

Clinton then came up with the idea of seeking Assad's help. He thought that if Syria would agree to return to the negotiating table—after some of Arafat's demands had been met—then probably the PLO would sluggishly follow suit. To make that happen, Clinton told Assad that he was willing to abstain from, rather than veto, the proposed UN resolution. The US president called up Damascus to discuss the idea directly with President Assad and then hurriedly dispatched Warren Christopher to the Middle East. Clinton was asking Syria for a favor, and in good faith President Assad acted accordingly, discussing the matter with King Hussein and Lebanese president Elias Hrawi. Assad asked them to give Clinton the benefit of the doubt. The two men agreed to Assad's request, and the White House announced that thanks to Syria, peace negotiations between the Arabs and Israelis were going to resume, as promised to the Syrian leader in Switzerland.

The Rabin Deposit

On April 30, the American delegation returned to Damascus, this time headed by Warren Christopher. They arrived at the palace early in the morning on May 1 with the famous Rabin Deposit. This deposit, Christopher explained, was based on the Egyptian example of 1978 and built on previous common ground reached in Geneva between Assad and Clinton. Among other things, it included the dismantling of settlements in the Golan and full withdrawal in three stages, which would take place over a five-year period. It listed security arrangements, early warning stations managed by the United States, and demilitarized zones. In exchange for peace, Rabin wanted open borders, an end to the boycott, free movement of people between the two countries, trade, tourism, the safeguarding of Israel's water supplies, and, of course, full diplomatic relations between Damascus and Tel Aviv. Rabin wanted "the depth of full withdrawal to reflect the depth of full peace." The agreement, we were told, would not be related to the Palestinian peace track and would be kept strictly confidential among Syria, Rabin, and the Clinton administration. The deposit did not say whether by "full withdrawal" Rabin was referring to the international borders of 1923 or the June 4, 1967, border that Syria had stressed at the Madrid Peace Conference. The two borders, after all, are very different. The Israelis were also seeking both secret and public diplomacy, similar to Anwar al-Sadat's diplomacy on his visit to Israel in 1977—to which President Assad was clearly not going to commit. "First we get our land back," he said, "and then we talk about everything else. How can I convince my people of the need to engage in any public diplomacy with the Israelis when they are still occupying the Golan?"[7]

The Israeli proposal included several points that deserve elaboration. In Phase I of the withdrawal, Israel troops and settlers would retreat to the "first defense lines, 2-3-4 miles from the disengagement line." Phase I would be a limited withdrawal that did not include the dismantling of settlements or setup of early warning stations. In Phase II, Israel suggested withdrawing to the middle of the Golan while dismantling "some of the settlements."[8] Rabin proposed that Phase III would involve full withdrawal from the Golan.[9] In his memoirs, *Chances of a Lifetime*, Secretary Warren Christopher wrote about his meeting with Assad when the Rabin Deposit was delivered that winter, saying, "From meeting to meeting, there were virtually no deviations in the routine, and no surprises, pleasant or otherwise. When he chose to talk substance, Assad's message—delivered, repeated, and reinforced—was clear. He wasn't going to begin negotiating until Rabin committed to full Israeli withdrawal from the Golan Heights. He was telling us the Israelis would have no secure peace, prosperity, or existence unless they met his non-negotiable demand."[10] After delivering the deposit, Christopher recalled, "I thought I detected a thin smile on Assad's face, but his only verbal response was a series of nitpicking questions and contentious pronouncements that I tried to answer without displaying my irritation."[11]

Christopher had first heard of the Rabin Deposit in August 1993 when, during a visit to Tel Aviv, he had been called into the prime minister's office for a closed meeting. Dennis Ross and the Israeli ambassador, Itamar Rabinovich, were both present when Rabin asked the secretary of state to pose a hypothetical question to President Assad: "What was Syria willing to do in exchange for Israel's full withdrawal from the Golan?"[12] According to Christopher, the questions included: "Was Assad willing to sign a stand-alone treaty with Israel, i.e., one without linkage to the Jordanian and Palestinian negotiating tracks? Was he willing to join in personal and public diplomacy to reassure the Israeli public of Syria's commitment to peace, including a meeting with Rabin? Was he willing to agree to a five-year timetable for Israel's full withdrawal from the Golan, with incremental normalization of relations between the two countries, such as exchange of diplomats, as the withdrawal progressed?"[13] Additionally, the Israelis wanted a new set of talks to start in the United States, where their ambassador Rabinovich would meet with our ambassador Mouallem, with Dennis Ross also participating. President Assad's argument against this tripartite committee, delivered in 1994, was the following: "If Rabin cannot solve this problem, then surely neither Barak nor Rabinovich can. Why delegate this work to less senior officials when Israel's top command cannot manage it?"[14] It should also be mentioned that when all this was conveyed to us in Damascus, no mention whatsoever was made of the various Palestinian factions that existed in Syria. In the years to come, when the negotiations entered murky waters, the Israelis and the Americans used this card as a pretext to accuse Syria of hampering the process. But as far as they were concerned, in 1993–1994 Hamas, Islamic Jihad, and the Popular Front for the Liberation of Palestine were not on their priority list when it came to trying to achieve peace with Syria.

Hafez al-Assad seemed not to be impressed by the deposit. Although he appreciated its importance, he did not see it as groundbreaking or great as the Americans thought it was. He saw many loopholes in all the suggestions, such as Rabin's request that Syria be divided into four districts: a demilitarized zone with no troops, a second zone with limited troops, a third with limited troops deep into Syrian territory, and a fourth zone with no limitation on the number of troops. The president sarcastically remarked: "You want to give us the Golan and occupy all of Syria instead? This means that disarmament would reach as far inland as Homs."[15] The suggestion seemed to have one objective, which was to reduce the power of the Syrian army. Assad then said: "You are talking about peace with the mentality of war. When we reach peace—

if it is genuine—none of these measures would be necessary."[16] Additionally, he did not like the term "normalization," instead preferring to use "normal peaceful relations," a term he had insisted upon since the launch of the Madrid peace process three years earlier. Christopher suggested keeping an early warning station on Mount Hermon and proposed that we keep one as well in occupied Safad. Assad, however, was unimpressed with the suggestion: "We don't want an early warning station in Safad—or in Mount Hermon. Just dismantle the one you already have and there would be no need for any other!"[17]

In looking back at the Rabin Deposit, I feel the need to comment on how the language of peace has deteriorated. In 1994, the Israelis were talking about "dismantling settlements." By the late 1990s, this had become "freezing settlements." At the turn of the twenty-first century, the same issue was discussed in terms of "slowing down the building of settlements." Then, in 2009–2010, the matter became "halting settlements for three months." Now in 2011, they are talking about "not building new settlements."

The main point that Christopher and Ross were trying to make was that Israeli public opinion was not convinced of Syria's readiness to achieve peace and was asking for something in return for the Rabin Deposit. US officials were seemingly more interested in publicity—giving an interview to an Israeli newspaper, for example, or allowing an Israeli journalist to visit Syria—than they were in substance. They always spoke as if Syrian public opinion didn't really matter. Because Hafez al-Assad was who he was, they believed he could make any decision he wanted, without first consulting with the Syrian people. That struck a particularly raw nerve with the Syrian president, who, clearly irritated, snapped back: "You are supposed to be honest brokers, speaking for both sides!" Assad was equally disturbed by Rabin's proposed five-year timetable for withdrawal and dismantling of settlements. "The Golan is a very small area," he said. "They don't need years. That's for sure."[18] Assad believed withdrawal could be achieved in thirty days. In one meeting with Warren Christopher, he said, "When we worked on the armistice agreement after the war of 1973, it took no more than fifteen days to complete. Why should withdrawal now require up to five years?"[19] Christopher, of course, did not have an answer to this, except to say that the 1974 disengagement agreement was limited and interim, whereas withdrawal from the Golan would be "final and total." President Assad ordered sandwiches and lemonade for his guest and advised him to sleep on it, visit Palmyra for some sightseeing, and then meet again the following day to discuss the subject further.

Twenty-four hours later, our response to the Rabin Deposit was ready, having been hammered out during the night by President Assad, in consultation with the army chief of staff Hikmat al-Shihabi, Defense Minister Mustapha Tlass, and Foreign Minister Farouk al-Shara. President Assad—contrary to what the Americans thought—was a very consensual leader who was very careful to consult with his top officials before reaching a strategic decision of such magnitude. The Syrian response was written on a piece of paper that President Assad read from. "Usually I don't read from a paper, but today I will. Of course, these are just ideas and suggestions; they are non-binding, but they reflect what is seen as in Syria's best national interest." The president put on his glasses and slowly began to read in Arabic, and I followed with the English translation: "Syria expresses satisfaction with the proposal of Prime Minister Rabin for the full withdrawal from all territories occupied by Israel, up to the borders of June 4, 1967." He welcomed the dismantling of settlements but questioned what borders were being referred to by Rabin. Were they the 1923 or 1967 borders? The time frame, he added, "should not exceed six months after the signing of the peace treaty." He then spoke of security arrangements, saying, "Each party should be able to avoid surprise attacks and have arrangements for self-defense. Syria is satisfied with the fact that Israel considers that these arrangements should be mutual. What happens on the Syrian front should be parallel to the Israeli one, in both land and arrangements. Equality is the key to success in any peace agreement, and has to be parallel and exact on both sides. No security measures should be taken for one side at the expense of the security or territorial integrity of the other."[20] He added that any deal would need "international guarantees that embody the will of the international community" in order to serve as "an important deterrent against any party that thinks of launching an attack on the other."[21] He said that Syria would agree to allow UN peacekeepers to patrol both sides of the border and that both Syria and Israel would have to agree on the mission, nationalities, size, and armaments of the UN forces. They would also have to agree on how long these forces would be mandated to remain on both sides of the Syrian-Israeli border.

President Assad then glanced quickly at his guests to see how they were reacting to his words and continued: "Syria sees no need for early warning stations once peace is signed. The presence of international forces is enough to ensure the security of both sides. Syria is ready to consider a joint military commission with the supervision of international forces to see the implementation of agreed security." He ended by saying, "Syria is also willing to work for a Middle East that is free from all nuclear, biological, and chemical weapons, and this has to apply to both the Arabs and Israel." Once peace was signed, he added, "the two sides agree to establish diplomatic relations on the basis of mutual letters between them, which would be an appendix to the actual peace treaty. We will do that after peace is achieved absolutely." He then summarized as follows: "The first phase starts the day the final peace agreement is signed. And it will end within six months. The area from which the withdrawal will take place will be specified. During this period, the Syrian committee is willing to implement the following: put an end to the state of war, with both sides acknowledging the sovereignty and territorial integrity of each other; end the economic boycott from the second and third degree; and pledge to participate in multilateral negotiations. The second stage will end with a full Israeli withdrawal to the 1967 borders, within the next six months.[22] The two sides will adopt confidence-building measures to prepare the appropriate climate for a just and comprehensive peace in the region."

Silence fell in the room as the Americans tried to digest what the Syrian president had just said. "Thank you Mr. President," Christopher said finally, "but it is already clear to me that your answer is not going to be readily accepted by Rabin."[23] The golden phrase used by Ross was: "We have proposed things, they have proposed things, and you have proposed things. Nothing is agreed upon until everything is agreed upon." Assad immediately added, "By the way, you cannot say anything to Rabin unless you are 100 percent certain that he has offered the June 4, 1967 borders."[24] When writing about the meeting in his memoir, *The Missing Peace*, Dennis Ross said that President Assad had been "cautious" about rushing into a deal with the Israelis that did not secure all of Syria's rights.[25] He was "mindful as the last true Arab nationalist that his deal—if there was to be one—had to reflect that Syria was not defeated. Syria must recover all its land. Having held out, he wanted to get what Egypt got—full withdrawal—and wanted to give less. He wanted to show that he could do better than Egypt. Moreover, Israel must neither gain nor be seen as gaining from the agreement—other than Assad's offering them an end to the conflict."[26] The president of Syria, he added, "was dead-set against giving anything away. Everything must be part of a deal." Ross described why Assad was such a skilled negotiator: "No detail in our discussion could be ever too small. He saw discussion as a kind of sport. Negotiations were an exercise in attrition. He could always hold out longer. He was never in a hurry. He was content to live without an agreement, especially if this agreement would not meet his standards of dignity and honor. He would never let anyone get the best of him in any way."[27]

Ross also referred to the famous 1915 correspondence between the prince of Mecca, Sharif Hussein Ibn Ali, and the British high commissioner, Sir Henry McMahon. During the exchange of letters, the Arabs promised to raise a rebellion against the Ottoman Empire in exchange for Arab rule over all Arab territories liberated once World War I came to an end. Ross said, "During the famous Sharif Hussein correspondences with McMahon, Hussein made it clear that 'any concession designed to give France or any other Power possession of a single foot of territory in those parts is quite out of the question.' Not surrendering a single square foot—something I was to hear often seventy years later from President Assad—reflected in Arab eyes that the land had almost a sacred quality."[28] How right he was—land was indeed sacred to President Assad, which is why he proved to be such a tough negotiator during the peace process—especially with regard to his acceptance of the Rabin Deposit. The major difference between what the Israelis were proposing and what President Assad was asking for was that he wanted total, full, clean withdrawal, and then the establishment of peace. The Israelis were speaking about building confidence and establishing contacts after the first phase of withdrawal. We, however, were saying that UNSCRs 242 and 338 do not mention those things and that our people are not going to accept full, normal relations so long as our land is occupied, with so many phases of withdrawal. This was non-negotiable, and the end of the argument as far as Hafez al-Assad was concerned.

Ross's assessment of the president deserves mention here. In addition to the aforementioned remarks, he wrote, "My relationship with him was unusual. At one level, he respected my knowledge and attention to detail. He was always asking me about the black binder I would carry into our meetings, into which I seemed to write everything that was said. He would say, 'That has all your secrets?' and I would say, 'Absolutely.' It was not all sweetness and light between us. I knew that Assad was also suspicious of me. Here, I am convinced, my being Jewish was a factor. In his eyes, that necessarily made me close to the Israelis. My arguments that he needed to reach out to the Israeli public no doubt further confirmed this view of me."[29] That is not true, of course—Ross being Jewish had nothing to do with the President's appreciation, or lack of it. Assad had dealt with numerous Jewish Americans in the past, ranging from Henry Kissinger to Martin Indyk, and it was their attitude, rather than their religion, that contributed to his assessment of his interlocutors. Another mistake that stands out in Ross's memoirs is the following statement: "Assad, as we were to find out in nine months, viewed all the territory that was in Syrian control on June 4, 1967, as Syrian. Rabin felt any territory beyond the putative international border—the one affixed as part of the British and French Mandates in 1923—should be Israeli. The difference in territory between these two lines was not significant, but for Assad every inch of the territory that he considered Syrian was 'sacred.'"[30] But it did not take Ross "nine months" to discover Assad's veto of the 1923 border—we made it clear on day one, over and over again, that Syria would never accept anything short of the June 4, 1967 borders. President Assad had made this very clear to Carter in 1977, Bush in 1991, and Clinton in 1994. It is a uniform demand that has been handed down from father to son, one that has been repeated by President Bashar al-Assad in all his talks with the Americans since he came to power in 2000. It did not take Ross nine months to discover this demand—he knew it all along.

Rabin's Response

Two weeks later, on May 15, 1994, the Americans were back in Damascus, having met Prime Minister Rabin in Israel and heard out his views on Syria's reaction to the deposit. Secretary of State Christopher was carrying a letter from Clinton, which President Assad refused to accept "until we agree [on what was said in response to the deposit]. I prefer to receive the letter at the end of the meeting. Let us see first what the Israelis have to say."[31] First, Rabin requested a direct channel with President Assad, which was immediately flatly rejected. Second, the Israelis expressed anger that "the Syrian response focused on the need for withdrawal and not on the needs of the State of Israel." This was only natural, the president told Christopher. "Syria focuses on what is in its best interest, not in the interest of Israel."[32] Rabin was unhappy with the fact that Assad wanted no normalization until full withdrawal had been achieved. He also "cannot accept that the depth of the area that needs to be demilitarized would be the same for both Syria and Israel, given that [Israel has] much less land than Syria."[33] When it came to the time frame for withdrawal, Rabin had told the Americans, "I could do it in less time if Assad is willing to allow Israelis living there to remain under Syrian sovereignty." President Assad laughed. "First you want me to let the Jews leave Syria and now you want them to remain!"[34] Here, of course, he was making reference to James Baker's repeated demands that Assad allow Syrian Jews to emigrate to Israel or the United States, back in 1991–

1992. Finally, Christopher once again lobbied for public diplomacy with Damascus, saying, "Rabin cannot understand why you are so hesitant about this point." Without even blinking, the president said to Christopher: "You are free; we are not going to walk in the fog. Personally this discussion has deepened my doubt about Israeli intentions and increased my belief that the talks are simply Israeli ideas, and they are neither serious nor concrete."[35] At this point, the president gave one of his famous analogies, "What you are saying is similar to the farmer who finds a big rock while plowing the land. He obviously cannot continue plowing until that rock is removed. What Israel is trying to do is continue plowing without removing the rock; [the rock] being occupation."[36]

When the Americans left the room, I walked up to the president and said, "Isn't it obvious, Your Excellency, that we go to a meeting and produce nothing. We go to another meeting and we also don't produce anything. We are producing nothing, so why are you wasting your time; Mr. President?"

With the stern look of a concerned father, Assad said to me: "Bouthaina, the entire international media is against us, and if at any point we want to say that these meetings are indeed producing nothing, they will accuse us of being the ones who ruined the peace process. However, the moment you agree to compromise principles, you can only go down the line!"

On May 18, Christopher and Dennis Ross returned to Damascus—yet again—to deliver a delayed letter from President Clinton. It included plenty of nice talk about how "happy" President Clinton had been to meet President Assad in Geneva "in order to end the conflict and transform the Middle East." Clinton wrote that if peace were to be achieved, "Israel would have to implement withdrawal; Syria would have to implement peace. Both sides would have to implement security arrangements. Obviously we would have to negotiate with the Israelis which elements of withdrawal would have to go with which elements of peace."[37] He then added, "I recall our historic meeting in Geneva and our joint commitment to achieve a breakthrough in your negotiations with Israel. You know that from the very beginning of my administration I have made that objective one of my highest priorities. In my meetings with Prime Minister Rabin he made it clear that he was genuinely interested in a comprehensive peace and agreed with me that Syria was key. I was gratified in our Geneva meeting that you shared this goal. With the statements you made afterwards, I became convinced that it can be done."[38] Considerable headway, he added, "has already been made."

At this point, President Assad told Christopher, "You are always using the phrase 'There is no time' or 'Time is not on our side.' Why are you in a hurry, Mr. Christopher? We have had this problem for decades."[39]

Christopher dodged the question with a rather undiplomatic answer: "We simply cannot wait: summer becomes autumn and autumn becomes spring. There are other events that will interfere in the peace process. And something might come that would have a negative effect on the negotiations and put them in jeopardy. You never know what lies around the corner in the Middle East."[40]

The Assad-Clinton Summit in Damascus

In mid-October, 1994, we began to prepare for a special event: Bill Clinton was touring the Middle East and was scheduled to stop in Damascus for a high-profile summit at the Presidential Palace. President Assad wanted to make sure that he received a prestigious welcome, being the first US president to visit Syria while in office since Richard Nixon's trip in 1974, exactly twenty years earlier. Nixon, however, had been a defeated president whose reputation had been tremendously damaged by the Watergate scandal. His trip to Syria took place during his final months in office, making Nixon effectively irrelevant to Arab-Israeli peacemaking, whereas Clinton was at the apex of his career, just completing his second year in office, and strongly eyeing his own re-election. Like no other US president, he was heavily involved in Middle East peacemaking and genuinely respected by the Arabs, especially the Syrians and Palestinians. I accompanied President Assad to Damascus International Airport that morning in October 1994, where the entire Syrian government was already neatly assembled at the red carpet, ready to welcome the president of the United States.

One week before the visit, a young Palestinian had detonated a bomb wrapped around his waist, killing twenty-one Israelis and one Dutch citizen in Tel Aviv. Although we abhorred the loss of civilian life, in Syria we posed the question: "Why has this young man resorted to ending his own life for the sake of putting an end to occupation?" For us the answer was anger, humiliation, and desperation—all on account of the Israeli Defense Forces. As far as the United States was concerned, however, the man was nothing but a "terrorist suicide bomber." Realizing that what had happened would place Clinton in a difficult situation, Assad swiftly condemned the attack to silence members of the

President Bill Clinton at Damascus International Airport in October 1994, being welcomed by President Hafez al-Assad. Standing next to President Clinton are Bouthaina Shaaban and Syria's ambassador to Washington, D.C., Walid al-Mouallem.

US Congress who would try to use the incident to denigrate the Damascus visit. In his carefully crafted statement, the president said, "Syria condemns the killing of civilians, whether in Beirut, Ramallah, or Tel Aviv."

On the day of Clinton's arrival, Hizbullah fired Katyusha rockets into northern Israel, which threatened to snowball into a major crisis. It did not, however, because no civilians were killed. The United States said nothing about what had occurred, and we neither condemned nor applauded the incident, although the entire world knew of our strong ties to Hizbullah and its charismatic young leader Shaikh Hasan Nasrallah, who at the time had been in power for less than two years. Dennis Ross incorrectly stated in his memoirs that US officials were silent about the Hizbullah attack because "we were relying on Assad's word that he would disarm Hizbullah once Israel had committed in a peace agreement to full withdrawal from Syria and Lebanon."[41] Now, at the time of writing, seventeen years after the Clinton-Assad Summit in Damascus, the minutes of all those meetings are piled on my office desk. There is not a single reference in any one of them to Assad promising to "disarm Hizbullah" if peace was ever signed with the Israelis. I accompanied the president on all his foreign visits and sat during every meeting with US officials, ranging from members of Congress to heavyweight politicians such as James Baker and Bill Clinton. Not once did Assad ever make such a commitment, which would have run contrary to

Presidents Hafez al-Assad and Bill Clinton, with Bouthaina Shaaban, at Damascus International Airport in October 1994.

all his principles, first of all as an Arab statesman but also as the Syrian president.

President Assad cracked a slight smile when Air Force One landed in Damascus. Here he was—despite all his previous suspicion of the United States—playing host to none other than Bill Clinton in the capital of the Umayyads. What made the situation all the more ironic was that Assad was actually excited that Clinton was in Syria, and, as we were to soon discover, so was Clinton. The chemistry between the two men and the mutual determination of purpose seemed to have defeated the troubled history and years of doubt in Syrian-US relations. It was music to our ears to hear the Syrian and US national anthems played, right after Clinton inspected the Syrian Guard of Honor.

It should be noted that, contrary to what was rumored at the time, First Lady Hillary Clinton did not accompany her husband on the visit to Syria. Many have argued that she actually came to Syria but did not get off the plane because the Syrian first lady, in mourning over the death of her son, was not at the airport to welcome her. That is simply not true and, for the sake of history, needs to be corrected.

Once the formalities were over, when we got into the car to drive to the Presidential Palace, Clinton said, "Since I was a child, I've read so much about Damascus at school and I cannot believe that I am actually here, in the oldest inhabited city on earth!" I was seated in the middle between the two presidents—one whom I viewed as a father figure, and another whom I respected and admired tremendously. The excitement in the automobile was high, mainly due to my personal satisfaction as I said to myself, "Way to go, Bouthaina! You have come a long way indeed!"

While walking through the palace, known as Qasr al-Shaab (the People's Palace), President Clinton was clearly amazed by the architecture and size of the building, perched on top of a hill overlooking Damascus. The pistachio colors added plenty of life to the palace, which had been designed a few years back by a brilliant Japanese architect, Kenzo Tange.[42] The marble floors, the huge chandeliers, and the beautiful gardens all contributed to its splendor—explaining, perhaps, why President Clinton was so impressed. It wasn't the White House, of course, but it emanated a sense of warmth, practicality, and pomp, being the seat of power of the city that Clinton had rightfully described as the oldest inhabited city on earth.

When we entered the meeting room, Assad and Clinton looked through a large window that gave a panoramic view of the Syrian capital. Assad began to point out historical landmarks in Damascus: "Over there is the Grand Umayyad mosque. If you look that way, there is St. Anania's Church, off the street called Straight, where St. Paul converted to Christianity. Over there is Mount Qassiun, where Cain killed his brother Abel." I couldn't help but think to myself: "If the president wants to show him all there is to see in Damascus, Clinton needs an entire month, not just a couple of hours in Syria!"

When we got down to business, Clinton went over the Rabin Deposit, wanting to find middle ground between Assad and Rabin. Present in the room, in addition to the two presidents, were Foreign Minister Shara, Secretary of State Christopher, Special Envoy Dennis Ross, and myself. President Assad agreed to two phases for Israeli withdrawal (previously, he had offered only one).[43] When it came to public diplomacy, however, he refused to budge on his previous commitment, saying, "Syria has already agreed that Foreign Minister Shara would grant an interview to Israeli television. What did we get in exchange for that? Nothing! But to tell you the truth, we expected and require nothing from the Israelis; what they should now do is withdraw from the Golan Heights, with no conditions!"[44] Any further gesture on public diplomacy, he added, would have to come only *after* a peace treaty is signed. President Assad seemed to be saying: "I accept the Rabin Deposit, with modifications." From where he saw things, UNSCRs 242 and 338 made no mention of public diplomacy, and the fact that Syria had already approved the Shara interview meant that Syria had taken more steps than it was required to do, even by the international community. "You cannot have public diplomacy when there is occupied land; occupation and diplomacy are not compatible, Mr. Clinton!" The president wanted withdrawal, security, followed by normal relations. Rabin, however, was after peace, security, and full withdrawal, in that order. Nevertheless, Assad was clearly trying to avoid disappointing President Clinton, while Clinton was equally keen to avoid disappointing President Assad. Both leaders were trying to avoid provoking or upsetting one another. They did not want disagreement to become a point of departure. They wanted leeway to arrive at a more or less substantive point. Clinton put it brilliantly: "Let us see if we can tango together, before we get married!"[45] The two men broke into laughter.

When the meeting was over, the two delegations went into another room, leaving Assad, Clinton, and myself. Clinton said, "I did not want to make too much about the time of withdrawal, but it seems to me that the Israelis insist they cannot do it during the time frame you specified." Assad walked up to his American guest, speaking to him in almost a fatherly tone, saying: "I understand how they are trying to score points, not because they are interested in real peace, but because it makes them feel stronger and better. I am going to give this to you, and not to the Israelis: sixteen months. Not twelve months, but I will give them sixteen months to withdraw from the Golan. This is really for your sake, and I would never have done it had you not been coming to Damascus to see me. I don't believe they need this time, however, as I have strongly stressed on so many occasions." This was more time than Assad had ever previously proposed to the United States and Israel. Sadly, however, even that amount of time produced no breakthrough in the Middle East. Indyk described President Assad's initiative, saying, "Sixteen months for the completion of the withdrawal (previously he had said twelve months) and an Israeli diplomatic presence, but not an embassy, four months before the completion of the withdrawal (previously, diplomatic relations were to come after Israel had completed its full withdrawal)."[46] Clinton was very pleased by the Syrian offer, promising to put his full weight behind it.

In his memoirs, Martin Indyk remarked, "Previously, in their discussions with the United States, Assad and Rabin had only referred to 'full withdrawal' from the Golan Heights. The detail-oriented Christopher noted that Rabin had not specified the June 1967 line in his proposal. Assad claimed (inaccurately) that Christopher and Dennis Ross had both previously affirmed that Rabin would withdraw to the June 4 line."[47] He adds that Christopher had taken the blame for the gap in interpretation between the 1923 and 1967 borders: "He had not been aware that there was a distinction between the international border and the June 4, 1967 line."[48] That statement, ludicrous as it may seem to anybody familiar with the Syrian-Israeli peace process, comes as no surprise. When that small, confidential meeting was finished, we stepped out and immediately headed for the press conference. I remember whispering to President Assad, "Please walk slowly to give me time to reach the translation booth." President Clinton expressed his determination to "achieve progress" in the Middle East peace process, saying that these views were shared by President Assad. When it was his turn to speak, Assad said, "It is my pleasure to welcome President Bill Clinton to Damascus, the oldest inhabited city in the world, the heart of a region that has witnessed humanity's oldest civilizations and the birth of all monotheistic religions. The people of this region, however, have suffered for too long, especially during this century, from the bitterness of war, conflicts, and bloodshed. Now we hope that they will live in peace and stability." He added that the talks with Clinton had been "positive and fruitful, focusing on different aspects of the peace process." The Syrian leader continued, "I express my deep satisfaction with the compatibility of our views regarding a comprehensive peace process based on UN Security Council Resolutions 242 and 338 and the principle of 'land-for-peace.' I stressed to President Clinton, based on the concept of full withdrawal for full peace, Syria's readiness to commit to the requirements of peace: normal peace relations with Israel in exchange for full Israeli withdrawal from the Golan up to the June 4, 1967 borders, and the South of Lebanon." He wrapped up his statement by saying, "Finally, I would like to greet the American people and thank President Clinton for his personal efforts, and those of his aides, and express my willingness to work with them in order to achieve a comprehensive, just, and real peace in the region."[49]

Speaking to journalists on the way to Israel, Clinton remarked that no peace was possible without the Syrians: "I think that President Assad wants peace and I believe he will achieve it." The Syrian leader, he added, was a "difficult negotiator who nevertheless is worthy of our trust because he lives up to his word." Syria and the United States, he added, "had reached a point in bilateral relations where there was no longer any mistrust between them." When asked if Assad gave him anything in private, Clinton said, "Yes, he did; we spoke in private about details of the negotiations and I do believe that we achieved a certain progress. We are satisfied with it."[50]

Depending on who one talks to about the Assad-Clinton press conference, it was either a great success or a failure—as Clinton's peace team described it. Dennis Ross, for example, was furious because when CBS News reporter Rita Bravis asked President Assad about terrorism, he accused Israel of being at the root of all terrorism in the region. Bravis, it must be noted, structured her question in a manner that seemed to be saying that Syria and the Palestinians were to blame for the acts of terror that were plaguing the Middle East. "This was a disaster," Ross said, adding, "Here was the President of the United States standing next to the President of Syria one week after a suicide bombing in Tel Aviv, and Assad was blaming Israel for acts of terror." Personally, I don't think the conference was negative in any way, but if Dennis Ross and Warren Christopher were expecting Assad to shower Israel with honeyed phrases and praise, they had another thing coming. Scratching beneath the surface, however, it becomes clear that the two leaders reached impressive milestones at the Damascus Summit, and these were described in a fairly straightforward manner at the press conference.

When we got in the car after the conference was over, President Clinton remarked, "I can't believe I actually got to Damascus and was unable to tour the Old City."

President Assad laughed. "It is the fault of your security, Mr. President. If you will agree, I can take you on a tour of Old Damascus where we can have lunch. And I give you my word that you will be very safe." At the airport, when saying good-bye, Clinton ended by saying: "I wish I could stay longer, but I have to go back to the United States because we have midterm elections."[51]

President Assad smiled at this, saying, "If only we could go back with you to America—we would vote for you in the midterms!" An image of President Hafez al-Assad lobbying on his behalf in North Dakota or Michigan probably formed in Clinton's mind—if only for a second—and he laughed, saying, "Well, that certainly would be great, Mr. President."

Notes

1. Ross, *The Missing Peace*, 91.
2. *Unpublished Assad-Ross Minutes*, February 1994.
3. Ibid.
4. Ibid.
5. Ibid.

6. Indyk, 112.
7. *Assad-Christopher Minutes*, May 1, 1994.
8. Ibid.
9. Ibid.
10. Christopher, *Chances of a Lifetime*, 217–218.
11. Ibid., 221.
12. Ibid.
13. Ibid.
14. Personal conversation with President Assad, May 1994.
15. *Assad-Christopher Minutes*, May 1, 1994.
16. Ibid.
17. Ibid.
18. Ibid.
19. Ibid.
20. Archives of the Syrian Presidential Palace, Assad-Christopher Papers, May 1994.
21. Ibid.
22. Ibid.
23. Ibid.
24. Ibid.
25. Ross, *The Missing Peace*, 142.
26. Ibid.
27. Ibid.
28. Ross, *The Missing Peace*, 31.
29. Ross, *The Missing Peace*, 143.
30. Ibid.
31. *Assad-Christopher Minutes*, May 15, 1994.
32. Ibid.
33. Ibid.
34. Ibid.
35. Ibid.
36. Ibid.
37. Archives of the Presidential Palace, Clinton-Assad Correspondence, May 1994.
38. Ibid.
39. *Assad-Christopher Papers*, May 15, 1994.
40. Ibid.
41. Ross, *The Missing Peace*, 232–233.
42. Kenzo Tange (1913–2005) was a world famous Japanese architect who came to Syria to design the Presidential Palace, blending a sharp Far East style with modernism. During his career he designed buildings on five continents, namely in his native Japan after the World War II atomic bomb attack in Hiroshima.
43. Archives of the Syrian Presidential Palace, the unpublished Assad-Clinton Meetings, October 27, 1994.
44. Ibid.
45. Ibid.

46. Indyk, *Innocent Abroad*, 141.
47. Ibid., 124.
48. Ibid.
49. Archives of the Syrian Presidential Palace, President Hafez al-Assad's Speeches and Interviews, October 1994.
50. Ibid.
51. Personal communication before Clinton's departure.

6

Rabin's Assassination and the Long Road to Nowhere

DURING THE LAST FEW WEEKS OF 1994 AND THE FIRST MONTH of 1995, several informal meetings took place at Dennis Ross's home in Washington, D.C., attended by Ambassador Mouallem and Israeli ambassador Rabinovich. The Americans felt that these informal gatherings would help break the ice in Syrian-Israeli relations, and President Assad agreed to them, rather begrudgingly, in order to please President Clinton. President Assad knew the talks were doomed to fail from day one: he was not going to make any further concessions, and the Israelis were uninterested in further advancing peace unless we engaged in public diplomacy. As far as we were concerned, what they were asking for was synonymous with committing political suicide. During those informal chats, Rabinovich proposed a two-step strategy. In Phase I, his government would partially withdraw from the Golan, in exchange for a number of steps such as academic or media exchanges between Syria and Israel. When Mouallem refused, Rabinovich even proposed that tourists from countries other than Syria and Israel who were visiting the Middle East be allowed to move freely between Damascus and Tel Aviv. Israel would withdraw from more of the Golan, he added, in Phase II, which would include face-to-face meetings between Syrian and Israeli officials and talks between business delegations from both countries. Israeli tourist groups, but not individuals, would be allowed to visit Syria, he suggested, and vice versa. Once again, Mouallem said no, fuming: "There is no way to have an Israeli flag flying in Damascus while Israel still occupies the Golan!" Rabin seemingly could not understand why Assad was refusing to do "all of the above" before the Golan was back under Syria's full control. "Egypt did it in 1978," Rabinovich said.

"Why can't Syria?"[1] When we received reports of those talks from the ambassador, I couldn't help but ask myself: "Was Rabin trying to be smart, or did he truly not understand Hafez al-Assad after all these years?"

The Shihabi-Barak Meeting at Blair House

Secretary of State Christopher then suggested, in December 1994, that he arrange a secret meeting between Syrian and IDF officers. This would take place in Washington, D.C., and would fit nicely with the informal talks under way between the Syrian and Israeli ambassadors. The IDF, he told us, was close to Rabin, and meeting with its top brass would be seen as a breakthrough by the Israeli public. He suggested a "warming up" meeting between Mouallem and a senior IDF officer. Wanting to walk the extra mile, the president agreed, mandating a meeting between his ambassador and IDF chief of staff Ehud Barak. The choice of Barak was no accident—he was the most senior of Israeli officials, and a heavyweight in Israeli politics who was set on replacing Rabin as prime minister. Although this was the first meeting between Barak and a Syrian official, we knew plenty about the man whom we were bound to eventually face at Shepherdstown, West Virginia, in January 2000. Barak had joined the IDF in 1959, shortly after President Assad graduated from the Homs Military Academy, and served as an officer for thirty-five years. His name was permanently associated with the April 1973 Israeli raid on Lebanon, which they called Operation Spring of Youth, in which several Palestinian commanders were surprised in their homes and murdered in cold blood, on his direct orders. Barak arrived at the Beirut shoreline in a rubber boat, dressed as a brunette, and then headed to the posh Verdun neighborhood, where he gunned down Muhammad Youssef Al-Najjar (Abu Youssef), Kamal Adwan, and Kamal Nasser. With such a bloody track record, it was only normal for us to be very cautious when dealing with our new "interlocutor."

After the meeting, which took place at Blair House, opposite the White House on the corner of Lafayette Park, Barak spoke of "creative ways" to solve the Syrian-Israeli conflict: "Israel understands the importance of land and the need to preserve Syrian dignity in any deal."[2] The meeting, needless to say, produced no breakthroughs, but it got the Americans excited, who came to us with yet another suggestion. Step II of these confidence-building measures, Christopher said, would be for a top Syrian military official to meet with Israeli ambassador Rabinovich.

Here Assad went a step further, saying that he would send Chief of Staff Hikmat al-Shihabi to meet the Israelis. General Shihabi, a decorated military officer who had served in the wars of 1967 and 1973, was also a trusted confidant of the president who had been closely following up on all military and logistical details of the peace process since 1991. He had been highly involved in the disengagement agreement with Israel following the October 1973 war. A ranking member of the Baath Party's Regional Command, General Shihabi was the most senior any Syrian official could get in the peace process. Sending him to the United States was indeed a breakthrough that caught all of us by surprise and undoubtedly angered all the optimists in Syria, who saw no reason to engage any further with the Israelis. If anything, however, it mirrored President Assad's genuine commitment to reaching a breakthrough for Middle East peace.

In my capacity as interpreter, I was asked to accompany the Syrian chief of staff to the United States, along with his top lieutenants, Basem Sheikh Koroush and Ibrahim al-Omar. Our first meeting was on December 19, where we met with the Israelis again at Blair House, a 170-year-old American home that has lodged various White House visitors since World War II. What I remember most about that meeting was how it revealed the true substance of General Shihabi. In Syria, we rarely saw him in public or knew anything about his private life. He was one of the least accessible officials, almost never appearing on television and giving no press interviews. In the United States, however, he came across as a tough, brilliant negotiator, a seasoned intellectual, in addition to being a very dignified military officer as well. When we walked into Blair House, General Shihabi was dressed in a Western suit rather than a military uniform. He was sending a message that he came to meet the Israelis "in peace," with no stars on his shoulder and no revolver strapped across his belt—as Arafat had done when signing the Oslo Accords on the White House lawn in 1993. The medals he would have worn on his uniform had been well earned from President Assad for the numerous wars he fought with the Israelis since 1967. General Shihabi calculated his steps very carefully, marching slowly into the meeting room, looking Ehud Barak straight in the eye. He had a stern expression on his face: sober, tough, and very serious. Here were two staunch enemies who had been at daggers ends for years, finally coming face-to-face within a two-minute walk from the Oval Office. Shihabi made his first statement by refusing to shake hands with Ehud Barak. Barak tried—yet again—to please the Syrian general, saying: "We believe that President Hafez al-Assad is the most important leader in the Middle

The Syrian delegation to the peace talks at the Oval Office, chatting with President Bill Clinton in December 1994. President Clinton is talking to Syrian chief of staff Hikmat Shihabi, Bouthaina Shaaban, and Ambassador Walid al-Mouallem. Standing behind the US president are Clinton's national security adviser, Sandy Berger, and his Middle East envoy, Dennis Ross.

East. Both Syria and Israel can play a very important role in the stability of the Middle East. Syria is the strongest neighbor of Israel, not only in military terms, and because of the role it plays, and the Arab nationalist flame that it carries, we understand that peace with Syria is going to be extremely important for us."[3]

Once again, Shihabi did not even smile . . .

Ehud Barak tried a third time. "It is very important to negotiate in great detail with the Syrians. We got the worst blows from the Syrian army [during the war of 1973]. You have brave officers, Your Excellency."[4] Warren Christopher interrupted, trying to shelter his Israeli guest from more embarrassment, telling us how he was planning to spend the Christmas holidays with his family in California, but how his plans had changed when the Syrian and Israeli generals arrived in the United States, signaling a major breakthrough in the peace process. Christopher advised us to be "brave and creative," noting that "the people gathered around this table can make peace. You have the will and the courage to do so, and we in the United States are willing to do all that it takes to achieve peace on the Israeli-Syrian track."[5] He then turned to Shihabi and said, "We are very glad to see you with us and this is a very clear sign of how serious the Syrian leadership actually is in its quest for peace." When it was his turn to speak, Shihabi began to explain, slowly and carefully, "My presence here is the result of a very important political decision, taken by the Syrian leadership, because peace—as agreed upon at Madrid—is very strategic for us." He recommended moving directly to security arrangements, which was music to the ears of both Warren Christopher and Ehud Barak. Shihabi stressed what had been agreed upon in August 1993, namely that "security is a legitimate need for both sides, and one country cannot have it at the expense of the other. It needs to be mutual and equal."[6] No security arrangement, he added, should "infringe on the rights, sovereignty, or territory" of the other, stressing however, that it applies to the June 4, 1967, borders.

Apparently, the Shihabi-Barak meeting not only surprised the Syrian peacemakers but vibrated strongly throughout the White House, pleasing President Clinton. Knowing perfectly well how committed Assad was to an Israeli concession on substance, Clinton saw this meeting as the opening of a private, high-level channel that might produce substantial movement in the negotiations. What Clinton did not know, however, was that Ehud Barak, senior as he may have been in the IDF, knew absolutely nothing of the Rabin Deposit. He came to the United States with no clue as to how far negotiations had reached between Assad and Rabin—a blunder on Israel's part—that no doubt resulted in yet another missed opportunity. He spoke a language that was seemingly now from a bygone era, refusing to acknowledge, for example, the difference in positions between the borders of 1923 and 1967. This prompted General Shihabi to angrily comment: "How can we speak of security measures if we have not decided on the border!"[7] Syria wanted mutuality in security arrangements, with limitations on forces applying equally to both sides. Barak was still worried about the geographic asymmetry of the two sides, arguing that Syria was a large country, whereas Israel was much smaller and its cities were closer to the border. He could not accept equality in limitations, although he would say yes to mutuality. Barak wanted the restriction of forces to apply to all territory from Safad to Damascus. Shihabi wanted the restriction to apply only from Safad to Qunaitra, the principal town in the Golan. The meeting, which lasted for two days, produced absolutely nothing. Barak tried to raise the issue of early warning stations, arguing that they would reduce the possibility of attack from the Syrian border. Shihabi responded, "My impression is that what you seek is war, not peace. An early warning station means you are preparing for war, Mr. Barak. As a military man, you know that early warning stations are very important when one is planning to wage war—not peace. We simply cannot reach any agreement if you are in this state of mind."[8]

After the meeting, it must be noted, President Clinton invited us to the White House at 4:00 P.M. on December 24. General Shihabi was given a private audience on his own, which lasted for five minutes, and when it was our turn to walk in, Clinton took me completely by surprise by addressing me directly—for the first time—by my first name. "How are you, Bouthaina? It's good to see you again." He added, "The next time you are in Washington, I would love you to meet my wife and daughter—I have already shown them your book." It was very nice of him to say that to me—but I never had the chance to meet Hillary or Chelsea during my upcoming visits to the United States, nor did I ever meet the US first lady when President Barack Obama appointed her secretary of state in 2009. I did, however, maintain a good relationship with Clinton and continued to respect him ten years after he left the White House. We even met twice after he left office, once during his "Clinton Initiative" in New York and once in Dubai. That was when I invited him to visit Damascus, after consulting with President Bashar al-Assad. Clinton welcomed the idea, expressing a desire to do so, but never did. We later found out that President George W. Bush did not let him and also tried to prevent President Carter from visiting Damascus in December 2008. After exchanging niceties with me back in December 1994, Clinton referred to a gift he had received from President Assad during his October visit to Syria, a mosaic-decorated multipurpose desk that serves as a chessboard, handmade by the gifted craftsmen of Old Damascus. "It is in my room," Clinton said to me, "but I have not had a chance to play with it yet, although I plan to do so during Christmas." He then touched on the peace process: "I am very grateful for President Assad and his wise decision to send you here. I welcome you all at the White House and express my belief that negotiations at this stage are very important. We are seeking a peace treaty that is 'in harmony' with your principles, and the United States is willing to exert whatever is needed to achieve progress on that track."

Sadly however, and despite Clinton's good intentions, Shihabi then left Washington empty-handed to visit his son in Newport Beach, who was studying nuclear medicine. Barak returned to Israel, where he was due to be replaced as chief of staff by Amnon Shahak on January 1, 1995. Ross frantically tried to arrange another meeting, this time with Shahak, in the first week of January, but Rabin was less enthusiastic, not wanting his top officer to leave Israel only days after assuming office, claiming that this would send the wrong message to the Israeli

A souvenir photo signed by President Bill Clinton, picturing him with Bouthaina Shaaban at the White House in 1994.

public. When President Assad read the minutes of the Shihabi talks in the United States, he too was unimpressed that Ehud Barak had been "deliberately misinformed" by Rabin. He may have felt that he had given too much and gotten very little in return, believing that Shihabi may have been too senior, giving the Israelis the wrong impression that Assad was caving in. That is the impression I got, which I conveyed to the president when we were back in Damascus. The president immediately wrote off the Blair House talks as imbalanced, dismissing them as effectively useless. To make a point, he kept Ambassador Mouallem in Damascus for six weeks, sending a clear message to the Americans, who had called for the "officers meeting" in the first place.

A Stormy Meeting in Latakia

On April 4, 1995, Dennis Ross came to Damascus for a meeting with President Assad, attended by Foreign Minister Shara and Ambassadors Allaf and Mouallem. The meeting took place in Latakia and lasted for five nonstop hours. Ross started on a light note, joking that a clairvoyant friend of his had just sent him a fax saying that he expected a Syrian-Israeli peace deal in 1995. This friend, Ross noted, cannot go wrong, telling us how he had predicted similar victories for San Francisco football and basketball teams in the past.[9] Assad smiled, clearly amused at the story, which if anything, mirrored a very vivid imagination. "Many world leaders have relied on clairvoyants and soothsayers in the past, including former US president Reagan," said the president. "We don't rely on such predictions, however, because they are frowned upon by Islam, and because clairvoyants base their predictions on visions rather than facts—and this might lead to a great illusion."[10] Taken a little aback by Assad's lack of response to the dry humor, Ross ignored his own previous remark and carried on saying, "I have with me a letter from President Clinton, who sends you his regards and says that it is now time to surpass differences and enter the stage of security details [for reaching a real peace]." President Clinton, effectively, was asking President Assad for more help to empower him vis-à-vis the Israelis.

"The government of the United States," Ross went on, "is still committed to what was started with former Secretary Baker; being no secret deals with any party at the expense of the other. When we say something to the Israelis, we tell it also to Syria, and vice versa."[11] Meaning, the Americans had delivered all of Syria's points to Prime Minister Rabin, who objected to several clauses in President Assad's response to the deposit. Rabin said that he had committed himself, through President Clinton in Geneva in January 1994, to the borders of June 4, 1967. The Americans had confirmed this in writing to President Assad, making it a de facto official American position as well. What Ross told us that April in Latakia was: "I have just come from Israel and I can tell you that at the end of the day, and as part of a package in which Israel's needs would have to be met, the United States understands that your needs would have to be met, and that therefore, the meaning of full withdrawal would be to June 4, 1967. This only has meaning if you come to an agreement on everything. If you don't come to an agreement on everything, it has no meaning. In any case, this [Rabin proposal] is in our pocket, not yours!"[12] Given all of the above, he added, why was Syria so worried about the terms of withdrawal outlined in the Rabin Deposit? President Assad braced himself to explain—for the millionth time in less than two years—the difference between the 1923 and 1967 borders, stressing that the Rabin Deposit made no explicit mention of 1967 but just spoke of "withdrawal."

Ross then suggested that Foreign Minister Shara visit Washington in the third week of April for talks with the secretary of state ahead of Rabin's upcoming visit to the United States. The minister's visit, he added, would send the right message to the American and Israeli publics that Syria was "still committed" to peace, regardless of the upheaval in Palestine and on the Lebanese-Israeli border. The Americans, it must be noted, were always very keen on bringing Syrian officials to the United States, regardless of whether there was anything important to discuss or not. For our part, we always said that we were not after a photo opportunity at the White House and would not make the trip unless there was something concrete to discuss. Back in 1992, it must be remembered, Baker had toyed with the idea of inviting President Assad to the United States, along with King Fahd of Saudi Arabia, King Hussein of Jordan, and Yitzhak Rabin. He knew that the chances were slim—if not none—so long as the Golan remained occupied, but according to Ross, "Baker thought it was worth a try." When asked whether Assad would make the trip, Ross replied, "Assad was the key. If Assad went for it, the others would do it. But it goes against everything Assad believes. It would mean giving the Israelis a huge concession for nothing in return. It would mean he would have to meet an Israeli leader without having gotten his land back. It would mean giving the Israelis the symbols they crave with no assurances of getting the substance he [Assad] wants."[13] We in Damascus knew of that suggestion only too well and wondered why Dennis Ross was now trying it again—although he knew perfectly well where the president stood on giving and getting "nothing in return."

"We are running out of time, Mr. President. We have upcoming elections that would consume our attention and energy, not only in the United States but also in Israel. We need to reach a peace deal this year, in 1995."[14] He added that there was a "psychological element" to the crisis, where all parties concerned needed to feel that they were making progress—any progress—in order to maintain momentum. Once again, President Assad was not amused, feeling that Ross was trying to corner him into granting more concessions when he had gone out of his way with the eighteen-month proposal in order to give peace a chance. He was adamant about not moving an inch forward unless he saw something concrete from the Israelis. "What we said, Mr. Ross, was complete withdrawal and complete peace. The entire world now knows what Syria is willing to offer. Rabin spoke to the Americans about full withdrawal. He told them that he accepts full withdrawal and asked that this message be conveyed to us by your diplomats. We then went into debate about the details of peace, but a very small circle of people know of these positions. Only a limited number of Syrians, Americans, and Israelis know of Israel's position, whereas the entire world knows where we stand and what we are willing to do for the sake of peace."[15] President Assad was trying to say that it was time for the Israelis to publicly acknowledge the need to withdraw from the Golan, in full, based on the June 4, 1967, borders, and to prepare world and Israeli public opinion for such a withdrawal. This could not happen overnight, and if Israel were truly interested in full withdrawal, its leaders should say that explicitly, loud and clear, regardless of how this would be perceived by the Israeli street. As far as the president was concerned, Rabin was still more interested in a "peace process" than a "peace treaty." How could we believe what Ross was saying when in his own memoirs, he described the Israeli prime minister's reaction to Syria's response this way: "Rabin exploded, saying that full withdrawal in his eyes had always meant to the international border, not the June 4, 1967 lines."[16]

The Americans, he now added, had suggested keeping the Rabin Deposit confidential. "We accepted, saying that leaking it would harm the peace process and therefore, harm Syria's national interests."[17] But now, he added, it was time for Israel to come out with a public statement about the need to withdraw from the Golan. "Peace is our utmost pleasure and we would not want it to remain secret."[18] The Rabin Deposit carries the same messages that have been going back and forth between Syria and Israel through Ross, Christopher, and Clinton himself. "What will Minister Shara's visit to the United States add to the process? Will Mr. Christopher hear more from Shara than he heard from me in Damascus? His mission there is not the same as Rabin's visit to Washington, D.C. Rabin has interests in the United States, and when he goes there, he is going to his second home. To be frank, such a visit would add nothing but give a wrong impression—that we are on the verge of achieving a peace agreement—which is not the case." With regard to military details, he added, "When the time is right, these need to be sorted out by military men. It is not right for me to negotiate them."[19] Again, this statement bears witness to President Assad's respect for institutions and the men in uniform that surrounded him during his long career. Although a former air force pilot and defense minister who since 1970 was constitutionally the commander in chief of the Syrian army, President Assad nevertheless felt that when it came to technical military details, they needed to be sorted out by the chief of staff, General Hikmat al-Shihabi.

"If I were to negotiate the details, it would mean immediate success or immediate failure—that is why this needs time, and the officers themselves have to get involved in the talks, and their details."[20] The job of the officers from both sides, he added, comes at a later stage, "after we have agreed on all hypothetical and political issues." Early warning stations on Mount Hebron, he reminded Ross, were still out of the question for Syria. "Israel recently launched an espionage satellite that can record even the license plates of Syrian automobiles. With such sophisticated equipment at its disposal, why does it still insist on early warning stations on the ground?"[21] Since Syria was offering Israel peace, the Israelis do not need extensive security arrangements, as asked for by the United States. He then firmly added, "Now you always tell me that we are running out of time. We are not in a hurry, Mr. Ross, if haste means relinquishing any of our rights simply for the sake of telling the world, 'We achieved a peace treaty.' You may be in a hurry, but the Israelis are not. They are the ones who have brilliantly wasted time since we went to Madrid—not us. We are not trying to gain time or waste time. We remain, as we always have been, committed to a just and comprehensive peace. We have done a lot when it comes to confidence-building measures—more than what was expected from us. We walked the extra mile, Mr. Ross."[22]

The 1923 and 1967 Borders

It might be useful here to underline the fundamental difference between our position and that of the Americans and Israelis on the borders of 1923 and 1967. During the first Palestine War of 1948, the Syrian army had seized territory to the west of the 1923 line in three areas, famously infuriating US president Harry Truman, who had staunchly supported the creation of the State of Israel. As part of the armistice, Syria withdrew from all three areas in 1949, under then-President Husni al-Za'im, returning to the international border of 1923, making those areas demilitarized zones. In 1967, Israel seized about two-thirds of the demilitarized areas. The difference between the two lines, 1923 and 1967, is about 66 square kilometers, and they are vital when it comes to water, especially at the Banias Spring and the shoreline of Lake Tiberias/Sea of Galilee. Rabin feared that a Syrian presence on Lake Tiberias would give Syria a share of what he claimed was Israel's only reservoir. President Assad would hear nothing of the argument, arguing that this was Syrian territory long before Israel existed and needed to be returned to Syria. Full stop! This was beyond negotiation. Whenever the Americans would tell him that Rabin "did not know" of the difference between both lines, he would reply, "If he did not know what the land was, then there is no point in negotiating [with him]!"

When the meeting ended, in thunder, President Assad tried to calm the tension by asking Foreign Minister Shara to take Ross out for lunch. Over a good meal, Shara told him, "If the Israelis will accept the principles [of what the president has said], we can be flexible on the details."

Notes

1. Archives of the Syrian Foreign Ministry, Dispatches from the Syrian Embassy in Washington, DC, December 1994.
2. Archives of the Syrian Foreign Ministry, Dispatches from the Syrian Embassy in Washington, DC, December 1994.
3. Archives of the Syrian Ministry of Foreign Affairs, Shihabi-Barak Meeting Minutes, December 19, 1994.
4. Ibid.
5. Ibid.
6. Ibid.
7. Ibid.
8. Ibid.
9. Unpublished Assad-Ross Papers, April 4, 1995.
10. Ibid.
11. Ibid.
12. Ibid.
13. Ross, *The Missing Peace*, 87.
14. Unpublished Assad-Ross Papers, April 4, 1995.
15. Ibid.
16. Ibid. Rabin said that "there was no map of the June 4 lines; it represented the positions of the two sides on the eve of the 1967 war." Anybody familiar with the Syrian-Israeli peace track realizes the folly of such a statement—we have presented, and continue to hold, the maps that Rabin declined to accept, showing exactly where the June 4, 1967, borders were marked after the Six-Day War.
17. Ibid.
18. Ibid.
19. Ibid.
20. Ibid.
21. Ibid.
22. Ibid.

7

The Legacy of Yusuf al-Azma

ON JULY 24, 1920, SYRIA'S THIRTY-SEVEN-YEAR-OLD MINISTER of defense Yusuf al-Azma put on his military uniform, hugged his baby daughter Laila, bid farewell to his young Turkish wife, and headed to the Presidential Palace in the al-Muhajreen neighborhood—the same palace that President Assad used back in the early 1970s, after he first came to power.[1] General Azma called upon the King of Syria, Faisal I, telling him that he was about to head to war against the invading French army. That army had landed on the Syrian coast in 1919 and was heading toward Damascus, mandated to colonize by the League of Nations. Azma knew that chances of victory were close to impossible, especially with an ill-equipped and poorly trained young Syrian army, which at the time, was barely one year old. He did not want history books to mention, however, that the French had passed through Maysaloun on the Damascus-Beirut highway without facing tough resistance from the Syrians.

The Battle of Maysaloun, a grand milestone in the history of Syria, began at 6:30 A.M., with General Azma heading 850 Syrian troops, 170 of them volunteers who were not prepared to fight a full-fledged war against the mighty French army. Their arms were outdated, being either leftovers from the Arab Revolt of 1916 or from the Ottoman army that left Syria in 1918. The French, however, had 11,000 soldiers, 48 cannons, 15 tanks, and 5 airplanes. Yusuf al-Azma died on that fateful day in Syrian history and has forever served as a source of inspiration to all Syrians who came after him—a man who sacrificed his life, at such a young age, in order for his nation to survive. Yusuf al-Azma, no doubt, achieved more for Syria in death than during his lifetime.[2]

He happened to be one of President Assad's many heroes. Assad, who spoke frequently and proudly of General Azma, probably saw himself as a natural extension of Yusuf al-Azma, especially because the latter had been minister of defense in 1920, forty-six years before Assad himself assumed the job in 1966. When Azma was appointed minister in 1919, he was only thirty-six years old. When Assad became defense minister in 1966, he too was exactly thirty-six. Azma had heroically led the Syrian army against the French during the Battle of Maysaloun; Assad had led the same army in 1967 against the Israelis. Assad's argument vis-à-vis the Israeli occupation of the Golan was identical to that of Azma during the 1920 conquest of Damascus. Both of them saw in defeat the chance for a nation to be reborn—a nation made morally and militarily stronger and wiser. Azma knew that history would not end on July 24, 1920, just as Assad fully understood that June 9, 1967—the day the Golan Heights fell to Israel—was only temporary in the history of Syria. The Syrians, both men believed, would one day rise from their defeat to reclaim victory and a long-denied justice.

On December 5, 1995, Dennis Ross came to Damascus, to speak to Assad, in the presence of Ambassador Christopher Ross, about the merits of Yitzhak Rabin—who as the entire world knows, was gunned down by an Israeli extremist in November of the same year. By his death, Rabin had given peace a tremendous push forward, Ross said, achieving more for Israel perhaps than during his entire political career. As Ross spoke very emotionally about Rabin, President Assad decided to tell him the story of Yusuf al-Azma. He too had achieved more for Syria by his death than during his short-lived political career. The meeting, which lasted for three hours and forty-five minutes, was attended by Foreign Minister Shara, Muwafak al-Allaf, Ambassador Mouallem, Dennis Ross, and me, serving as the presidential interpreter. The Syrian team nodded as Assad explained to Ross how heroic a leader Yusuf al-Azma had been, adding, "By doing what he did, he actually created thousands of Yusuf al-Azmas in Syria."[3] In addition to countering the Rabin argument, Assad was trying to tell his American guest that the "culture of resistance" was not exclusive to him or the ruling Baath Party. Syria's positions, although hard-line, reflected what day-to-day Syrians thought on the street. This is why at every juncture since the peace process started in 1991, Assad had insisted on taking any detail, no matter how small, to the Syrian street, claiming that he could not take a unilateral decision on peace, that he needed their approval.

The Peres Era

When they got down to business, Ross admitted that "things had been slow" during the Rabin era because the late Israeli prime minister had tried to contain rather than provoke Israeli extremists who—at the end of the day—ended up killing him.[4] Things were going to be different, he added, with Rabin's successor, competitor, and lifelong friend, Shimon Peres. On November 5, President Clinton had headed a large and impressive US delegation to Rabin's funeral, partly because of the president's respect for Rabin's efforts at Oslo, but also because Clinton was interested in seeing whether Peres would pursue Rabin's peace policies with Syria. For his part, Assad had made it clear that he was willing to give Peres the "benefit of the doubt." Although old and ailing at the age of seventy-two, Peres was one of Israel's most seasoned politicians, having served in the Knesset nonstop since 1959. Additionally, he had been a member of over ten cabinets, fought in the war of 1948, was a heavyweight from the Labor Party, and had co-won the Nobel Peace Prize in 1994, along with Yasser Arafat and Rabin. He knew the peace process inside-out, but his weakness—as far as the Syrians were concerned—was that Rabin had kept him in the dark about the famous Rabin Deposit. Peres heard about it only after Rabin's death, when he discovered "computer printouts and secret documents" in one of Rabin's safes at the Ministry of Defense, outlining his proposal on the Syrian Golan to Presidents Clinton and Assad.[5] Rabin had conducted all talks with Assad, via the Americans, personally and in strict confidentiality. Only a handful of aides had been informed of progress on the Syrian track, and apparently Peres was not one of them. That story, it must be mentioned, was published in a biography of Peres entitled *The Man Who Could Not Win*, written by Israeli journalist Orly Azulay-Katz. Excerpts appeared in the mass-circulation Israeli daily *Yediot Aharanot* on September 13, 1996. Although furious at not having been informed of the deal, in his capacity as Rabin's deputy and foreign minister, Peres nevertheless promised to honor it. Elections were scheduled in Israel for October 29, 1996, and Peres realized that if he could come to a deal with President Assad, then his chances of becoming a real prime minister—rather than one "by accident"—would be very high. He sincerely believed that he could "sell peace with Syria" to the Israeli public, thereby building his own legacy in Israel rather than feeding off that of Rabin. When meeting with President Clinton in Washington, D.C., on December 10,

Peres expressed his readiness to engage in talks with Syria's Assad, be they "fast or slow, broad or narrow."[6]

To do so, Peres argued that he needed strong US involvement in the Syrian-Israeli talks. We found that rather strange; the Americans were already playing the role of sponsor, facilitator, mediator, and participant. A stronger role meant outright interference in Syrian affairs and would ultimately overwhelm rather than help the peace process. Peres asked the Americans for a meeting with President Assad, either in Jerusalem or Damascus. Washington, he told Dennis Ross, would be a third option. Only such high drama, he added, would convince the Israeli public that he was as good as—if not better than—Yitzhak Rabin, delivering to them what Rabin had failed to achieve: Hafez al-Assad in their midst or Shimon Peres in the heart of Damascus. Both options, needless to say, were completely out of line for President Assad. The Syrian president, according to top Israeli negotiator Itamar Rabinovich, "felt he had been used and misled [by Rabin]. In his own views, he who 'had made Madrid possible' was the only participant who had, so far, failed to benefit from it. Assad believed that Rabin did not want to conclude an agreement before the elections [of October 1996], but Peres did. Assad wanted to come to an agreement in 1996 but this agreement had to be different from everybody else's."[7]

Assad welcomed Peres's commitment, saying to Ross: "It was not us who killed Rabin. It was an Israeli extremist."[8] Peres should understand that peace needed brave decisions, Assad explained, "and somebody who could deliver and honor his commitments." It also required somebody "who could sell peace to the extremists and hard-liners within Israel itself"; in other words, Assad was asking Ross if Peres had that kind of character.[9] Peres seemed "softer" on the issue of time frames and security than Rabin had been and was unencumbered by most of Rabin's reservations about signing a peace agreement with the Syrians. He lacked charisma and leadership traits, however, which was very worrying to President Assad. When Ross failed to convince him of the need to meet with Peres face-to-face, he came up with another "creative idea" in public diplomacy: a tripartite meeting in Washington, D.C., with Assad, Clinton, and Peres. That also failed to win President Assad's approval. Once again, Assad flatly rejected the idea. Ross then mentioned Lea Rabin, the prime minister's widow, who had recently expressed her commitment to her late husband's peace efforts with the Arabs. It would be advisable, Ross noted, "if Your Excellency builds upon that heritage, which is very popular in

Israel today, by sending her a cable of condolence. It would show commitment to peace and to Yitzhak Rabin's legacy."[10] Once again, Assad said no, prompting Rabinovich to comment in his memoirs a few years later: "Syria's direct response to Rabin's assassination was, at best, heartless!"[11]

What Assad did agree to do, as a gesture of goodwill toward Peres, was use his considerable influence in Lebanon to talk Hizbullah into ending its armed attacks on northern Israel. "This needs to be mutual," he told Ross, "because you should not forget that Peres is more in control of his army than we are in control of Hizbullah."[12] Ross, glad to have secured something from Assad, immediately grabbed it, asking: "Can I say this explicitly to Peres, that you are committed to calming the situation in South Lebanon? I have not discussed this with him, but I will raise the issue accordingly." Smiling, President Assad said, "Please do! But please make sure that the IDF stops shelling southern Lebanon."[13] That was bound to give peace a strong push forward, Ross noted, creating a strong foundation upon which Peres could fortify himself within Israel.

I recall that while I was doing the interpretation, Christopher Ross and Dennis Ross commented upon one word (I cannot remember which) I had just translated from English into Arabic. I explained my choice of words, but President Assad cut them short, sternly saying: "Okay, you are Americans, but you don't have a PhD in English Literature like Bouthaina!"

Stalingrad and al-Qunaitra

In mid-December 1995, Warren Christopher came to Damascus after having visited Peres in Tel Aviv, carrying a ten-point program from the Israeli prime minister. Point I was that the substance of any Syrian-Israeli deal "should be" more important than a time frame for withdrawal from the Golan. Other points included water rights, early warning stations, public diplomacy, limits of withdrawal, demilitarized zones, and, of course, the Lebanese-Israeli border and Syria's relationship with Hizbullah. Most of the points were not new, having earlier been raised, one way or another, by Yitzhak Rabin.[14] What was new was that they were now coming from his successor. Warren Christopher, having just returned from the Balkans where US peacemaking was at its peak, tried to talk President Assad into responding positively to Peres's eagerness, once again asking—in fact begging—for a Syrian-Israeli summit. When Assad rejected that idea—for the millionth time since Madrid—Christopher asked: "Can you at least, Mr. President, think of a suitable place for such a meeting?" I looked at President Assad for any signs of boredom or frustration at the suggestion, but he seemed as calm as ever. "I can think, yes, but that doesn't mean I will ever go to such a meeting unless the Golan Heights are returned in full to Syria."[15] He then added, "Tell Peres we are ready and have put a great effort to bringing peace to the Middle East, but so far, we have found that all doors are still closed."[16]

Christopher then suggested bringing an economist from the State Department for back-to-back visits to Syria and Israel in order to advise both governments how to prepare their economies for peace and for bilateral trade, once an agreement is signed.[17] President Assad found that to be a strange suggestion, asking: "What is the use of her visit if nothing tangible has yet been achieved on the fundamentals of peace? We are not even close to signing an agreement with Israel if we have not yet agreed to what borders they are going to be withdrawing!" Assad, rather offended by the suggestion, added, "I am negotiating peace because I believe in it, not because I need money for my country or because I am seeking economic assistance from the United States."[18] Syria is a self-sufficient country, he added, that does not need foreign investment for agricultural or economic development. He made reference to an early twentieth-century saying by the Arab writer Khalil Gibran: "Pity the nation that wears a cloth it does not weave, eats bread it does not harvest." Foreign aid, he added, comes with strings attached, pointing to Egypt since 1978, which because of American aid had lost its independent voice not only in the Arab-Israeli conflict, but in the Arab family at large. Assad then continued:

> Just before the Israelis withdrew from Qunaitra, the principal town in the Golan Heights, they completely destroyed it. This was rare in politics, where an occupied city is destroyed after it is captured—not through war, but by systematic destruction. [Henry] Kissinger came to me back then, after the disengagement agreement of 1974, with an offer to rebuild Qunaitra: $100 million USD. Qunaitra, I told him, was not destroyed during the war of 1967. It was destroyed while the Israelis were withdrawing from the city after the October War of 1973. They ransacked the city and set it ablaze, destroying it with full conscience of what they were doing and in cold blood. What Kissinger really wanted was not to help Syria rebuild Qunaitra. That was the last of his worries. What he wanted was to erase the memory of what the

Israelis had done with their explosives and bulldozers. I know what a city that has been through war looks like; I visited Stalingrad during one of my many trips to Russia. There were symbols of war everywhere; bullets, shrapnel . . . all harsh memories and wounds that the people of Russia had a hard time forgetting. Obviously Stalingrad had been through war, but its buildings remained standing and its infrastructure remained intact. That was not the case with Qunaitra, which was destroyed beyond imagination by the Israelis, in a very cruel and inhuman manner. We decided not to rebuild Qunaitra, so every Syrian child would see what the Israelis did to their land—not during war, but during a supposed truce, or cease-fire. No, Mr. Christopher, I will not accept US financial or economic assistance for the sake of peace. The only thing that we would welcome is if the United States stops provoking us and tarnishing our image within the international community, with sanctions and an ongoing media war. Once that stops, the Syrian economy will thrive on its own, believe me. It is a virgin economy and does not need foreign investment.[19]

The words of Hafez al-Assad, published for the first time in this chapter, sound—as far as a Syrian reader is concerned—like something Yusuf al-Azma would have said in 1920.

Notes

1. This was the same palace in which I met President Assad for the first time back in 1971. He used it temporarily in the early 1970s before moving to the Rawda Palace and then the People's Palace overlooking the Syrian capital.

2. For more on Yusuf al-Azma, please see Malcom Russell, *Syria Under Faisal I* (Minneapolis: Bibliotheca Islamica, 1985).

3. Archives of the Syrian Presidential Palace, Minutes of the Assad-Ross Meeting, December 5, 1995.

4. Ibid.

5. Rabinovich, *The Brink of Peace*, 5.

6. Ibid., 206.

7. Ibid., 204.

8. Archives of the Syrian Presidential Palace, Minutes of the Assad-Ross Meeting, December 5, 1995.

9. Ibid.

10. Ibid.

11. Rabinovich, *The Brink of Peace,* 208.

12. Archives of the Syrian Presidential Palace, Minutes of the Assad-Ross Meeting, December 5, 1995.

13. Ibid.

14. Assad-Christopher Meeting Minutes, December 15, 1995.

15. Ibid.

16. Ibid.
17. Ibid.
18. Ibid.
19. Ibid.

8

The April Understanding

THE MOOD IN THE MIDDLE EAST CHANGED RATHER DRAMATI-cally when, in February 1996, four attacks rocked Israel over nine days, killing many civilians and damaging—perhaps beyond repair—the reputation of Shimon Peres in the eyes of the Israeli public. Coming just three months after Rabin's assassination, the multiple attacks exposed Peres as a weak and rather colorless leader who had all of Rabin's weaknesses and none of his strengths.

As a young man, Peres had worked as an assistant to Israel's first prime minister, David Ben Gurion, helping him to establish the Israeli Defense Ministry from scratch, but in 1996 young Israelis considered him "too soft" on security because he had never actually served in the IDF. Had he been tougher on security, they argued, the attacks would never have happened in Israel, right under the prime minister's nose. Any initiative made by Peres toward peace with Syria would now spell political suicide—especially given that the Palestinian group Hamas, which had its political offices in Damascus, had claimed responsibility for three of the attacks, while the fourth was claimed by the Damascus-based Islamic Jihad. For Peres to return to the negotiating table, he first had to polish both his nationalist and military credentials at home, and something dramatic had to happen in the Middle East to salvage the Syrian-Israeli peace process.

The Clinton White House ultimately threw a life jacket to him. In late February, Dennis Ross suggested bringing world leaders to a peace summit, where Arab kings and presidents would face the prime minister of Israel. It was proposed that President Clinton himself would chair the assembly and that collectively these leaders would condemn the bombings and formulate an "action plan to combat terrorism." This would empower Peres within Israel, give peace a strong nudge, and, according to Ross, "demonstrate to the Israeli public that pursuing peace was transforming the region and that Israel was not alone in fighting the terrorists." Secretary Christopher welcomed the idea, although President Clinton's top adviser, George Stephanopoulos, vetoed it.[1] The latter argued that the president of the United States would look silly before the American and Israeli public if yet another Palestinian attack took place while the summit was in session, or immediately after it ended. Rather than help Peres, Stephanopoulos claimed Clinton would actually be further damaging his credibility at home if the Palestinians decided to escalate their attacks. This was a likely option, given that Arafat's ability to uphold Oslo was diminishing, while hard-liners such as Islamic Jihad and Hamas were gaining the upper hand in the Palestinian Territories.

It was a big risk, no doubt, with minimal chances of success, but President Clinton—always a proactive optimist—decided to go ahead with a summit, which was scheduled to be held in Sharm al-Shaikh, a beach resort on the Red Sea, in March 1996. Egyptian president Hosni Mubarak pledged to host the "Summit of the Peacemakers," while Saudi Arabia's foreign minister Saud al-Faisal confirmed attendance, although his country did not have diplomatic relations with Israel.[2] Eventually, twenty-nine world leaders went to the beach resort, fourteen of them from the Arab world. But President Assad refused to attend—still arguing, just as he had done at Madrid back in 1991—that he would not sit face-to-face with an Israeli leader "so long as the Golan Heights were not restored in full to Syria." He was amazed by the invitation, and said to us: "It is strange indeed that they still don't get the message!" As far as the Syrian president was concerned, the entire event was nothing but a Kodak moment, staged for the sole purpose of drumming up international solidarity for Israel, and Hafez al-Assad was not interested in being part of the photograph. There was no sense in attending the summit, he argued, so long as the peace process was in limbo, Arab lands were still occupied, and several regional heavyweights (Iraq, Libya, and Iran) had not been invited to join the "Summit of the Peacemakers." Lebanese president Elias Hrawi also refused to participate, to avoid signing a statement that condemned resistance groups such as Islamic Jihad, Hamas, and, of course, Hizbullah.

Since Rabin's assassination in November 1995, we in Syria had felt that we were constantly being asked to do things against our wishes with the sole purpose of helping Shimon Peres gain credibility and legitimacy. It started with Assad being asked to meet with Peres in December, followed by a suggestion that he should send a condolence cable to Lea Rabin. Now the United States was asking us to attend a summit with Peres—to make him look good in the international community and to his own constituency inside Israel. By mid-1996, we began to feel that although we had had nothing to do with Rabin's assassination, we were paying a price for his death by being constantly asked to walk that extra mile and make that extra gesture to reach peace and "uphold Rabin's legacy."

The April War

The pressure accelerated during the first few months of 1996 and reached new heights in April during the Lebanese-Israeli war, known in the West by its Israeli code name, Operation Grapes of Wrath. Arabs, however, prefer to call it by its Arab name, the April War, which was coined by the Hizbullah chief Hasan Nasrallah. The sixteen-day campaign was ostensibly launched by the Israelis to halt Hizbullah missile attacks into northern Israel—with 1,100 Israeli air raids over Lebanese territory and a salvo of 25,132 shells landing on Lebanese homes, farms, and civilians. Shamefully, the IDF struck a UN building in Qana village during the battle, with five 155-millimeter howitzer shells, killing 118 civilians in what has since been called the first "Qana massacre" (the second one happened during the 2006 Israeli war with Lebanon). An entire generation of young Arabs—the same age as my two daughters—recalls that massacre with a shiver running down their spine. It was one of the most brutal attacks in the history of the Arab-Israeli conflict and will remain imprinted in the minds of very many generations of Arabs for years to come. In his memoirs, however, Martin Indyk, described it as "accidental," claiming that the IDF had spotted Hizbullah rockets at the site, which left them with no choice but to attack. Indyk, it should be noted, was at the time serving as Bill Clinton's ambassador to Israel. Amazingly, Warren Christopher does not even mention the Qana massacre in his memoirs *Chances of a Lifetime*; neither does he make any reference to the marathon negotiations that he led to bring an end to the crisis, which came to be known as the "April Understanding." Dennis Ross does indeed acknowledge the gravity of Qana and admitted: "We muted our criticism of the Israeli action, striving instead more visibly to produce a cease-fire."[3] Israel was very slow to express regret for the loss of innocent lives. Initially, IDF deputy chief of staff Matan Vilnai said that the rockets had hit the UN building not because they were off target but because the IDF had outdated maps of the area. Peres himself remarked, "We did not know that several hundred people were concentrated in that camp. It came to us as a bitter surprise."[4] IDF chief of staff Amnon Shahak added, "I don't see any mistake in judgment. We fought Hizbullah there [in Qana] and when they fire on us, we will fire at them to defend ourselves. I don't know any other rules of the game, either for the army or for civilians."[5] US State Department Spokesman Nicolas Burns stated that, "Hizbullah is using civilians as cover. That's a despicable thing to do, an evil thing."[6] But as far as we were concerned in Damascus, the Qana massacre and how both the United States and Israel reacted to it was a human tragedy and a diplomatic disaster for the peace process. Nobody in their right mind would talk to an Israeli prime minister who had so much Lebanese blood on his hands. The Qana massacre proved that Shimon Peres was no different from Ariel Sharon, Menachem Begin, or Yizhak Rabin; indeed, President Assad always told us that Arab blood was "sacred," whether it was Lebanese, Palestinian, or Syrian.

Since their 1978 invasion of South Lebanon, the Israelis had not had a single day of peace and quiet on the Lebanese border. This, of course, was thanks to the resolute Lebanese people, along with various elements of Lebanese resistance that started with the Syrian Social Nationalist Party (SSNP), the Amal Movement, the Lebanese Communist Party, and Hizbullah, which emerged after the 1982 invasion of Beirut. In 1985 the IDF established what it called a "Security Buffer Zone" in South Lebanon. Eight years later, in August 1993, it launched a major offensive—which it called Operation Accountability—aimed at breaking Hizbullah, but with no luck. That campaign ended with a cease-fire and verbal agreement that both sides would cease to target civilians, with Syria keeping a watchful eye on things. Tel Aviv had violated this agreement in April 1996 with yet another military campaign aimed at subduing Hizbullah. The new battle started on March 30, when two men were killed by an IDF helicopter while working on a water tower in Yater in Lebanon. A roadside bomb then went off in the south, killing a fourteen-year-old Lebanese boy in the village of Barashit and injuring three civilians. Hizbullah responded by launching twenty missiles into northern Israel on April 9. Two days later, on April 11, the Israeli government began Operation Grapes of Wrath, ostensibly in response to Hizbullah rockets that had injured six Israeli civilians. The famed Hizbullah rocket—the Katyusha—was not a lethal weapon, and nobody knew that better than the Americans and Israelis.

In the early morning of April 11, Israeli aircraft and artillery began an intensive bombardment of southern Lebanon as well as targets in the Beirut area and in the Bekaa Valley. The declared objective of these attacks was to put pressure on Prime Minister Rafiq al-Hariri to clamp down on Hizbullah border attacks. Israel conducted air raids on targets that included Katyusha launchers, Hizbullah installations, schools, ambulances, and plenty of other civilian targets. In one instance the IDF struck at a two-story building in the Nabatiyeh village in South Lebanon, killing nine civilians in their sleep. No fewer than 500,000 residents of southern Lebanon were forced to flee their homes because of the Israeli attacks. The caravan of refugees aroused international anger, but by no means did it halt the Israeli offensive. On April 12, Israeli airplanes attacked a Syrian military post, killing one soldier and injuring twelve others. By April 13, the IDF had blocked off the ports of Beirut, Sidon, and Tyre. On April 14, the IDF attacked the Beirut power stations in the Jumhour neighborhood of the Lebanese capital, cutting off its electricity supply and sending Beirut into haunting darkness. Approximately 170 Lebanese were killed in the April War, including 106 civilians, and 350 were wounded. That number—small when compared to what happened in 2006—was definitely larger than the 62 civilians killed in Israel by Hizbullah missiles. The damage to Lebanese infrastructure was significant as major bridges and power stations were destroyed. According to Human Rights Watch, 2,018 houses and buildings in South Lebanon were either completely destroyed or severely bombarded. Lebanon's total economic damage was estimated at $500 million, according to the Lebanese Center for Policy Studies: $140 million for rebuilding damaged infrastructure, $30 million for assisting those displaced, $260 million in lost economic output, and $70 million in losses due to delays in economic projects.[7]

Cease-Fire Talks

US diplomats rushed into the region to broker a cease-fire based on the 1993 verbal understanding that prohibited the targeting of Lebanese and Israeli civilians. The Israelis, however, were operating as if there were no 1993 agreement protecting civilian territories in South Lebanon. Shimon Peres had no other choice but to behave thus—he had to show that he was tough on security or lose the upcoming Israeli elections scheduled for May. Nevertheless, desperate for a cease-fire that would hold, he asked the Clinton team to talk President Assad into using his influence with Hizbullah to get them to stop firing rockets at northern Israel.

The April Understanding talks in Damascus in April 1996. Heading the US delegation on the left side of the table is Secretary of State Warren Christopher. On the right side (from left to right): Mikhael Wehbeh; Adnan Omran, assistant secretary-general of the Arab League; Foreign Minister Farouk al-Shara; President Hafez al-Assad; Bouthaina Shaaban; Nasser Qaddour; Syria's ambassador to the United States, Walid al-Mouallem.

Peres knew that Syria was a staunch supporter of Hizbullah but realized that to obtain even a modicum of peace and quiet on the Israeli-Lebanese border, Syrian cooperation was vital. No deal would hold, he told the North Americans, unless it was supported by Hafez al-Assad.

Warren Christopher was in the Far East when the April War started. Dennis Ross was in Washington, D.C., conducting diplomacy over the telephone with the Syrian foreign minister Shara, the Lebanese, and the Israelis, frantically asking all parties to abide by the 1993 agreement. Lebanese prime minister Rafiq al-Hariri flew to Paris, desperate for a cease-fire to save his country from ruin, and enlisted the help of the French president Jacques Chirac, who was a personal friend. Peres wanted US diplomats to come to Syria to secure a written agreement from President Assad. He told them that a verbal agreement, like the one in 1993, would no longer hold with the angry Israeli public. Shara told him that the Syrian president, in principle, did not mind a written commitment "if the Lebanese government would also be party to such an agreement."

Ross arrived in Tel Aviv on April 19 and met with Israel's top political and military leaders, including Defense Minister Ehud Barak. They argued that Syria and Hizbullah were "certainly not losing in the crisis" and that the IDF was in no hurry to end the fighting. This, however, was against the wish of Prime Minister Peres, who by now was seriously contemplating an Israeli withdrawal from South Lebanon to get the entire Hizbullah "nightmare" out of his crosshairs. The only condition, Peres said, was that it could not be effected until a cease-fire was hammered out, and not under the humiliating pressure of Hizbullah missiles. If the IDF withdrew, he added, this would deprive Hizbullah of a pretext to keep its arms, thereby "damaging its resistance rationale." Syria, he argued, would be cornered into a situation in which it could not but back Israel's decision to withdraw from Lebanon. Assad, Ross explained to him, "would not let Israel live easily in Lebanon so long as the Golan Heights remain occupied."[8]

President Assad, of course, understood what was contemplated in the upper echelons of power in Tel Aviv. Had Peres lived up to his idea in 1996, Assad's requirement would have been that the withdrawal be immediate and unconditional, based on UNSCR 425. The Israelis would not be given the luxury of "waiting for calm" before they left South Lebanon. Peres's message, conveyed to us by the United States over the next few days of shuttle diplomacy, was that he was willing to lose the Golan or the upcoming Israeli elections—but not both.

On April 20, the US team arrived in Damascus, headed by Secretary of State Christopher and Dennis Ross, for what was to be the first of four long meetings with President Assad. The top US diplomat had one clear argument: "Israel has the right to fire back at whatever source of fire is targeting northern Israel, regardless if it was civilian or not."[9] This, of course, sharply contradicted the 1993 agreement, which prohibited any attack on civilian territory. Hizbullah warriors firing the rockets, Christopher argued, were "hiding" in civilian towns and villages in South Lebanon, from whence they were firing rockets into northern Israel. The IDF was being left with no choice but to strike back at the "source of fire," regardless of whether it came from a civilian or military base. What follows is an account of the first meeting, taken from the official unpublished papers of President Assad:

ROSS: The Israelis were brought to believe, back in 1993, that the Lebanese attacks would continue from within the security zone, but not from civilian towns and villages in southern Lebanon. Today the Hizbullah attacks are taking place from outside the security zone, and we believe that the IDF has the right to fire back at the source of the attack—as stated by the 1993 agreement.

CHRISTOPHER: Let me try to explain what happens: a Katyusha rocket is fired into northern Israel, and I get on the phone and call Damascus, objecting to this. My good friend Farouk [al-Shara] listens to me attentively, and then says that Hizbullah did that because the IDF was firing at civilians north of the security strip.

Assad: Yes, that is true . . .

Christopher: But in reality, Mr. President, the Israelis are not firing at the villages, but rather at the source of fire that happened to come from the villages themselves.

Assad: From a military point of view, this analysis is flawed. First of all, the Katyusha rocket is small, and, after firing it, the fighter immediately moves from one location to another. It does not ground him to a particular base or village, and this is why we see a lot of commotion between the security zone and civilian districts in southern Lebanon. The Israelis have a long military history, and they know very well that when they fire at a particular village they are hitting the village and not the person who fired the rocket at them, regardless of whether or not he was based in the village itself or not. And even if the Hizbullah fighter struck from within the village, he probably would have left the village after completing his attack. This means that when the IDF strike at a village they are actually destroying the village and punishing its civilian population, not the Hizbullah fighter who fired at them, who is the real "source" of the attack. The source in this case is not the village but the person who fired the rocket. Obviously what the 1993 agreement lacks is a mechanism to determine who opened fire first, where this fire came from, and what justifies retaliation against the "source" of the attack.

Christopher: If we address this issue, can we reach a solution?

Assad: In theory, yes, we can, but there needs to be a proper mechanism, a proper monitoring of the border, and, of course, accountability that applies to both sides.

Shara: This would also create relative calm . . .

Assad: When you spoke with Mr. Shara over the telephone, he suggested that Syria and the United States assume joint responsibility for what happens on the border. Once the truce comes into effect, we need a proper monitoring committee mandated by all parties to judge which side is responsible if there is a violation of the cease-fire. This committee would then conduct an investigation, within a period of twenty-four to forty-eight hours. Until that investigation is complete, neither side would have the right to open fire on the other.

Ross: If that is agreed, can we speak about a negotiated withdrawal once calm is restored to the Israeli-Lebanese border?

Assad: This "negotiated withdrawal" is not new; it has been raised before, many times, even before the peace process began. The Israelis used to say that they would need a period [of time] to test the calm, but the Lebanese would never accept such a probationary period.

CHRISTOPHER: That is correct . . .

ASSAD: I don't believe the situation has changed.

SHARA: The day before yesterday, Peres suggested a negotiated withdrawal once calm is restored, conditional on a probationary period to see if border security holds and is sustainable.

ASSAD: I have not heard that from Peres, but this is what all his predecessors have asked for in the past.

CHRISTOPHER: Do you think we can all now concentrate on a cease-fire to bring an end to the killing?

ASSAD: What we can do is try to protect civilians on both sides of the border. This has always been our objective. Let us be a little realistic here. It is impossible to ask fighters, from either side, suddenly to trust each other. After peace is achieved, this may become possible as time goes by. But for somebody whose land is occupied, for him to keep watching the occupier—while at the same time doing nothing about it—is very difficult and unjust. No country in the world can prevent its citizens from standing up for their national rights and working to restore occupied land. The Israelis are sensitive about civilians—we understand and respect that. Every country in the world is keen to protect the lives of its civilians, and Israel is no exception. But when a country tries to prevent its citizens from fighting an occupying force, the problem will immediately transform from fighting the occupier into fighting each other. Meaning, now Hizbullah fighters are trained [to fight] against Israel. If the Lebanese government tries to prevent them from doing so, they will start to fight each other, and the Lebanese government itself. The Lebanese government simply will not be able to stop them from leading a resistance movement against Israel. You all know that Lebanon has just emerged from a very bloody civil war—a war that all parties concerned, including the United States, worked hard to bring to a halt. If today you pressure the Lebanese government to restrict the activities of Hizbullah, you will actually be pushing Lebanon into a civil war.

CHRISTOPHER: Do you suggest a partial cease-fire, Mr. President, where fighting can continue, but only in the security zone?

ASSAD: The word "cease-fire" is usually used in connection with an official war between two countries when there is a war led by governments. But here we are talking about a nonstate player, Hizbullah, fighting a guerrilla war with an official army, the IDF.

CHRISTOPHER: No, [the term] "cease-fire" has been used in different contexts, even when no official armies are involved, as is the case in Bosnia.

ASSAD: In that instance, it was a war between different parties within Bosnia. I am not objecting to the term "cease-fire," but I am insisting that we must be clear about whaever phrase we use, to avoid any future misconceptions. Clarity is vital to us, Mr. Secretary.

CHRISTOPHER: What kind of cease-fire do you think is possible on the Israeli-Lebanese border?

ASSAD: The same formula we agreed upon in 1993, but with some guarantees. Why was that agreement, which was seen as positive back in 1993, suddenly viewed as flawed by the Americans and Israelis?

CHRISTOPHER: We can reach a cease-fire, but what you are asking for is a total understanding between Israel and Hizbullah.

SHARA: Yes, but not before a cease-fire is achieved . . .

ASSAD: And what happens after the cease-fire?

SHARA: After the cease-fire, we can talk about other details . . .

ROSS: In other words, a cease-fire comes first, followed by an understanding. An understanding would help strengthen the cease-fire.

ASSAD: I suggest a temporary cease-fire for now. Yesterday, our foreign minister had a meeting with ten people from Hizbullah. We had a hard time tracking them down and assembling them for the meeting. They listened attentively to what we had to say but did not commit to anything. I am not sure what they will say to all of this, but I am optimistic that they will agree. I cannot speak on their behalf, however, because I am not a member of Hizbullah.

CHRISTOPHER: If this happens, we can put it in writing.

ASSAD: We can put it in writing only after we reach a mechanism for monitoring and accountability. We must not leave room for any vagueness. As I have just said, clarity is vital. We have always suffered from vagueness in our dealings with the Israelis.

ROSS: Can we get a final say from you, Mr. President, before Secretary of State Christopher leaves for Israel?

ASSAD: First let him go to Israel; we can speak further when he gets back.

CHRISTOPHER: They say that time is vital in times like these.

SHARA: Indeed, time is gold . . .

CHRISTOPHER: We need to agree on what will happen when Israeli soldiers are targeted outside the security zone. If we don't agree on that beforehand, I simply will not be able to get the approval of the Israelis to anything decided upon in this room.

ASSAD: One option is for them [the Israelis] to retaliate with individual weapons; for example, a rifle with a range of 100–200 meters. Meaning that under no circumstances will they be allowed to use long-range weapons against civilian targets in Lebanon. The point here is not to protect the fighters but the Lebanese civilians. A fighter is a fighter—he knows how to defend himself. According to the UN Charter, all people living under occupation have the right to defend themselves against foreign occupation. I cannot think of a single case in history where people have been prohibited from combating an occupying force. Don't forget that the Lebanese fighters are not targeting Israeli soldiers for the sake of creating trouble along the border; they are doing so because the Israelis occupy southern Lebanon.

CHRISTOPHER: Part of the agreement needs to include a clause on what to do when confronted by fire coming from a civilian area. The Katyusha rockets, after all, are being fired from civilian neighborhoods.

ASSAD: In the 1993 agreement, all parties agreed on the right to strike back at any source of fire. But this cannot in any way mean entire towns and villages. It means the right to fire at any person who initiated an attack, but not collective punishment of an entire civilian neighborhood or town. Let them fire at the person who fired at them, not at the geographical territory from where a missile was launched.

There will be another session tomorrow—let us discuss this further then.

ROSS: We need to speak about the proposed negotiated withdrawal from Lebanon.

ASSAD: Occupation did not come through negotiation, and therefore I don't think withdrawal needs to come through negotiation. If the Israelis want to leave, they should be encouraged to do so without negotiation. Negotiation means there is something else sought after under the table. What is it that you want the Lebanese to give in exchange for withdrawal?

ROSS: The Lebanese have to present something . . .

ASSAD: Every country is responsible for its own borders. All they [the Lebanese] are asking for is restoration of their occupied land. I cannot dictate anything to the Lebanese.

CHRISTOPHER: I will raise all these points when I travel to Israel tomorrow. We have to move early because we have a long trip ahead of us. Of course, you haven't visited that country in a long time, but it takes a while to reach Jerusalem, where Peres is now based, from Tel Aviv Airport, where we will be landing.

ASSAD: That is their responsibility, not ours. Why did they move the airport in the first place?[10]

Mr. Secretary: President Assad Is Unavailable

The meeting ended with the US team traveling to Israel but planning to reconvene in Damascus on April 22. In fact, Christopher arrived unannounced in the Syrian capital on April 21 and requested a meeting with the president. Benazir Bhutto, prime minister of Pakistan, was in town, and President Assad had already scheduled a long meeting with her. Also on that day, the French foreign minister Herve de Charette, his Russian counterpart, and the Iranian foreign minister Ali Akbar Velayati were all in Damascus, as well as the US secretary of state and the Pakistani prime minister. What I remember most about that day was that it was very long and filled with back-to-back meetings with the president, during which I did all the interpretation for him.

During his session with Bhutto, a woman whom he admired greatly, the chief of protocol walked in twice, each time carrying a note saying that Warren Christopher was at the US embassy in Damascus and "needs to see President Assad immediately." The president looked at me in surprise, somewhat offended that Christopher had the nerve to drop in on us without an appointment and yet expect an immediate audience with the president. It sounded like something the French high commissioner might have done in Damascus back in the 1930s but seemed bizarre for a seasoned diplomat like Christopher, who knew more than most North Americans that such behavior strikes a raw nerve in Syria.

"I cannot see him today as I also have a state dinner for Prime Minister Bhutto," the president mumbled. Then he looked back at his Pakistani guest and smiled, apologizing for the interruption.

More news came in, on yet another yellow note, that read that "Warren Christopher was furious" and "might leave now and not wait until tomorrow."

President Assad did not even blink. "Then let him leave; it is up to him!" I could tell from the look in his eyes that if he had previously been toying with the idea of wrapping up the Bhutto meeting to receive Christopher, the secretary's arm-twisting had killed that idea. The chief of protocol sent a note to Christopher to say that President Assad is "busy with a full schedule" and wouldn't be able to receive the top US diplomat. What the president seemed to focus on now was not Christopher but Asif Zardari, Bhutto's husband, who was seated right next to me. So that the official talks could start, Zardari (now president of Pakistan) had to leave the room because he had no official reason to attend his wife's summit with President Assad. Zardari, however, did not seem

A dinner in honor of Pakistani prime minister Benazir Bhutto in Damascus in 1996. From left to right: Prime Minister Mahmoud al-Zoubi, Prime Minister Bhutto, Bouthaina Shaaban, President Hafez al-Assad, Assistant Foreign Minister Abdulfattah Ammura, Asif Zardari (Bhutto's husband and the current prime minister of Pakistan), Vice President Abdul Halim Khaddam.

to be getting the message, so the president continued with the meeting in his presence.

Somewhere on the other side of town—probably at the Sheraton Hotel where he stayed while in Damascus—was Warren Christopher, furious at being "snubbed" and "dressed down" (as the US press was saying) by the Syrian president. The US secretary of state ended up swallowing his pride and spending the night in Damascus to attend an 11:30 A.M. meeting with President Assad on April 22. Christopher arrived carrying his brown briefcase, packed with papers and notes. He was obviously tense, and his face was swollen and crimson red, as he had failed to "cool off" from the previous day.

After the good morning niceties, he asked for a private meeting with the president. Assad nodded and the three of us moved into a nearby room with one sofa and a few chairs. The president signaled for him to take a seat. Christopher's hands and lips were still trembling as he put his hands around his briefcase, saying, "Mr. President, I want to know why you were so intent on insulting me and my country, the United States of America, yesterday?"

Keeping his composure, President Assad looked him straight in the eye, before saying, "And in what way did I make that happen, Mr. Christopher?"

Christopher then exploded, nevertheless politely. "I have been asking to see you since yesterday and [up until now] you have refused to see me. More than once I thought of leaving!"

Again very calmly, the president explained the reason for his being unable to see Christopher. "We did not have a time set for our meeting. You simply arrived and wanted to see me immediately, while I was seeing the prime minister of another country whose visit was scheduled and planned beforehand. You wanted me to leave her and meet with you? Why did you take my being unable to see you as an insult, rather than as a natural way of behaving? Whether it is the United States of America or any other country in the world, be it large or small, powerful or weak, all countries are equal when it comes to integrity. All people, Mr. Christopher, should enjoy the same human dignity. I acted according to the rules of protocol and diplomatic behavior, and you have no right to feel insulted or angry."

Christopher, somewhat reassured by the president's words, rejoined, "Everybody is saying that you kept me waiting and refused to see me!"

Assad smiled rather affectionately at his US guest, speaking now more like a father addressing a teenage son who has just finished a temper tantrum: "No matter what they say, I am sure you know that I was right. Now let's join the rest for the meeting!"

Strangely enough, in his memoirs, Warren Christopher made no mention of this episode with President Assad, and neither did President Clinton.

The only senior US official to give his version of what happened in Damascus—which is very flawed and blatantly wrong—was Dennis Ross. He wrote: "American pundits were asking: How could we put up with this? And for some time, this episode became an enduring image of Warren Christopher's term as Secretary of State. That is unfair, because the real story was that we had not gone to Damascus to see Assad but to stage a surprise, unannounced helicopter flight to Beirut as part of our shuttle diplomacy. Since Baker's time, all trips to Lebanon had been by daytime motorcades from Damascus. For security reasons, we need to keep our plans unknown until the last minute. With our delegation assembling and the press contingent ready to leave the hotel, we learned that the US commander in Europe had turned down approval of the helicopter flights, citing unspecified security reasons. We were stuck in Damascus. It was too late to organize a motorcade to go to Beirut. At this point, we sought a meeting with Assad but he proved to be 'too busy.' There is no question that Assad liked the suggestion that he would see the Secretary of State only on his terms.

Secretary Christopher had every right to walk away at that point. He could have postured and made himself look good. However, this would have jeopardized the cease-fire and we would have ultimately had to go back to Assad to produce one. The situation would lead the Israelis back into Lebanon north of the security zone and subject them to a continuing guerrilla war. In these circumstances, Warren Christopher chose not to take the easy way out."[11]

Concluding the Understanding

Back in the meeting room, it was business as usual for President Assad and Secretary of State Christopher. Christopher suggested calling what was agreed between him and the Syrians on one front, and the Israelis on another, an "understanding." He had come back to us with a draft document, written by Ross, the principal notetaker in all our meetings, suggesting that this "understanding" was not a substitute for a Lebanese-Israeli peace process. It was agreed, and stressed, that civilians from both sides would not be targeted. President Assad asked for a chance to read the proposed document, telling Christopher: "We will be flexible; we won't be biased toward our interests—I can assure you."[12] That is what I respected about the president. He was a very smart man, very outspoken in his views, but at the end of the day he was someone who was both fair and sensible. We broke for recess, reviewed what had been written, and then returned to discuss it with the US personnel. The president read the preamble out loud in Arabic, and then I continued the rest of the understanding. Syria had three main amendments to the document that it insisted upon and that need to be emphasized. One was to include France on the monitoring committee, despite Washington's original objection. Christopher then argued that this might upset other countries in Europe, but Assad insisted, arguing that nobody would object given the historical relationship between Paris and Beirut from the days of the French Mandate in Lebanon. He added that French president Chirac felt a deep-rooted desire to be part of the solution in Lebanon. President Assad thought that the French president would be an honest broker in Lebanese affairs and wanted to give him that role.

Syria's second amendment was that it did not want to be mentioned as the main negotiator of the agreement, out of respect for the Lebanese, asking that reference be made only to "consultations with Syria."[13] Third, Assad insisted that no mention of Hizbullah be made in the agreement, respecting the wishes of Lebanese prime minister Hariri and

Nabih Berri, the powerful speaker of parliament and head of the Amal Movement, who was a strong ally of President Assad. The two men had visited him the previous day, making sure that the Lebanese government was mentioned by name in the agreement. "Hizbullah is not Lebanon," Hariri told the Syrian president, stressing the same point to Christopher when they met in Shatura, a sleepy town on the Lebanese-Syrian border. If the two sides wanted, they could write "popular movements" or "military groups" but certainly not militia or terrorist organizations—as the Israelis would have wished—or Hizbullah by name, as the United States was suggesting. Assad strongly supported their argument, saying to Christopher, "I agree to every word they said."[14] Although anti-Syrian figures in Lebanon spoke out against Syria's handling of the April War, claiming that President Assad was practicing hegemony over the Lebanese, the truth is that he was very keen to consult with top Lebanese officials at every juncture of the April Understanding negotiations. Rafiq al-Hariri, Nabih Berri, and Hizbullah had the ultimate say in the agreement. Assad only facilitated the talks, standing up for what the Lebanese wanted and articulating what they perhaps could not articulate or deliver as strongly as he could.

There was the thorny issue of where and when to announce the cease-fire. Assad suggested Lebanon, whereas Dennis Ross proposed Israel. It was then decided that the announcement would be made simultaneously in both Lebanon and Israel, to keep all sides happy. Then came the second bottleneck: April 26—the day of the cease-fire announcement—fell on a Friday. The Sabbath, the most widely observed ritual in Judaism, which mandates "rest" according to the Ten Commandments and is strictly observed in Israel, begins at sunset and ends at nightfall—meaning that Shimon Peres would not be able to do or say anything after leaving his office on Friday. "All of Israel comes to a grinding halt after 6:00 P.M. on a Sabbath," Christopher told us, suggesting we change the time to 5:30 P.M.

President Assad was not impressed by what he was hearing, but he chose to say nothing about it in order to finalize the cease-fire, wondering nevertheless what would have happened had it been the other way round: with Israelis being killed by Hizbullah and the United States asking us to implement a cease-fire on a Friday.

By the fourth round of talks with Christopher, the president could see that the US delegation was desperate for a cease-fire, but he was not going to agree to this unless he got what he wanted—a new understanding with Israel that offered de facto recognition of Hizbullah and also secured civilian areas in southern Lebanon. Before members of the delegation left, President Assad decided to play his final card and extract one last concession that was very dear to his heart. He raised the issue of the naval blockade of Lebanon, saying that unless it was lifted, he would not accept the agreement. End of story! President Assad, although exhausted by the talks, was now suddenly full of life as he now spoke for the sailors and fishermen of Lebanon, the working people that he as a socialist always identified with far more strongly than he did with world leaders or heavyweights from the corporate world. Needless to say, the US delegation was infuriated by Assad's last-minute suggestion. Christopher got up, buttoned his coat, and looked at Ross, saying, "Dennis, we are leaving!"[15] The Secretary of State was clearly angered at having his arm twisted, yet again, by the Syrian president. What made it worse was that he knew how much he needed the Syrians to seal off any agreement. But no matter how angry he was with the issue of the naval blockade, he could not but agree to lift it to keep Hafez al-Assad happy.

I was doing the interpretation and was taken aback by Christopher's outburst. I looked at the president for some kind of signal as to what I should do or say. He leaned over and whispered softly to me: "Stay seated. They will come back." His body language was completely at ease with what he was saying; his hands gently resting on the oriental sofa on which he was seated, his face calm and relaxed. Surely enough, a few minutes later, Christopher and Ross returned to the room, having come to their senses, and resumed the talks as if nothing had happened. The April Understanding was announced in both Lebanon and Israel on April 26 and went into effect at 4:00 A.M. on April 27, 1996. It included all President Assad's suggestions—every single one of them.

The April Understanding reads as follows:

> The United States understands that after discussions with the governments of Israel and Lebanon, and in consultation with Syria, Lebanon and Israel will ensure the following:
> 1. Armed groups in Lebanon will not carry out attacks by Katyusha rockets or by any kind of weapon into Israel.
> 2. Israel and those cooperating with it will not fire any kind of weapon at civilians or civilian targets in Lebanon.
> 3. Beyond this, the two parties commit to ensuring that under no circumstances will civilians be the target of attack and that civilian populated areas and industrial and electrical installations will not be used as launching grounds for attacks.
> 4. Without violating this understanding, nothing herein shall preclude any party from exercising the right of self-defense.

A monitoring group will be established consisting of the United States, France, Syria, Lebanon and Israel. Its task will be to monitor the application of the understanding stated above. Complaints will be submitted to the Monitoring Group.

In the event of a claimed violation of the understanding, the party submitting the complaint will do so within 24 hours. Procedures for dealing with the complaints will be set by the Monitoring Group. The United States will also organize a Consultative Group, to consist of France, the European Union, Russia and other interested parties, for the purpose of assisting in the reconstruction needs of Lebanon.

It is recognized that the understanding to bring the current crisis between Lebanon and Israel to an end cannot substitute for a permanent solution. The United States understands the importance of achieving a comprehensive peace in the region.

Toward this end, the United States proposes the resumption of negotiations between Syria and Israel and between Lebanon and Israel at a time to be agreed upon, with the objective of reaching comprehensive peace.

The United States understands that it is desirable that these negotiations be conducted in a climate of stability and tranquility.

This understanding will be announced simultaneously at 1800 hours, April 26, 1996, in all countries concerned.

The time set for implementation is 0400 hours, April 27, 1996.[16]

Conclusion

In an article published in the *Journal of Palestine Studies* (Fall 1997), President Assad's biographer Patrick Seale wrote: "Assad saw Grapes of Wrath as directed primarily against him. He could not fail to see it as a replay, albeit on a more modest scale, of Operation Peace for Galilee, Menachem Begin's invasion of Beirut in 1982." The ultimate goal of the operation, Seale added: "was to undermine Hafez al-Assad in Lebanon and drive a wedge between him and Iran."[17] In reality, however, the exact opposite happened. Grapes of Wrath and the April Understanding were turning points in the history of diplomacy in the Arab-Israeli Conflict, and a cornerstone of Syrian foreign policy. They did for President Assad's reputation as an international statesman what the Camp David Accords did for President Carter's. If anything, they made Assad stronger, firmer, and more committed than ever before to saying "No" to the United States. After all, the April Understanding talks proved that, unlike what everybody believed, the United States does not get what it wants every time in the Middle East. Myth is one thing, but political reality is another. The new political reality imposed following the April Understanding was that Hizbullah was now there to stay, and that, unlike before, it was internationally recognized—without that perhaps being stated—by the United States and France, who served on the monitoring committee for the understanding. In addition to being the man who "snubbed" Warren Christopher, President Assad proved to be somebody who could deliver and honor his word. The April Understanding—as far as Hizbullah's commitment—held for 120 months, right up until July 2006, when Israeli prime minister Ehud Olmert decided to kill it by launching the second Lebanon War in 2006. It was Hafez al-Assad who made the understanding happen for ten years, even though for six of those years he was not around to make sure that it held ground. He created a viable system and proper mechanism that lived longer than he did.

Notes

1. Ross, *The Missing Peace*, 246–247.
2. Ibid., 247.
3. Ibid., 251.
4. Human Rights Watch, *Civilian Pawns*.
5. Ibid., 93.
6. Ibid., 94.
7. Wright, *The Looming Tower: Al-Qaeda and the Road to 9/11*.
8. *Tishreen*, April 20, 1995. See also Ross, *The Missing Peace*, 252.
9. Archives of the Syrian Presidential Palace, Minutes of the Assad-Christopher Talks, April 1995.
10. Ibid.
11. Ross, *The Missing Peace*, 253–254.
12. Archives of the Syrian Presidential Palace, Minutes of the Assad-Christopher Talks, April 1995.
13. Ibid.
14. Ibid.
15. Ibid.
16. Archives of the Syrian Presidential Palace, The April Understanding, April 27, 1996.
17. Seale, "Asad's Regional Strategy," *Journal of Palestinian Studies*, 26, no. 1 (Autumn 1996): 27–41.

9

The Not-So-Secret Lauder Talks

THE SECOND HALF OF THE 1990s WAS DIFFICULT FOR PRESIdent Clinton and, therefore, challenging for the moribund peace process. By mid-1995, Clinton was already immersed in the US presidential campaign and focused entirely on the November 1996 elections. He had very little time anymore for the Middle East, and most of the talking—no matter how repetitive—was done by his aides, supervised by the outgoing secretary of state, Warren Christopher. Clinton was eventually reelected with 49.2 percent of the popular vote, defeating the Republican Bob Dole and independent candidate Ross Perot, and was thus sworn in for another presidential term in January 1997. Clinton became the first incumbent Democrat since Lyndon Johnson to be elected to a second term at the White House. Arab Americans celebrated his reelection, and leaders throughout the Middle East rejoiced. Since 1993, Clinton had proved that he was somebody with whom they could do good business.

Life was not as rosy as it seemed, however, since the Republicans retained control of both the House and the Senate, thus providing Clinton with a constant headache when it came to the Arab-Israeli conflict. What made things much worse was the infamous scandal that exploded in Clinton's face in early 1998—his affair with twenty-two-year-old White House intern Monica Lewinsky, dating back to his first term in office. That story nearly got him impeached, and very greatly affected his reputation both in the United States and throughout Arab and Muslim countries.

The world remembers only too well how Clinton addressed the people of the United States on January 26, 1998, when he said, with his wife at his side: "Now, I have to go back to work on my State of the

Union speech. And I worked on it until pretty late last night. But I want to say one thing to the American people. I want you to listen to me. I'm going to say this again: I did not have sexual relations with that woman, Miss Lewinsky. I never told anybody to lie, not a single time; never. These allegations are false. And I need to go back to work for the American people. Thank you."¹ What was so ugly about that statement, which sadly has become one of the most memorable soundbites of his presidency, was that Bill Clinton had indeed lied to the American people in order to save his career, his marriage, and his reputation before millions of people around the world, who looked up to him as a role model.

In looking at newspaper archives and notes from the 1990s, I have to pause for a moment to comment on Hillary Clinton, a woman who inspired confidence in those who watched her as the first lady of the United States during the difficult months of her husband's trial. Hillary stood by Bill Clinton until the curtain fell on the Lewinsky affair. When speaking to NBC on January 27, 1998, she famously said: "The great story here for anybody willing to find it and write about it and explain it is this vast right-wing conspiracy that has been conspiring against my husband since the day he announced for president."² Today, however, in her capacity as secretary of state, Hillary Clinton no longer uses the word "conspiracy." She frowned on the Palestinians when they used it to explain US bias toward Israel before, during, and after the 2008 war on Gaza. She harangued them when they claimed that an "international conspiracy" was obstructing their UN call to nationhood in September 2011. And in Syria, when we used the word "conspiracy" to define part of what was happening on the Syrian streets since mid-March 2011, Hillary Clinton insisted that there was no "conspiracy" being hatched against the Syrian government. Conspiracies do happen—it's only natural in politics. Some of them succeed but fall short of destroying their target, as was the case with the Lewinsky affair. Others fail, and are written off in history as lessons to be learned.

At any rate, as Syrian officials, we were completely undaunted by the Lewinsky affair and stood firmly behind President Clinton, whom we considered to be a friend. With all that was happening in the Occupied Territories, our media made only passing mention of the scandal, reckoning it, more or less, to be a domestic North American issue. Our response, though, was very different from how the Libyan, Iraqi, and Iranian media tackled it, as they often gloated about the US president. But President Assad was very careful to sidestep any mention of Clinton's personal life in his meetings with foreign visitors, always claiming that Clinton's life was none of our business. As far as we were concerned, what mattered to us was his position regarding the June 4, 1967, borders of Israel, and his ability to restore the Golan Heights—in full—to its rightful owners. At one point when receiving American guests in the summer of 1998, President Assad even said: "We believe President Clinton has fallen victim to a conspiracy [the Lewinsky scandal] because he tried to achieve something concrete and fair in the Arab-Israeli conflict."

As if the Lewinsky affair were not enough to divert Clinton's attention from Middle East peacemaking, we also had a change of leadership in Israel. As most analysts had predicted, despite his declared commitment to peace, Shimon Peres had very little substance to make him a prime minister of choice rather than a prime minister by accident. He had originally called for early elections to give his government a popular mandate to advance the peace process with the Syrians and Palestinians, but a series of events made him an easy target for his opponents, namely bombings within Israeli cities and towns on March 3–4, 1996. A total of thirty-two Israelis were killed in these attacks, making Peres's victory close to impossible. Likud's candidate, Benjamin Netanyahu, was strong and popular, however, although he had never yet served as prime minister. He was only age forty-six—the youngest person to hold the post since 1948—whereas Peres, already at seventy-three, was way past retirement age. Netanyahu campaigned for office in May 1996 as the man to put an end to Palestinian attacks on Israeli civilians and as the man who did not trust Yasser Arafat. His campaign slogan was: "Netanyahu—making a safe peace."

Prior to the May 1996 elections, Peres went to Washington, where he was received with red carpets at the White House. President Clinton desperately wanted him to continue as prime minister because the Israeli leader embodied the continuation of the Rabin legacy and commitment to peace with Syria. Peres's survival meant that Oslo would survive, but his demise threatened to destroy everything Clinton had worked for since his election in 1993. It had become clear that Netanyahu was uninterested in agreeing to all of Clinton's ambitions in the Middle East. According to Dennis Ross, "Clinton, a hero in Israel since the Rabin funeral, sought to transfer his own credibility to Peres, and in so doing, 'save' Labor and the peace process."[3] During his Washington meetings, Peres requested that the Clinton administration move its embassy from Tel Aviv to Jerusalem, saying that this would help him to win votes in the elections. Warren Christopher supported the idea, but Sandy Berger, the US deputy national security adviser, rejected this flatly unless it was "absolutely necessary" for the elections.[4] The administration had somehow been brought to believe by its embassy in Tel Aviv that Peres was going to win, although only just, by 51 percent to 49 percent in the Knesset.

As prime minister, Netanyahu immediately opened fire on the Oslo Accords, claiming that too much had been given to Arafat in exchange for too little. Netanyahu said that the concessions only gave extra encouragement to "extremist elements like Hamas and Islamic Jihad, being that terrorism pays well." To prove his substance as a hard-liner, in 1996 Netanyahu opened an exit from the Western Wall Tunnel into the Arab Quarter in Jerusalem, setting off three days of Palestinian riots. Peres had instructed the exit to be put on hold for the sake of peace. Later Netanyahu came out with his three "Nos," which mimicked the Arab position after the war of 1967 that said "No to peace with Israel," "No to negotiations with Israel," and "No to recognition of Israel." Netanyahu's "Nos" were the following: "No withdrawal from the Golan Heights," "No discussion of Jerusalem," and "No negotiations under any preconditions." He then sent Clinton a letter saying that he intended to abide by the Rabin Deposit "at this time." That declared position softened gradually, however, until another window of opportunity emerged for peace in 1998.

Secret Diplomacy

One of the interesting "secrets" in Middle Eastern diplomacy, which managed to remain confidential for many years, was the visit by Netanyahu's friend Ronald Lauder, a US businessman, to Damascus for nine meetings with President Assad in the summer of 1998. A small circle of people attended these talks, and nobody knew about them in Syria, except for Foreign Minister Farouk al-Shara, Ambassador Walid al-Mouallem, and, of course, the president and myself. We were told that Netanyahu initiated this back channel within one year of assuming office to ease US pressure on the Tel Aviv government. Clinton was furious that no breakthroughs were being made in Middle East peace on account of the bad blood between Netanyahu and Yasser Arafat. If nothing was in the pipeline on the Palestinian front, the least he could do was to tackle the Syrian talks. Netanyahu told Washington that he was "more attracted" to Hafez al-Assad than Arafat. According to Dennis Ross, "Assad was everything Arafat wasn't—he commanded a real state, with a real army. . . . He was a tough enemy, but one who kept his word."[5]

Netanyahu probably believed that a certain deal could be made with Assad, asking Lauder, who was a newcomer to the Middle East, to be the go-between. In future years, however, the Israeli prime minister would deny all claims to the Lauder mandate for talks with Assad, even though many insiders in the Netanyahu team knew everything about the Lauder visit. One of those who knew was Netanyahu's former defense minister Yitzhak Mordechai, who by mid-1999 was challenging him for the premiership on a minority party ticket. In a televised debate that April, Netanyahu declared that he would not give President Assad "what Ehud Barak had been willing to give the President of Syria." Angered by this statement, Mordechai coldly dared Netanyahu to repeat what he had just said: "Look me in the eye, Bibi . . . look me in the eye!"[6] He was, of course, referring to Ronald Lauder's Damascus visits, and Netanyahu knew that only too well. The latter did not repeat his earlier statement, fearing that Mordechai would reveal "untold secrets" to the Israeli electorate. Those briefed on the Lauder talks on the Israeli side were the prime minister's adviser Uzi Arad; Danny Naveh, his cabinet secretary; Mordaechai; his aide Yaakov Amidror; and General Shimon Shappira, the military secretary to the Israeli prime minister.

In his memoirs, Dennis Ross claims that the Track II talks were the brainchild of Lauder himself, who approached ambassador Mouallem in Washington with the idea. Lauder asked for a "secret, private channel to Assad" and said that he had been sent to Mouallem by "Bibi."[7] These talks, he added, would be "very intensive and very unofficial." According to Martin Indyk, "Bibi had made it a condition of the negotiations that neither side should inform Clinton."[8] After obtaining an initial okay from the Syrian Embassy, mandated at the highest level by President Assad back in Damascus, the talks were also approved by the Clinton team, which thus sheds doubt on Indyk's statement. "We have no problem with their coming up with something on their own—if they could," Ross said in his memoirs.[9] Clinton's new secretary of state, Madeleine Albright, was not too excited about the Lauder visit, "given the sensitivity" of the Syrian track, and neither was Sandy Berger. They both asked Ross to "sit in on one meeting" and tell them "if this is for real or not." In Damascus, we were certain that something of that magnitude would not pass in Washington without the direct approval of Clinton himself. Ronald Lauder was an energetic man, full of life and humor, but he knew very little about the Middle East and almost nothing about Syria. His warm personality, however, created an immediate positive chemistry between him and President Assad—views that were shared by me personally, as I sat in on all of his talks at the Presidential Palace in

Damascus. We got along so well that at one point he even jokingly offered me a job as his office manager. A few years ago, *Forbes Magazine* listed him as one of the world's richest people, worth an estimated USD$3 billion. What we knew about him in the late 1990s was that he was the son of the founder of the international cosmetics brand, Estée Lauder Companies. Educated in Paris and Brussels, he had worked with the family business for years until President Reagan appointed him US ambassador to Austria in 1986–1987. A staunch Republican, a high-profile millionaire, and heavyweight American Jew, he had run for mayor of New York City in 1989 but lost to Rudy Giuliani in the Republican primary. According to what Ambassador Mouallem told us, he had the ear of Netanyahu, and his mediation efforts certainly would contain something new and groundbreaking from the Israelis.

Lauder arrived in Damascus on August 7, 1998, and was given an audience with the president the very next morning. Joining the New York–based businessman on his Damascus trip was his aide Allen Roth and George Nader, editor and president of the Washington-based *Middle East Insight*. Lauder broke the ice shortly after entering the room, saying: "Syria is such a beautiful country. My ancestors came from Aleppo 1,200 years ago!"[10] In customary fashion, Assad welcomed him to Syria, saying that he could always consider the country his home, and then noted that "all previous talks had been too complicated with too much paper," hoping that Lauder had brought with him something "different" from Prime Minister Netanyahu.

"Contrary to what you might believe," Lauder replied, "Netanyahu can make peace and is interested in peace with Syria."[11]

Assad smiled—he had heard this only too often about Shamir, Rabin, Peres, and now Netanyahu. "Clinton is sincere about peace," he said, "but there are people around him who don't want breakthroughs in the Middle East."[12]

Lauder's sense of humor surfaced as he chuckled, saying, "They are Democrats. They can't achieve peace. Only the Republicans can make peace, Mr. President."[13]

Assad, surprised by the unusual humor, which was strange for stiff peace negotiations, gently pointed out: "Republicans or Democrats, it makes no difference to us. We judge people by their deeds and actions, not by their political affiliations."

The president then explained what Syria had achieved during President Clinton's first tenure, but Lauder interrupted him, saying, "Please, Mr. President, I beg you, don't compare me to Warren Christopher. What have I done that you compare me to *him*?"[14] We all laughed—this round of peace talks was clearly going to be different from all those that had preceded it.

Lauder said that the Israelis were willing to withdraw "from all Syrian lands" without specifying the June 4, 1967, borders.[15] President Assad explained the obvious, yet again setting out the difference between the 1923 international borders and the 1967 borders. Lauder clearly did not understand why the Syrians were making such a fuss over the two borders, given that the 1967 line gave Syria only 25 additional square miles of land. He failed to realize that for Hafez al-Assad, land was sacred from a nationalist point of view. Also, from both the military and political points of view, the additional miles were not only symbolic but gave Syria access to the Banias, Yarmouk, and Jordan Rivers, in addition to Lake Tiberias, which accounted for nearly half of Israel's water supply. "This is our land," the president added. "You cannot impose conditions and then imply that this is an Israeli concession. I want to remind you, Mr. Lauder, that the Golan is Syrian, not Israeli."[16]

Lauder then spoke about Israeli withdrawal from Lebanon, saying that in theory this would start three months before the IDF withdrew from the Golan. In return, he wanted Assad to commit himself to the disarmament of Hizbullah and prevent further attacks on northern Israel from South Lebanon.[17] Lauder was clearly very excited and wanting to jump ten steps further than all his American predecessors, saying, "We can agree on a declaration of principles within one week; that should be easy. You and Netanyahu can then go to Washington to sign the declaration at the White House. Once that is done, we can talk about all the details."[18]

The idea of him showing up in Washington for a loose and meaningless declaration of principles was inimical to President Assad: absurd, outrageous, and completely unacceptable. "Look at what they did to Arafat," he said very firmly, reminding Lauder that Arafat had signed an agreement with the Americans and Israelis that, five years down the road, was still nothing but a distant reality as far as Palestinian nationhood was concerned. "If you want to achieve peace, why don't we just sit down and talk about what is important regarding withdrawal and time frames? Why limit the discussion to a declaration of principles and not a peace agreement?"[19] Assad, of course, felt that Lauder was after high drama rather than a sustainable peace between Syria and Israel. Lauder wasn't trying to be smart or bluff the Syrians. He simply knew too little about the peace process—and nothing about Syria. Assad, a strategist, was worried about how future generations would judge any Syrian-Israeli peace carrying his name, whereas Lauder was after a Kodak moment of Hafez al-Assad, Benjamin Netanyahu, and Bill Clinton together on the White House lawn. Trying to be polite, Assad gently told his American guest, "It's not as easy as it seems." Assad requested the minutes of the previous talks with the Americans since Clinton came to office and handed them to Lauder, asking him to read them thoroughly before a second round was scheduled between them on August 11.

When Lauder came in for his second meeting, carrying the piles of paper with him, he looked at the president and grumbled, saying, "These papers proved better than sleeping pills. I tried to read them but fell asleep. They are so damn boring!"[20] We all laughed—how right he was. To think that we had gone through this process, with nothing having been achieved for eight long years, spoke volumes about the peace process.

President Assad then got down to business, saying to Lauder, "Now that you have read them, let us talk about security—security of both sides. I want to be fair, and I want you to be fair as well."[21] He then added, "Each step by the Israelis will be reciprocated by a step from our side, carried out in equal proportions. I am willing to give up all the arms Syria has if Netanyahu is willing to give up a third of the arms Israel has."[22] The Israelis, of course, hated the idea of reciprocity, arguing that Israel's territory was much smaller than Syria and that therefore demilitarized zones could not be equal in both territories. This was not new; we had heard this argument before from both James Baker and Warren Christopher.

To facilitate the peace process, Assad agreed to two new terms, but only after Netanyahu had committed to withdrawal up to the line of June 4, 1967, not to the 1923 border. One was Syria's readiness to accept a US presence in early warning stations. Assad said, "I personally don't want a warning station inside Israel and would prefer to have no Israeli station inside Syria."[23] But if that would make the United States happy and the Israelis feel secure, then it was something he was willing to consider. The second concession was an extended timetable for Israeli withdrawal. When Clinton had come to Damascus in 1994, Assad had allowed four extra months for the Israelis to withdraw.

Up till then, Lauder had only been listening and conveying Israeli messages while constantly telling us: "I am not entitled to make decisions; I am here just to relay messages from Netanyahu." That actually gave him an advantage in the talks; he didn't have to absorb anything—all he had to do was to dictate what had been said to him by the Israelis.

But when Assad's new terms surfaced, Lauder knew that he had been told something worthwhile and asked to take the matter directly to Netanyahu. He left Syria that same afternoon and headed to Israel for talks with the prime minister. Before leaving, he jokingly said, "I will be back and will see you when I return. You certainly don't have anything other than us to deal with, right, Mr. President?"[24]

At this Assad laughed, saying, "It seems as though I have nothing except the Americans to deal with these days! That is exactly what is happening with me! I am doing nothing else!"

Before he left, Lauder looked up at Assad and added: "By the way, Mr. President, has anybody ever told you that you are less difficult than Netanyahu? I have seen you smile and laugh many times in two days, but I saw him laughing only once—when he won the latest elections."[25]

Assad appreciated the joke: "That means he laughs only once every four years!"

Lauder then said, "If this fails, it will be Bibi's fault, not yours!"

When he returned to Syria, Lauder commented on how spacious the Presidential Palace was and asked Assad, "Do you have halls that are larger than this? It makes for a good morning's workout."[26]

Assad smiled, saying, "Yes, whenever I have some time between two meetings, I walk back and forth. It provides good walking exercise." He then said to Lauder, "How old is the White House?"

Lauder beamed. "It was built in 1814. This means that it is 184 years old. But I am not a Democrat, so I have never slept there!"[27]

Assad repeated an earlier line: "I don't want to get involved between Democrats and Republicans. What I care about are principles. There are good and bad people in both the Democratic and Republican Parties."

Lauder roared with laughter. "No, Mr. President, all good people are only Republicans!"[28]

Lauder brought along a ten-point document entitled, "Treaty of Peace between Israel and Syria," which had been co-authored by him and Netanyahu in Israel. There was a short preamble, saying that the two countries, Syria and Israel, had decided to establish peace based on "security, equality, and respect for the sovereignty, territorial integrity, and political independence of each other." Lauder tried, with little luck, to replace the word "equality" with "comparability" but we firmly said no, arguing that such a word does not exist and that it was not part of the dictionary of peace. The Syrian public, Assad said, would never accept it because it was purely meaningless and served nobody's interests but Israel's.

Article One, the document read, would be "termination of the state of war" upon signing a Syrian-Israeli peace treaty. Article Two stated that Israel would withdraw from Syrian lands up to the border of June 4, 1967. When presenting this document to Clinton, however, Lauder slightly changed what had been written in Article Two to "a commonly agreed border based on the international line of 1923." Article Three maintained that the withdrawal would be in three stages, based on Assad's time frame of eighteen months. Article Four stated that "simultaneously with the Israeli-Syrian deal, Lebanon would sign an agreement with Israel, and the Syrians would make every effort to ensure that no further paramilitary or hostile activities would be launched against Israel from Lebanon. There would be three zones that limited the deployment of forces, a demilitarized zone, a zone of limited arms, and a zone free of 'offensive weapons.'" Assad wanted them less than 10 kilometers wide. Finally, the existing early warning and monitoring stations would remain on the Golan but would be run by a multinational presence of Americans, French, and Syrian personnel. Additionally, "normal relations" would follow the signing of an agreement, and "water rights would be addressed in accordance with international norms." The normalization would include ambassador exchange at the beginning of the withdrawal and full normalization at the end. Assad agreed to all of the above, on the condition that Lauder return to Israel and return with a map signed by Netanyahu, showing exactly what border line would apply to the Syrian-Israeli peace. If he could provide no such document, then everything that had been agreed upon was "null and void." At this point, Lauder's mission became an absolute mess. He knew that Netanyahu would never commit to the 1967 borders and that Assad would refuse to meet him again if no such map was forthcoming. According to Martin Indyk, the Israeli prime minister toyed with the idea of "drawing a line with a thick marker pen on a small map in order to leave room for negotiations about the exact positioning of the border."[29] He could not produce this, however, without involvement of the IDF. Such a map required the approval of Defense Minister Mordechai, who would never accept such a lame attempt from Netanyahu, which, according to Mordechai, made Israel look weak and silly before the Syrians and Americans. Mordechai said no to such an idea, and Foreign Minister Ariel Sharon seconded his veto. If Netanyahu went ahead with his doctored map, it would have probably brought down his entire cabinet. Years later, a journalist in *Haaretz*, an Israeli newspaper, wrote that Sharon "told fellow Likud members that he torpedoed the third-party efforts with Syria," adding that when Sharon learned of the Lauder talks, he confronted Netanyahu, saying that there was "not enough of a basis for Israel to put forward any withdrawal map."[30] The Lauder talks collapsed because no map was produced.

Once back in the United States, Lauder told US diplomats that Assad had shown flexibility "on borders, on security arrangements, and on early warning monitoring stations."[31] But Ross took that with a grain of salt: "I pulled out a map and asked him [Lauder] to show me the flexibility on the border, and he pointed out that Assad was prepared to draw the border off the Sea of Galilee and off the Jordan River. Second, I asked what 'basically reached an agreement' meant? His answer was that what he would show the President [Clinton] was 99% agreed [with Assad]. Did the 1% represent disagreement on any of the core issues—meaning the definition of the border, the concept of security agreements, including early warning, the content of peace, and the timing for carrying everything out? Lauder believed there was no disagreement here."[32] The Clinton team thought that Lauder's document was "too good to be true" and doubted that Assad had approved the 1923 border—given his determination in every single meeting since 1990 to abide by the 1967 border.[33] Ross asked: "Did I think Lauder was lying? . . . No, he is sincere and I believe he believes much of what he is saying. But I am afraid he is not precise and what he considers minor differences are not so minor. Moreover, I think there is some real wishful thinking here. Where did I have the gravest doubts? I knew that the 1923 line was a complete nonstarter with Assad; in Assad's eyes, those were the colonial borders, and he would never accept them in a document. I was also highly dubious that Assad would ever acknowledge, much less accept, an Israeli presence in the early warning stations on the Golan Heights after Israeli withdrawal."[34]

Dennis Ross knew the Syrian president well; Ronald Lauder apparently did not.

The Lauder talks—like all those before them—were buried right there and then following their collapse in the autumn of 1998. Three years later, the Israeli newspaper *Yediot Aharonot* ran a photograph of Lauder's draft, "Treaty of Peace Between Israel and Syria," on April 13, 2001.[35] It clearly showed, in Article II, that Lauder had proposed "Israel withdrawing from the Syrian lands taken in 1967, in accordance with Security Council Resolutions 242 and 338." That document, the paper added, had been delivered to President Clinton by the

US mediator on November 17, 1998. Years later, in June 2004, Lauder spoke to *Haaretz* about the "leak," saying that the views expressed in the document were his personal views only—repeating what he had said to President Clinton in late 1998—and adding that Netanyahu had flatly rejected the proposal because he "wanted a border that would give Israel more than either the 1923 border or the June 4, 1967, lines."[36] In looking back, I think that Lauder was correct on his last point. It was true that Benjamin Netanyahu did not want to commit to the 1967 border. He wasn't lying; he was telling the truth, the whole truth, and nothing but the truth—as far as Israeli officialdom was concerned.

Notes

1. "Clinton Accused," *Washington Post,* January 17, 1998.
2. Guernsey, *Hillary Rodham Clinton*, 83.
3. Ross, *The Missing Peace*, 256.
4. Ibid.
5. "The Syria Temptation," *Wall Street Journal*, March 6, 2009.
6. Daniel Pipes, "The Road to Damascus: What Netanyahu Almost Gave Away," *New Republic*, July 5, 1999. Netanyahu's nickname is "Bibi."
7. Ross, *The Missing Peace*, 510–511.
8. Indyk, *Innocent Abroad*, 246.
9. Ross, *The Missing Peace*, 510.
10. Archives of the Syrian Presidential Palace, Classified Assad-Lauder Minutes, August 7, 1998.
11. Ibid.
12. Ibid.
13. Ibid.
14. Ibid.
15. Ibid.
16. Ibid.
17. Ibid.
18. Ibid.
19. Ibid.
20. Ibid.
21. Ibid.
22. Ibid.
23. Ibid.
24. Ibid.
25. Ibid.
26. Ibid.
27. Ibid.
28. Ibid.

29. Indyk, *Innocent Abroad*, 459.
30. Pipes, "The Road to Damascus."
31. Ross, *The Missing Peace*, 511.
32. Ibid.
33. Ibid., 512.
34. Ibid.
35. "Treaty of Peace Between Israel and Syria," *Yediot Aharanot*, April 13, 2001.
36. Pipes, "The Road to Damascus."

10

The Shepherdstown Debacle

WITH THE FAILED LAUDER TALKS BEHIND US, WE PUT THE PEACE talks on hold, waiting to see if Netanyahu would still be prime minister of Israel after the 1999 elections. His chances were slim, even according to the testimony of his closest aides, and we were glad that he was seemingly going to be history, given his ruthlessness with the Palestinians and his double-dealings with Syria. The Israeli left wing had begun to criticize Netanyahu openly for his talks with PLO chairman Arafat—which, by the way, never achieved anything for the Palestinians—and Labor Party politicians were working around the clock to bring him down and replace him with their candidate, Ehud Barak. Ordinary Israelis also parted ways with Netanyahu on account of a long chain of scandals, with Israeli police recommending that he be tried for corruption for services he had obtained for free from a government contractor that were worth $100,000.

It came as no surprise, therefore, that Benjamin Netanyahu was voted out of office and replaced by Barak, who back in 1995 had served as minister of internal affairs under Yitzhak Rabin. He then became foreign affairs minister under Peres and subsequently had replaced him as leader of Labor after Peres's defeat in the 1996 elections. As mentioned earlier, Barak had briefly been part of the Syrian-Israeli talks, when he had met Chief of Staff Hikmat al-Shihabi at Blair House. The youngest prime minister in Israel's history, Barak was, like his mentor Yitzhak Rabin, a decorated officer in the IDF who had plenty of Palestinian blood on his hands. In fact, Madeleine Albright described him as "the most decorated soldier in his nation's history." Having defeated Netanyahu by a wide margin, Barak had come to power in strength and decided to form a coalition cabinet with the ultra-Orthodox party Shas, which had won an unprecedented seventeen seats in the 120-seat Knesset. This was very worrying to us in Damascus, given Shas's declared positions on peace with the Arabs—especially with Syria. (They eventually left the coalition when they couldn't agree with Barak on how much power their deputy minister of education should have in the new Israeli cabinet.) Barak's choice of allies was alarming, to say the least, and completely overshadowed his campaign promise to end twenty-two years of occupation in South Lebanon and to jumpstart peace talks with the Syrians. Albright, however, did not even attempt to hide her pleasure at Barak's election, saying that it was greeted "with smiles from the Oval Office" and the State Department. She claims that when she first met him in 1997, when he was still leader of the Israeli opposition, she hoped that one day Barak would become prime minister of Israel.

We therefore had no choice but to deal with Ehud Barak, after receiving much-needed assurances from the Clinton administration that he would abide by the Rabin Deposit and all that had been agreed upon since Madrid. Barak agreed to resume talks with the Syrians, on the condition that negotiations needed to be "intensive" and "high-level." He added that they absolutely had to be sheltered from all media coverage to protect him from Israeli hard-liners. We gave him assurances to that effect; we had never leaked any of our talks to the media, not even the Lauder talks, which would have played out in our favor against Netanyahu. President Assad was a man of his word, and when he promised that no leaks would happen, it meant that Syria would tolerate no leaks. We could not be held responsible, however, for what made its way into the press based in the United States or Israel. Barak requested a $23 billion compensation package for withdrawal from the Golan, and a memorandum of understanding (MOU) with Washington that elevated Israel's standing to that of a "strategic ally" of the United States.

In private, however, Barak was horrified at the thought of giving up land, realizing that Israel depended on the Sea of Galilee for 40 percent of its freshwater needs. He wanted to retain enough territory to ensure Israel's control over that water, and in order to do that he needed to stall as much as he possibly could any breakthrough with the Syrians. Although he had criticized Netanyahu for relying too heavily on the Americans in his peace talks with the Palestinians and us, Barak eventually did exactly that which had been done before, requesting that any talks with Syria be held under American auspices. He was worried, however, that the Americans were beginning to develop a "soft spot" toward the Arabs and that after years of back-and-forth talks in Damascus, Gaza, and Ramallah, they were starting to sympathize with Arab grievances. He wanted the Americans to remain firmly focused on his needs and his needs only, not those of the Syrians or Palestinians.

Newspaper Diplomacy

In June 1999, veteran British journalist Patrick Seale visited Syria and Israel shortly after Barak's election. Seale was an old friend of Syria, having published a biography of President Assad back in 1988 entitled, *Asad: The Struggle for the Middle East*. He had lived in Damascus during the Mandate period and wrote his master's thesis on Syria in the 1950s. He was also married to the daughter of Sabah Qabbani, our ambassador to the United States in the 1970s. In short, he knew Syria well and had access to President Assad. Prior to his visit to Syria, Seale had traveled to Israel for a joint lecture with Itamar Rabinovich, the Israeli ambassador to the United States and our former negotiating partner, at the Moshe Dayan Center. Additionally, Seale had met Prime Ministers Shamir, Peres, and Barak and had toured the occupied Golan Heights with IDF officers. Barak told him, on the record, that he sought the "peace of the brave" with Syria. That term was the brainchild of President Assad and was later copied and used endlessly by Yasser Arafat, thereby becoming part of the Middle East peace vocabulary. The only path for sustainable peace in the Middle East, Barak told Seale, was through an agreement with Syria. "My policy is to strengthen Israel's security by putting an end to [our] conflict with Syria."[1] This statement, of course, became a front-page headline in the London-based *al-Hayat*, where Seale wrote a weekly column. In Damascus, Seale spoke with the president, obtaining a brief interview that was also a front-page story in *al-Hayat*. The headline read: "Assad: Barak Is Strong and Sincere. He Wants Peace [with Syria]."[2] This was the first time that the president of Syria and the prime minister of Israel had exchanged messages of good faith through the media—noticeably in one of the mass circulation Arab dailies that is widely read throughout the Arab world. Assad's interview was published on June 23, 1999, and it carried a strong message to the United States, showing just how committed Syria was toward real peace in the Middle East. Assad said that peace was not a new choice for Syria, stressing that he had called for peace as early as 1975. When asked about Barak, Assad said: "I followed his statements. He seems to be a strong and sincere person. Based on election results [in Israel] he seems to enjoy wide support. It is clear that he wants to achieve peace with Syria."[3] Barak's election, he added, indicated that something had changed within Israel because the situation under Netanyahu was, in Assad's own words, "hopeless."

After the president's *al-Hayat* interview, President Assad gave Clinton his trust yet again, for the ninth time since 1993, and on December 21, 1999, it was announced that Shepherdstown, West Virginia, would host the upcoming round of Syrian-Israeli talks, attended by Syrian foreign minister Shara and Israel's new prime minister. I was part of the Syrian delegation in my capacity as adviser at the Foreign Ministry. Perhaps it should be mentioned that back then, although I had been by President Assad's side for almost a decade, I was still officially an adviser to the foreign minister and a professor at Damascus University. I kept my teaching hours because I loved my job.

The choice of Shepherdstown puzzled many. Only seventy-five miles from Washington, D.C., it was a small, rural town, just off Interstate 81. The only activities it ever experienced were annual fairs that visited the place in the summer—which was nothing, of course, when compared to the international media attention it would be getting once it hosted the Syrian and Israeli delegations. Dennis Ross described it as "old, quiet, and sleepy." The Israelis asked that the talks be cut off completely from the outside world: no press delegations and no cellular phones. Ross added that Barak wanted the Syrian, Israeli, and US delegations to live in a "virtual cocoon." The Syrian delegation was not preoccupied with these matters. We had no secrets, and we felt that we had nothing to hide. Three Syrian journalists came to Shepherdstown, but they were not part of the official Syrian delegation. The United States tried to persuade us to hold the talks either at Wye River or Camp David, but we turned down both venues because they were permanently associated with Yasser Arafat, who had been to Wye, and Anwar Sadat, who had hammered out the ill-fated Egyptian-Israeli peace treaty at Camp David back in 1978.

Shepherdstown had a large hotel to lodge us, located just outside the town center, and a beautiful retreat owned by the US Fish and Wildlife Service, which hosted our meetings. Additionally, it was close to the White House, and President Clinton could fly in by helicopter in twenty to twenty-five minutes.

When we arrived in West Virginia in January 2000, we were told that the Americans were preparing a draft agreement, one that would acknowledge and build upon the Rabin Deposit. National Security Adviser Sandy Berger had briefed the US peace team on President Clinton's position—we were told—before the pocket (BP) and "after the pocket"

(AP). Clinton told them that "nothing was possible BP" but that a real breakthrough was possible "AP." Ross mentioned in his memoirs that the US position "was that the June 4, 1967 lines should be the basis of the negotiations on the border."[4] That is what we believed when we landed in the United States that January. The reality, however, we were soon to discover, was very different.

Barak and Shara first met at the White House on December 15, 1999. We accompanied the foreign minister to that meeting, where they both gave a brief statement to the press from the Rose Garden before heading off for talks at Clinton's guesthouse, Blair House, which paved the ground for the Shepherdstown talks. Located directly across Pennsylvania Avenue, facing the White House, Blair House was where former US president Abraham Lincoln had stayed while the White House was being renovated, back in the nineteenth century. What I remember most about that day was the cold, icy weather and the mud in the Rose Garden. Before appearing in public with Barak and Clinton, Shara told Albright that he would not shake hands with the Israelis. He would stand next to Ehud Barak, if that were absolutely necessary, but would not allow a handshake.

Originally it was agreed that only Clinton would speak at the event, but that quickly changed into allowing a few minutes for both Barak and Shara to say something. The US delegation was angry that Shara spoke for ten minutes, while Barak confined his speech to a few minutes, as explicitly requested by President Clinton. I recall that the Syrian foreign minister used the opportunity to emphasize Syria's position to the international media assembled at the White House garden that morning. The Americans were unimpressed, but I think the speech he gave was valid, since there were very few opportunities for Syrians to talk to the international media on account of the constant media war against us, whereas the Israelis had open access to television networks and newspapers all year long, twenty-four hours a day.

Clinton's anger at the relatively long Syrian speech, however, was quickly overshadowed by the physical collapse of General Yusuf Shakkur, our delegation's military expert, probably because of fatigue experienced during the press conference. Shakkur, who had served as chief of staff of the Syrian army during the October War of 1973, was a strong, firm man but was more than seventy years old. He was standing beside me when he began to sway, left and right. At first, I thought this was because of the muddy soil beneath us, so I turned to help him stand up straight, but I quickly realized that he was beginning to lose consciousness. Shakkur was immediately taken to the medical room at the White House and cared for by President Clinton's doctors.

Before the talks began on January 3, 2000, which happened to coincide with the holy month of Ramadan, our foreign minister was invited to walk along Shepherdstown Bridge, over the Potomac River, with President Clinton and Barak. It was a Kodak moment for photographers. Clinton shook hands with the Syrian delegation and walked ahead of us with his two guests, while Ross, Indyk, Albright, and I walked at a distance behind them. Madeleine Albright was walking beside me, wearing a lion brooch, the one she had worn during her first visit to Damascus in September 1998. She showed it off, as she had done previously, because it was in the likeness of a lion, which is what "Assad" means in English. "We just clicked, you know," she said, referring to her two earlier meetings with President Assad. "I believe we are all working for a noble cause. I do hope we will succeed, Bouthaina." Meanwhile, an army of photographers was busy taking pictures of the historical meeting between Syrians and Israelis in Virginia.

When the walk ended, Albright began her meeting with Shara, while Clinton sat for a one-on-one talk with Barak. Farouk al-Shara, I recall, was clearly satisfied by how things were going, and that gave the Syrian peace delegation confidence that light might be visible at the end of a very long tunnel. During those early hours of talks, President Clinton telephoned President Assad to brief him on developments. Assad agreed to allow a US team of experts from the Pentagon, accompanied by a rabbi, to exhume bodies from four graves in a cemetery in Damascus, which Israelis believed were the remains of IDF soldiers killed in a battle with Palestinians in the Bekaa Valley in Lebanon back in 1982.[5] Assad's humanitarian gesture, it has to be noted, was never mentioned either in the US or Israeli media.

Back at Shepherdstown, General Ibrahim al-Omar was designated for the borders and security meetings, and Riad Daoudi, the Foreign Ministry's legal adviser, was appointed head of the Syrian group discussing water-related issues with Israel. Ambassador Mouallem was appointed to the "Committee for Implementing Normal Relations." General Omar's counterpart in the security meeting was Shlomo Yanai, chief of planning in the IDF, and Uri Saguy was his counterpart in the borders meeting. Barak wanted the security committee to meet before the border demarcation committee, to show the Israeli public that he was putting Israel's security before Syria's border and water needs. He told President Clinton, "I have only one shot and I can't afford to make a single mistake."[6] Too much time had been "wasted" on the border

THE SHEPHERDSTOWN DEBACLE 177

A souvenir photo, taken during the Shepherdstown talks in January 2000, signed personally by Secretary of State Madeleine Albright.

issue, he said, and we "needed to reach a balance" on all issues related to peace.[7] The security committee held its first meeting on January 5, 2000. Yanai proposed security zones, areas in which forces would be separated and their arms limited, a suggestion we had heard before from various different US envoys. These zones, he added, would be closer in size to what the Israelis had in mind than to what the Syrians had been asking for since 1994. He proposed changing the original ratio that General Shihabi had agreed at Blair House from 10:6 to 10:5, meaning that the zones on the Syrian side would be twice the size of those on the Israeli side.[8] We reminded Yanai that Damascus was only 60 kilometers from the June 4, 1967, border. The Israeli position made no reference to the scope of withdrawal, simply reading: "The border needs to be mutually agreed upon." General Omar accepted Israeli's proposal for "extensive, active, and passive monitoring" using cameras in different bases. The first obstacle, however, was Barak's request that any commitment to the Rabin Deposit should go hand in-hand with Syrian support for Lebanese-Israeli peace talks. Albright quickly came to his rescue, claiming that the Lebanese track was "an orphan track" that had been neglected for far too long in favor of the Syrian-Israeli and Palestinian-Israeli tracks. After discussing the matter over the phone with President Assad, Shara sent word that if progress were to be made at Shepherdstown, then Lebanese-Israeli talks would take place at a later stage.

In the first round of talks, nothing was achieved between our team and the Israelis, reminding us of the rigidity we had witnessed back in 1991 with Yitzhak Shamir's envoy, Yossi Ben Aharon, at Madrid. Eight years of endless talks were seemingly going down the drain—until the Americans came up with what they claimed was a "creative solution" to bridge the gap between Syria and Israel. Barak was going around in circles, trying to tell us indirectly that the Rabin Deposit was apparently not going to be a Barak Deposit. One of his remarks, for example, was about an "old synagogue" on the Golan, which, he claimed, was one of the reasons why the Israelis found it difficult to withdraw from the territory they had occupied in 1967. Shara calmly replied that there are old synagogues in Damascus as well, ironically inquiring if that therefore entitled the Israelis to control Damascus.[9] Barak then backed down, telling us—as if we did not know—how important Syria was to all three monotheistic religions, breaking into a long (and boring) history of religion. He then added, "I hope that no other religion comes to Earth, because if it did, then it would have to come to Syria first!"[10] The most memorable statement said on day one was this one from Albright: "If it were not for the trust between Presidents Clinton and Assad, this would never have happened." I remember that the negotiating mood on that day was exactly like the temperature in the room, which was totally out of control. We were about to faint from the heat, which turned cold—very cold—when the heating level was adjusted at our request by the Americans.

President Clinton, always the visionary, said to us: "Every one of us should sit back for a moment and ask himself/herself, how they want things to look like 5 years from now. What do you all want the future to look like, for yourselves and for your countries? Even as President of the United States, I ask myself daily where I want to be 5 years from now, and today, I pose that question to all of you." He then looked across the room at each of us and said, in typically informal American fashion, "If you guys continue to talk more, you would agree more. I am sure!" Dennis Ross proposed that the US delegation draft a working paper outlining what they understood as each party's real, rather than official, negotiating position. It would be a non-binding paper, they added, that would commit neither party to any position. They shared their draft with Barak, who nodded approvingly and then mentioned the idea to our colleague Riad Daoudi—without showing him the actual draft. Madeleine Albright and Ross then decided to sit down with Shara and me on January 6 to explain their new strategy. There was a white board in the room on which Ross drew two columns, scribbling down Syria's position on peace in one column and that of Israel in the other. On the border, he said that Israel's position was "full withdrawal from the Golan except for a narrow strip along the northeast part of Lake Tiberias, and a small narrow strip along an area of the Jordan River, above the lake." Syria's position, we reminded him, was full withdrawal. Period! We had never accepted anything short of that in any of the talks since 1991.

On security, the Israelis wanted a limited presence in the Mount Hermon early warning station for a specific period after the IDF withdrew from the Golan. They also wanted three zones of demilitarized, or limited deployment, areas for Syrian forces extending "at least" to Damascus. Israel would not, however, accept demilitarized zones on its side of the border. We said that Syria would accept an international presence on Mount Hermon for a period of five years after withdrawal, but no Israeli presence. Regarding actual peace, the Israelis wanted the establishment of full diplomatic relations to be implemented together with the first phase of their withdrawal from the Golan. We, however, maintained that no embassies would open until the Golan was restored, in full, to its rightful owners. Israel wanted three years to complete its withdrawal, but we said that the withdrawal should be completed within eighteen months. When it came to sovereignty over Lake Tiberias, Ross said, many years later, that Shara had told him this: "The Israelis would have sovereignty over the Lake; the Syrians would have sovereignty over the Lake, at least all the land to the east of the 10 meters off the shoreline."[11] That, of course, is not true—the Syrians never recognized divided sovereignty over the lake, as I shall show in my description of the last Assad-Clinton Summit in Geneva, which I discuss in Chapter 11. I was present at the meeting, and although there were no minutes for that particular encounter, I can assure readers that the foreign minister never spoke of "shared" sovereignty over the lake. This presumed single statement was to arouse plenty of controversy, as the Americans used it with Barak, telling him that "the Syrian position has softened." Foreign Minister Shara, however, strongly denied ever having made such a statement. On the contrary, he always used to tell Yasser Arafat that when the Europeans drew up the 1923 borders, Lake Tiberias had been included in what came to be known as Mandate Palestine. "Let us get it back," he would say to Arafat, "and then we can discuss who has access to the Lake's territory, and who has access to its waters, Syria or Palestine. That is an internal matter that we will sort out as Palestinians and Syrians. What is certain is that it was never the property of Israel."

Albright's Chick Channel

Madeleine Albright was a fundamental player in the Shepherdstown talks. She made a strong impression on us when we first met her in 1997, and that impact was mutual. "I was determined," she wrote six years later, "upon reaching Assad's Palace, to make a strong impression."[12] She recalls having been taken aback by the number of satellite dishes on the rooftops of homes in Damascus, which meant that the people of Syria were well exposed to the outside world, and by the amount of marble at the People's Palace overlooking the Syrian capital. "The marble was more than you could imagine and, of course, in that part of the world, the carpets are splendid. There were sweeping stairways and you could envision James Bond exiting right, pursued by scimitars. Assad received me in a huge, sparsely furnished room with sofas, and two carved wooden chairs with cushions. Before sitting down, he drew back the curtains to reveal a spectacular view of his capital, one of the world's oldest cities."[13] During that meeting, Assad spoke of the need to uphold the 1994 Rabin Deposit, telling Albright, "I cannot settle for anything less. If I did, then the person who just served us coffee might—and will—assassinate me."[14]

Two years later, Assad still held that exact same position, and nobody knew this better than Albright herself. She approached me during the Shepherdstown talks for a private one-on-one, for what has since then been coined the "Chick Channel." Albright walked up to me and asked, very politely, "Can we get together for some girl talk?" I nodded, realizing that she must have something important to say. I respected the secretary of state as a hard-working, serious woman who had vision and character. At least, that is the view I had of her back then, although it was to change when we met again in Geneva two months later. From what I had seen of her in our previous four meetings, she was a woman who refused to get bossed around by men and someone who took her job very seriously. I remember that during our first meeting in Damascus she was wearing green, and stood at the gates of President Assad's office at the Palace carrying a briefcase rather than a lady's handbag. I made a mental note: "Good idea; we should carry briefcases, just like men do, and not designer handbags as women do on a casual outing." During that meeting, she told President Assad, "I am impressed to see that you have a woman adviser, Mr. President." Assad smiled and explained to her that women had held senior government offices since 1970, thanks to a long struggle for women's emancipation that had spanned the twentieth century. That topic, needless to say, was personally very dear to my heart.

The 1950s were fervent years of pan-Arabism with a monumental impact on the women of the Middle East, Assad explained. Ever since his first meeting with Henry Kissinger in the 1970s, Assad loved to tell US envoys—especially university professors such as Kissinger and Albright—about the history of Syria. The Communist Party and the Baath Party were also very attractive to Syrian women because they broke the socio-religious fetters on those who enrolled in them. The majority of these women held university degrees, and they were encouraged to unveil, work in public, and free themselves, both psychologically and financially, from the dominance of men. President Assad told Albright: "I have been pushing hard for the empowerment of women, to shatter the glass ceiling that limits their professional and social mobility, and have always been confronted by hard-liners in my own party, who still refuse to give this natural role to women. They like to see them—and keep them—at home, but still feel threatened by them in the Syrian workforce."[15] There was no doubt that that was music to my ears, coming as it did from a man who had enough dignity and good sense to criticize the party that he headed because some of its members still operated from a medieval mentality when it came to women's rights.

In his memoirs, Ross described me as one of those many Syrian women:

> Bouthaina was surely an unusual woman. She had written books on the role of women in Islamic societies. She was highly critical of Islamic regimes that repressed women. She was an academic by training and had secured a postdoctoral fellowship to a small university in Michigan for the Fall Semester. Since she had become Assad's interpreter she appeared increasingly confident in his presence. According to Gamal [Helal], she was an expert interpreter, but took liberties in her translating. While being precise with Assad's words she offered editorial commentary in her translation of what we said to him. If she had any uncertainty about her position, she would not dare to take such liberties. In addition, as Assad's health declined, she would fill out Assad's thoughts when he had difficulty expressing himself in phone calls with the president. In a sense, I believed she had become an additional pair of eyes and ears for Assad.
>
> I liked Bouthaina and had side conversations with her. She was very intelligent, easy to converse with, and always professed her commitment and desire for peace. But I had no illusions about her: her loyalties were to her regime and to its leader. She would not reveal anything her president did not want revealed. She would not, in my judgment, suggest any areas of flexibility or openings as a way to push the negotiations unless she was authorized to do so. The "Chick

Channel" as Madeleine Albright dubbed it, would not be a vehicle for us to influence the Syrian position; instead I believed it would be a channel for the Syrians to influence us.[16]

When we sat down for our one-on-one, Albright began her conversation by saying: "Bouthaina, we are stuck. I need your help." I sat tossing around ideas about what was needed to push the process forward, investing in President Clinton's determination to achieve a breakthrough on the Syrian-Israeli track before his term expired in 2000. Albright said: "When I became Secretary of State, they told me I would have a difficult time dealing with the Middle East. It is the place that fascinates me most, however. The image of Arabs and Muslims has been distorted tremendously in the United States and it needs to be corrected."[17] She suggested that we work on some joint academic effort to achieve that, to which I nodded affirmatively. "People say we care so much about Israel, but that is not true." What she said then, however, was also not true. No one challenged this statement better than Albright herself, when she wrote in her memoir *Madam Secretary*, published in 2003: "I had always believed that Israel was American's special ally and that we should do all we could to guarantee its security." During the 1967 war, she added, "We [the Americans] had helped Israel preserve regional military superiority so that its enemies couldn't destroy it." After a brief talk about women's issues and Middle East politics in general, Albright got down to business, saying that the United States wanted to know if Farouk al-Shara had the authority to negotiate, after having suffered a heart attack in the fall of 1999. I said that President Assad had absolute faith in his foreign minister and that he knew everything there was to know about Syria's position, having headed the negotiations since 1991 and sat in on almost every single one of President Assad's talks with US envoys. The US delegation clearly wanted to use Shara's illness to bypass the foreign minister and open a direct channel with the president, presumably through me, despite the fact that the foreign minister had fully recovered. "Don't undercut Shara," I told Albright very firmly. "He is very important for President Assad. Instead, try to empower him by giving him something that would lead to a breakthrough." I emphasized that he had to have something along the June 4, 1967, lines if the Shepherdstown talks were to succeed. I asked Albright whether the United States could put in writing that President Clinton had spoken to Barak about the Rabin Deposit, and that, if anything were to be achieved, the deposit needed to be upheld. She liked the idea and said that she would take it up with her colleagues and the president. Ross later commented, "It was not an unreasonable request."[18] I added that Barak's positions were creating a problem for Syria. The Americans were convinced I was honest and speaking in what was in the best interest of the peace process as a whole. During my meeting with Albright, she said to me, "Unless we are in an official meeting, please feel free to call me Madeleine." In her memoirs, however, although she dedicates twelve pages to the Syrian-Israeli talks, she makes no mention of the Chick Channel, acting almost as if she had never known me.

When we had finished our talk, I went straight to the foreign minister to report my meeting with Albright. He was surprised that she had used the word "stuck" when referring to the US position and was clearly worried that she was trying to use me to open a direct channel with the president. Looking back, I am surprised that Albright said that she went to Shepherdstown with the purpose of finding a "common definition of what returning the Golan Heights actually meant." In her memoirs, the ever-contradictory Albright admits that Assad "wished to recover the Golan on the *right terms*."[19] She adds that "land was a matter of honor" for Hafez al-Assad.[20] The central question, she added, was "Where was the boundary? Where was the line that existed before the June 1967 war?"[21] Foreign Minister Shara and I firmly believed that Albright knew exactly where that line was, having heard it an endless number of times from both of us, as well as from President Assad: it extended to the eastern banks of Lake Tiberias and also to the River Jordan. As far as the Syrian delegation was concerned, that part of the talks was non-negotiable. Martin Indyk, however, offered a different story, claiming that Shara had told him that "sovereignty on the lake is Israel's; sovereignty on the land is ours." Indyk added: "He [Shara] also repeated that on the northeast shoreline, the line would be the same as the 1923 international boundary [which Syria had never recognized, seeing it as a colonial border]. That is, Syria would be at least ten meters off the shoreline."[22]

President Clinton welcomed my proposal and instructed his aides to begin working on the letter. Before sharing the document with us, however, Clinton felt the need to share it first with Barak. According to Ross, when they met him, "Barak was intrigued with the channel and agreed that presenting the letter to Shara was a good idea." When Barak read the letter, however, he immediately objected to the wording. Originally, it read, "Barak has told mc [Clinton] that he will not withdraw the Rabin Deposit." The new wording, at Barak's request, read: "It was the President's understanding that Barak did not intend to withdraw the Rabin Deposit."[23] This was to imply, of course, that Clinton was free to believe whatever he wished. At the end of the day, the person calling the shots would be Ehud Barak.

That evening, Shara met Clinton, who brought the letter with him. The US president spoke briefly about what the letter contained and then presented it to Shara, who read it carefully and then looked up and described it as "very important and good." Albright commented on the mood at Shepherdstown that evening, saying, "The Syrians had agreed to begin talks with only an indirect commitment from Barak on this point but expected something explicit as soon as the talks began. We had expected it too. Instead, Barak backed away."[24] Barak, we immediately found out, was terrified at the thought of giving up the Golan, claiming that an entire generation of Israelis had grown up "believing that the Golan Heights were essential for defending Israel."[25] Additionally, there were 17,000 Israeli settlers on the Golan whom Barak felt he could not cross—otherwise, they would vote him out of office. Third, more than 1 million Russian Jews had recently immigrated to Israel from the former Soviet Union, and Barak felt the need to keep more land to accommodate them. Fourth, hard-liners in Israel, such as Shas and Likud chairman Ariel Sharon, were already criticizing him for going to Shepherdstown. In fact, Sharon had recently accused him of "total surrender" for sitting down for talks with Foreign Minister Shara.[26] As a result, when he received Clinton's proposal in Shepherdstown, Barak requested a few days to study the paper. President Clinton agreed, but reminded him that half-finished peace agreements "rot like bananas and do not grow better with age like cheese."[27]

In her memoirs, Albright claims that both the Syrians and Israelis genuinely believed Shepherdstown would bring about a breakthrough. Both sides, she argued, felt that at the very last moment President Clinton would intervene to bridge the gap on unresolved core issues. "I did not doubt the President's skills, but I didn't see how even he could perform magic tricks."[28] How right she was. At the end of the day, Clinton could only maneuver if the Israelis armed him with something concrete. Despite his good intentions, Clinton was unable to deliver more than what the Israelis wanted to give. In looking back, nearly twelve years later, I can safely say that Israel was unwilling to give up anything at Shepherdstown, and with hindsight and experience, I can also add that we should not have been surprised by Barak's attitude in West Virginia that winter. It was standard for the Israelis to back out on any breakthrough, at the very last moment. They did so in 1991 under Shamir, and did so yet again after the Rabin Deposit was made in 1995. This time, Barak simply disappeared after the Clinton letter was delivered.

We never heard back from him at Shepherdstown, and at Albright's request the talks ended with no joint press statement.

One episode still needs to be mentioned, which back then aroused plenty of controversy and was blamed—by the Israelis—for the collapse of negotiations. A story appeared in the London-based *al-Hayat* outlining the draft US peace paper, carrying the byline of the newspaper correspondent in Damascus, Ibrahim Hamidi. The Israelis cried foul play, claiming that Syria had leaked the document through Hamidi, a seasoned, respected Syrian journalist who had been present at Shepherdstown. Hamidi strongly denied any leak, claiming that the *al-Hayat* story was what he had envisioned the US draft document to be, rather than what it actually was. That article, it has to be said, stressed Assad's demand for complete Israeli withdrawal from the Golan. On January 13, an Israeli newspaper, *Haaretz*, published the entire draft text that Clinton had given Shara and Barak on January 27, with a report claiming that Farouk al-Shara had granted more concessions to Israel than at any previous point during the Syrian-Israeli talks.[29] Not surprisingly, the *Haaretz* report said nothing about Israel's withdrawal from the Golan, and, not surprisingly, public opinion polls in Israel were showing that 73 percent of Russian Jewish voters and 63 percent of Shas voters were opposed to Israel giving up the Golan. That fit in nicely with a story on the front page of *Haaretz*, saying that Barak would never give up the Golan. The person who leaked the story to *Haaretz*, it was later revealed, was Nimrod Novik, a former foreign policy adviser to Shimon Peres in the 1980s.[30] According to Barak, Novik had received a copy of the draft from a member of the US team, Dennis Ross's deputy, David Aaron Miller.

We immediately distanced ourselves from both articles, claiming that no leak had been made by the Syrian delegation and that neither article was accurate in showing what Syria's full negotiating position had been at Shepherdstown. Because of the leaks, however, and domestic hard-line pressure within Syria, the second round of negotiations was canceled, and the Shepherdstown talks came to an abrupt end. President Assad was at first reluctant to take a call from President Clinton, upset by the entire ordeal at Shepherdstown, but eventually did on January 18 (see Appendix 7). Barak left West Virginia claiming that, as the newly elected prime minister of Israel, he could not stay out of the country for more than one week. Bill Clinton, as is well known, was furious with him. Before the Israelis left Shepherdstown, Clinton told the Israeli prime minister, "You've gained from this round, but another round like this and it will be a wholesale disaster for you, and for me!"[31]

Notes

1. *Al-Hayat*, June 23, 1999.
2. Ibid.
3. Ibid.
4. Ross, *The Missing Peace*, 551.
5. Archives of the Ministry of Foreign Affairs, the Shepherdstown File, January 2000.
6. Indyk, *Innocent Abroad*, 258.
7. Ibid.
8. Archives of the Ministry of Foreign Affairs, Shepherdstown File, January 2000.
9. Ibid.
10. Ibid.
11. Ross, *The Missing Peace*, 554.
12. Albright, *Madam Secretary*, 603.
13. Ibid.
14. Archives of the Syrian Presidential Palace, Minutes of the Assad-Albright talks, September 1997.
15. Ibid.
16. Ross, *The Missing Peace*, 555–556.
17. Ibid.
18. Archives of the Ministry of Foreign Affairs, Shepherdstown File, January 2000.
19. Albright, *Madam Secretary*, 473.
20. Ibid.
21. Ibid.
22. Indyk, *Innocent Abroad*, 259.
23. Ross, *The Missing Peace*, 557–560.
24. Albright, *Madam Secretary*, 605.
25. Archives of the Ministry of Foreign Affairs, Shepherdstown File, January 2000.
26. Ibid.
27. Albright, *Madam Secretary*, 478.
28. Ibid., 609.
29. *Haaretz*, January 13, 2000.
30. Ross, *The Missing Peace*, 566. Ross claims that he heard this argument from Martin Indyk.
31. Archives of the Ministry of Foreign Affairs, Shepherdstown File, January 2000.

11

The Man Who Did Not Sign

IN EARLY MARCH 2000, PRESIDENT ASSAD RECEIVED A PHONE call from Clinton at his home. I was there to do the translation, and we pressed the speaker button to hear what the US president had to say.

"Mr. President, I have what you want," Clinton boomed proudly. Assad looked at me with a puzzled expression, as if to say, "What does he mean? What is there to say that has not already been said by the United States?" Assad was still furious about the failed talks at Shepherdstown, and he doubted whether Clinton really had anything to offer after Ehud Barak had failed him—and us—so badly only two months previously, in January. The Syrian leader realized, however, that it was Clinton's last year in office and that he was desperate, in every sense of the word, for a breakthrough in Syrian-Israeli talks. We knew that he wanted to win the Nobel Peace Prize that he had worked so hard for during his eight years in office. Assad also knew, however, that it was Ehud Barak's first year in office and that the Israeli prime minister was in no rush to return the Golan Heights to Syria—which was very clear given his walkout at Shepherdstown.

Clinton was preparing to visit India and Pakistan and proposed to meet the Syrian president prior to his Far Eastern trip. Assad gently said, "I am in the midst of forming a new government in Syria, and I don't think it would be advisable for you to come to Damascus at this time, so that it won't be misread."

Assad was indeed in the process of formulating a new government, to be headed by Prime Minister Mohammad Mustapha Miro, which was to replace the jaded administration of Mahmud al-Zoubi, who had been in power for over a decade. In his conversation with Clinton, however,

Assad was endeavoring to make two points. In the first place, he did not want the US president to appear to be associated with any microlevel politics in Syria. US politicians had frequently shown up in the Occupied Palestinian Territories since 1994, providing Arafat with a lifejacket whenever his relations soured with Hamas or scolding him whenever he appeared too soft on Israel's security. Assad would have none of these shenanigans in Damascus. It has to be remembered that this was Assad's thirtieth year in power, and by this time the man could do just about anything he pleased—domestically—with no questions asked by the Syrian people. Nobody would doubt his wisdom and nationalist credentials if Clinton showed up in Damascus while incoming prime minister Mohammad Mustapha Miro was forming his cabinet. Syrians in the past had had their doubts about certain aspects of the president's foreign policy, questioning the wisdom, for example, of his support for Iran after the 1979 Islamic Revolution or for Operation Desert Storm in 1991. By March 2000, however, the majority of ordinary Syrians believed that Assad knew what was in their best interest and trusted him wholeheartedly when it came to foreign affairs. All the decisions—even unpopular ones—Assad had taken since 1970 eventually played out in Syria's favor. This applied even to Syria's decision to send troops to Lebanon in 1976, the decision to refrain from supporting Saddam Hussein in his long war with Iran, and, more recently, in Assad's firm decision to take part in the international coalition to establish the liberation of Kuwait. Nobody would criticize the president for hosting Clinton while a new cabinet was being formed in Syria, but Assad himself was very sensitive about how his love-hate relationship with the United States would be perceived by the overwhelming majority of Syrians who still did not trust the United States.

The second point the Syrian president was trying to make was that his patience was running out; he was losing faith in the entire peace process. Assad was politely indicating to Clinton that Syria was no longer in a rush to achieve anything with Israel. This, it should be noted, was at a time when international media, especially US and Israeli newspapers, were running wild stories about Assad's health, claiming that he was "desperate" for a peace treaty to secure a smooth transition of power to his son, Bashar al-Assad.

Assad's Health

The story of Assad's poor health is a crazy myth that the United States created and eventually believed; all speculation that he was not as sharp or aware at Geneva as he had been previously proved to be totally untrue, as I will show later in this chapter. In his memoirs, Martin Indyk recalled: "The warning signs had started to emerge in March, when Clinton tried to call Assad to arrange for the summit meeting in Geneva. Ostensibly, this was exactly what Assad had been waiting for, yet the call had been repeatedly delayed. At the time, Assad was engaged in a shakeup of his regime, but if he was so preoccupied with domestic issues that he could not meet with Clinton to negotiate peace, it was a clear indication of how his priorities had shifted."[1] Indyk was very negative regarding his portrayal of President's Assad's health in all his briefings to President Clinton prior to Geneva. In his memoirs he recalls the following encounter, which needs to be both quoted and challenged. He says:

> We found Assad was a sick man, his emaciated face almost skeletal, his handshake bony and weak. As he greeted me he said: "Mr. Indyk, I haven't seen you in years. You should visit us more often." He clearly could not remember our encounter seven months earlier. His memory failed him in more important respects, too. Once able to enthrall secretaries of state with his intellect and hold court for hours recounting events in Arab history from Saladin's defeat of the Crusaders to Sadat's supposed perfidy at Camp David, he could no longer distinguish between Clinton and Barak. He seemed so confused that, at one point, Gamal Helal leaned over and whispered to me: "He doesn't understand what we are talking about."[2]

Perhaps because of this very flawed assessment, which, I want to stress, is misinformation promulgated on purpose rather than by mistake, Clinton was keen to meet Assad that March, with his aides assuring him that Assad would bend easily because of poor health. Other reasons, no doubt, were the reports Clinton had been receiving from some of his friends in the Arab world, who were speculating on Syria's readiness for peace on US terms. On January 22, 2000, for instance, President Mubarak of Egypt came to Syria and, after returning to Cairo, told Clinton that the "mood was ripe" for peace with the Syrians. Saudi Arabia's ambassador to Washington, Bandar bin Sultan, who arrived in Damascus a few days later, echoed that view. Bandar told Clinton that "President Assad wants to reach an agreement with Israel in one decisive round." Having by then been very close to Assad for a long time, I can assure readers, nearly twelve years after he died, that all three assessments—Indyk's, Mubarak's, and Bandar's—were totally inaccurate.

Instead of welcoming Clinton to Damascus, as he had previously done in October 1994, Assad suggested they meet in Geneva after Clinton returned from the Far East. Clinton agreed, but a few minutes later, his national security adviser, Sandy Berger, called our number again, asking to speak with me directly. I was still with President Assad in the room when Berger told me that President Clinton was very keen on keeping the matter "strictly confidential for now" and not announcing it to the Syrian media. This was so that the upcoming summit would not be killed stone dead before it even happened. "No third party will be present," Berger told me, clearly referring to the Israelis. We agreed that the two leaders would meet at the Intercontinental Hotel on March 26, 2000, where they had first met six years previously.

By then, we had plenty of reasons to believe that Clinton was serious about peace, but, unfortunately, the same could not be said for all members of his peace team. When he first met Albright in September 1997, Assad had said to the US secretary of state, "How can we talk peace with an Israeli government that does not recognize what is in the Americans' pocket [that is, the Rabin Deposit]?"

Albright replied, "The United States is not in a mood to waste its time, and that of everybody else in the region. If you want to do business, Mr. President, then we are ready."

Assad had responded to this by saying, "The first thing the Israelis have to do is to acknowledge the Deposit. Then they have to resume negotiations from where they stopped. I cannot give you anything in terms of public diplomacy or so-called confidence building, because that would disappoint everybody in the Middle East, including peace activists in Israel. I cannot give something to an Israeli government that is giving me nothing in return!" Israel was still violating the Lebanese border and air space, was still building settlements in Palestine, and had been coming up with creative theories like Netanyahu's "peace in exchange for security, not land." None of this had changed by the time Ehud Barak came to power in 1999, and the failed talks at Shepherdstown were testimony to how stagnated the waters of Syrian-Israeli talks had become. Looking back, I don't think Assad had the slightest hope that anything could be achieved in Geneva. He went to Switzerland for Bill Clinton's sake, which was probably a last "opportunity" for the US president to succeed in the Middle East.

The Final Failure: Geneva 2000

We arrived in Geneva in March 2000. Prior to the meeting, Clinton's interpreter Gamal Helal told me that the US president was worn out by the Far East trip and ill, ostensibly because of some Asian food that he'd eaten, and that he might need to walk out of meetings to go to the bathroom. Helal was saying this to see if President Assad considered this offensive, and asking the Syrian leader's permission for Clinton to do this. I smiled, clearly seeing through Clinton's alibi, and said to Helal, "If President Clinton needs a certain medicine and cannot find it, we would be glad to provide it for him." Clinton might have been ill that day, but his walkout excuse was certainly not to go to the bathroom, but rather to call Ehud Barak and brief him about how the talks with Syria were progressing. Regardless of this, however, we told Helal that President Assad would not mind Clinton's occasional walkouts and wished him a "speedy recovery."

I then walked up to President Assad's suite, twenty minutes before the meeting, to convey what I had heard from Helal. He was resting in bed, wearing blue pajamas. Whenever he traveled, President Assad would spend long hours at his hotel, never going out for sightseeing or dinner at a restaurant. This was not always the case, however: back in the 1970s, he used to travel around whatever city he happened to be visiting, seeing its monuments and landmarks. By the late 1990s, however, Assad was visiting cities he had already been to, sometimes numerous times, and preferred to concentrate on work rather than sightseeing. Realizing that somebody was at the door, he waved his hand as if to say "Come in," telling his aides, "Let her in, Bouthaina is like my daughter." I greeted him respectfully and told him the story I had just heard, at which he smiled, saying, "I don't think they have anything to offer. I can feel it." He repeated the same words as we were in the elevator, heading down to the meeting from the tenth floor. He even remarked, "We shouldn't have come here. It is a waste of time."

When we arrived at the conference room at 3:00 P.M., an army of reporters was waiting for us. President Assad walked right by them into the main room, while President Clinton, for security reasons, came through the kitchen. He did not look at all ill. Clinton walked up to President Assad, shook his hand, and said, "Good afternoon, Mr. President. I have not seen you in a long time."

Assad smiled back, saying, "I would have loved to have seen more of you—I see you on TV here and there, but you fail to come to Damascus, Mr. Clinton."

There was no round table for the talks, just couches neatly arranged in a small room, with a coffee table in the middle, decorated with a colorful assortment of flowers. Present in the room, in addition to the two presidents, were Secretary of State Albright, Dennis Ross, Foreign Minister Shara, and myself. Clinton started the conversation, saying, "As agreed, I would like to work in smaller groups."

Assad nodded and, signaling his team to walk out, then looked at me and commanded, "You stay." He then quickly added, "Farouk [Shara] as well."

Clinton continued talking: "I have been working with Barak for many weeks, in order to bring about a deal that can be accepted by President Assad. He wants to take what he described as 'big Ben Gurion–size decisions.' We will go over them point by point and ask you to accept, reject, or modify and suggest." Clinton then asked that the flowers placed on the table be removed, so that he could show us a map. It was a big satellite map of the Golan and the valley beneath it, marked in red. We later found out that Dennis Ross and Barak's chief of staff Danny Yatom had worked on the talking points, as well as on Clinton's map. As he unfolded the map, Clinton continued, "Israel wants full sovereignty over the Jordan River and on Lake Tiberias. This is their major freshwater reservoir. They want the lake and are willing to trade some land, somewhere else. They also want to keep the Syrians away from the Jordan River." In return, Barak wanted Syria to give Israel a sovereign corridor of 10 meters on both sides of the lake, from the springs of Banias in the northern Golan down to Lake Tiberias. The Israeli prime minister, who had personally drawn the line, wanted the line to be drawn 500 meters from the shoreline to allow for the construction of a road. Barak proposed giving Syria the right to fish in the lake, in return for Israelis being able to visit the hot springs of al-Hamma. The 500-meter adjustment around the lake, which was more than the 100 meters that Barak had previously requested, was presumably based on what the Israelis claimed to be Shara's concession at Shepherdstown. The lake, it should be noted, had been reduced over time by 470 meters at the northern tip from whence it emanated from the Jordan River, narrowing gradually to 50 meters at the south end of the northeastern sector of the lake. Barak, the US president told us, had "limited his requirements to his country's vital needs" and was prepared to withdraw to "a commonly agreed border based on the June 4, 1967 lines." Assad immediately stopped the translation, asking, "What are these words, 'commonly agreed borders'? I don't accept them!" The president was fuming as he looked toward me and asked, rather angrily, "What are they talking about? Territorial swaps? That part of the lake is ours and has always been ours. I myself used to swim in it, with my colleagues, before the war. How can we give that up?" He then looked up at Clinton and spoke to him in Arabic, which I quickly translated as, "This is the property of my people!"

Albright said to Assad that Barack was offering him 90 percent of the Golan, and that he might never receive this offer again; therefore it was worth thinking about.

Assad then looked across the room at everybody present, saying, "Even if we cannot restore it now, we will leave that to future generations, but we will never give it up. What you are saying to us is that Barak simply does not want peace."

Clinton then explained that no previous Israeli prime minister had ever set out a detailed offer of full Israeli withdrawal or presented a line of withdrawal on a map—regardless of how flawed it was to us Syrians. But it was no use; President Assad was no longer listening.

Trying to calm Assad, Clinton said, "Mr. President, even pro-peace politicians in Israel now no longer want to return the Golan Heights to Syria. They are saying, 'Just conclude a deal with the Palestinians, and leave the lake in Israel's possession forever.' And they can do just that. They feel they can hold on to the lake for a very long period of time. Nobody in Israel wants peace anymore. The only two people who want peace are Ehud Barak and myself!"

Assad was clearly no longer interested, completely ignoring Clinton's remarks and grumbling, saying, "We are not ready to sign peace and give away territory."

Clinton added, "By accepting this agreement, you would be getting 90 percent of the Golan. And without it, Mr. President, you might get nothing back whatsoever."

Assad was yet again furious, looking at me while I translated those words, which, I imagine, must have been very difficult for him to hear. "How can anybody ask us to give up our land? That land that is very dear to us, and we inherited it from our forefathers." He then added, "The Israelis were never there before the war! How can they claim that this territory is theirs?"

Clinton gently interjected, "They know that it is yours, Mr. President. They just feel that they need it for security."

At this Assad snapped, "If everyone thinks that simply by wanting something they can get it, only the law of the jungle will prevail."

Clinton tried to explain, begging the president to "understand him." Assad said, "I neither understand nor do I want to understand. That is not my job. I'd better leave!"

Assad began to get up, but Clinton urged him to stay, saying, "I respect your feelings toward your people. I don't want you ever to make a decision that will be embarrassing or humiliating to you. And I will not be offended if you get up and leave, while saying no to what I have offered, because at the end of the day I am an honest mediator."

Assad looked back at Clinton, implicitly begging him to understand Syria's position. "I cannot do it, Mr. President. If I do, I will not be president for more than two days!"

At this point, Albright tried to make herself useful but actually complicated things further by saying, "You know, Mr. President, we are offering you at least 85 percent of the Golan. There will never be a time when you can get anymore."

Assad, upset by the US personnel trying to corner him from two sides, snapped, "I don't have to get it back, and I don't have to sign [up to] giving anything away!" He then pointed to the map laid out before him. "What am I going to do with this land that you propose to give me instead of my land? I know the area well. You want to take water and the territory's finest land, giving me rocky mountains instead?"

I had to rely on my personal notes to recall what was said during that stormy meeting in Geneva. The conversation between Assad and Clinton, after all, was not officially recorded from our side. Dennis Ross was taking notes, and he promised to make us a copy. Today, twelve years later, we still have no official written account of what happened at the final Assad-Clinton Summit, namely because Ross never sent us anything. We also never received a copy of the proposal the US delegation were reading from as they claimed the copy "was not clean." Clinton asked Ross to give us a clean copy, but that too never arrived.

President Clinton described the meeting in his memoirs, *My Life*, saying:

> I flew to Geneva to meet with President Assad. Our team had been working to get Barak to make a specific proposal on Syria for me to present. I knew it wouldn't be a final offer, and the Syrians would know it, too, but I thought that if Israel finally responded with the same flexibility the Syrians had shown at Shepherdstown, we might still be able to make a deal. . . . It was not to be.
>
> When I met Assad, he was friendly as I gave him a blue tie with a red-line profile of a lion, the English meaning of his name. It was a small meeting: Assad was joined by Foreign Minister Shara and Bouthaina Shaaban; Madeleine Albright and Dennis Ross accompanied me, with the National Security Council's Rob Malley serving as notetaker. After some pleasant small talk, I asked Dennis to spread out the maps I had studied carefully in preparing for our talks. Compared with his stated position at Shepherdstown, Barak was now willing to

accept less land around the lake, though he still wanted a lot, 400 meters (1,312 feet), fewer people at the listening station, and a quicker withdrawal period.

Assad didn't want me to even finish my presentation. He became agitated and, contradicting the Syrian position at Shepherdstown, said he would never cede any of the land, and that he wanted to be able to sit on the shore of the lake and dip his feet in the water. We tried for two hours to get some traction from the Syrians, all to no avail. The Israeli rebuff in Shepherdstown and the leak of the working document in the Israeli press had embarrassed Assad and destroyed his fragile trust. And his health had deteriorated even more than I knew. Barak had made a respectable offer. If it had come at Shepherdstown, an agreement might have emerged . . . After we parted in Geneva, I never saw Assad again.[3]

We decided to go into recess, during which President Assad went up to his room for some rest. The first meeting had not lasted for more than thirty minutes.

As the two leaders were walking out of the conference room, Clinton said to the Syrian president, "I would like you to continue working for peace."

Assad replied, "I am the one who wants you to work for peace."

Clinton smiled, saying, "We certainly have to continue our efforts because if we don't, Dennis will not know what to do with his life."

Dennis was walking behind the two leaders, with Martin Indyk. Assad looked back at him and then said to Clinton, "So long as Dennis is working on peace, we will never reach peace!"

A second meeting took place at 8:00 P.M., followed by a one-on-one meeting between Shara and Albright. When we finished, we went up to our rooms to work on a joint press statement, but this was rejected by the United States, who were unhappy with what had been achieved in Geneva, thinking that it made President Clinton look silly in front of the Israelis. Clinton tried to save the situation by saying that he could not provide a joint statement without having first consulted with Barak.

After we packed our bags to return home, the Intercontinental Hotel management presented President Assad with a Swiss watch, in appreciation for choosing the hotel as the venue for all his summits with US presidents since his first meeting with President Carter. As we walked out, Arab journalists were all over the hotel, hoping for a statement from President Assad. He waved hello and then whispered to me, "See, we did not get a chance to see them." The only Arab journalist briefed by the Syrian team, it should be noted, was Sati Nour al-Din, who sat down with Foreign Minister Shara and me after the two presidents met that afternoon. While heading back to Damascus on the plane, President Assad—contrary to what many may have believed—said nothing about his failed summit with Clinton. Rather, he discussed Syrian domestic issues because he was concerned about the upcoming conference regarding the Regional Command of the Baath Party, scheduled for late June 2000. We talked about the new government, about what people expected from the conference, and then he said to me, "Bouthaina, would you like to become ambassador?" I was taken aback by his sudden question, which was out of context, yet this showed how concerned the president was with my professional development. "They tell me you would like to become a cabinet minister or get posted as an ambassador; is that correct?" Shyly, I replied that I wanted to stay right by his side, learning from him and making myself useful in his talks with foreign leaders. I had no political, social, or financial ambition other than being, what Bill Clinton describes as, "an additional pair of eyes and ears" to the Syrian president. President Assad was satisfied with my reply, gently commenting, "In your absence, I always tell them how good you are."

A few days earlier when taking President Clinton's call in Damascus, Foreign Minister Shara had told him that I had received an offer to teach at Eastern Michigan University for the fall semester. Assad looked hard at him and said, "No, no, Bouthaina would never leave us."[4]

I did not leave him, but sadly, only three months later, Hafez al-Assad left us.

A Sad Day in Damascus

Nothing much happened in Syria, or in Syrian-US relations, during the last three months of President Assad's life. Once again, contrary to press reports, he went ahead with his day-to-day life, going to the office every morning as he had done for the past three decades and receiving whatever foreign dignitaries were seeking an audience in Damascus. He was certainly not "clinically dead" by May 2000, as the Israeli press reported that summer. One morning he got up early for a routine check by his doctors. They gave him a clean bill of health, telling him and his wife, "You are in perfect shape, Mr. President."

On the very same day, while he was getting dressed for work, the telephone rang; it was Lebanese president Emile Lahoud on the line from Beirut. Assad liked Lahoud and treated him like a son, having supported his bid for president back in 1998. Lahoud was credited with keeping the Lebanese army united in the final years of the Lebanese

Civil War and for supporting Hizbullah, which had liberated most of South Lebanon by May 2000, a heroic feat. Assad had instructed Syria's top officials, and all the country's allies in Lebanon, to attribute the liberation of South Lebanon to the Lebanese themselves—namely to Lahoud and Hizbullah—and not to Syria. "This is their achievement, not ours," he would often say to me during his final days. We don't know what the Lebanese president said to his Syrian counterpart that morning, but what I do know is that his last sentence to Lahoud, according to what Assad's wife told me, was, "We owe it to future generations." (They were talking about the liberation of South Lebanon by the resistance on May 25, that is, a few days earlier.) In mid-conversation, Assad suffered a stroke and yelped, calling for his wife, the first lady. Mrs. Assad was in a nearby room counting out money that she was planning to send to poor families in rural Syria, an alms practice (*zakat*) that is one of the main pillars of Islam. She did not interrupt her money counting, thinking that her husband was calling for her to help him remember a certain name or date. When she eventually went into the room he was in, however, she found Assad collapsed on his bed, with the telephone and its cord dangling loosely to the ground. Lahoud later told us that Assad was talking to him about "future generations" and about making the Middle East a peaceful part of the world, free from war, death, and conflict. It was Hafez al-Assad's final words and last wish. He died that morning on June 10, 2000, four months before reaching his seventieth birthday.

I did not immediately know what had happened that morning, as I had been busy in my own home, preparing my daughter for her baccalaureate exam. If she passed the dreaded examination with high grades, I had promised I would introduce her to President Assad. Then one of my neighbors, an officer in the Syrian Army, called me up, saying, "Is anything wrong in the country? There is unusual commotion on the streets." I had seen the president only a few days earlier. He seemed to be in perfect shape, as mentioned earlier, and was busy preparing for the upcoming Baath Party Congress. I called the Presidential Palace to speak to his bureau chief, Abu Salim Daaboul, but he did not answer my call, which I thought was strange. Then I called up the president's family but was unable to reach his daughter Bushra. I got dressed and went to my office at the Ministry of Foreign Affairs in al-Muhajreen, with disturbed thoughts floating around in my head. There was an empty feeling in my stomach, a fear that something terrible had happened, but I didn't want to jump to any wild conclusions. The streets of Damascus were unusually crowded; it was an unusual crowd—one that masses on the streets rather chaotically before dispersing rapidly. People were in a rush, and they looked worried and uncomfortable. Everybody seemed to have reached the same conclusion as I had; something major had happened in Damascus, and it wasn't good. There was no army deployed on the streets, however, not even in al-Muhajreen, which is a few minutes' walk from the Presidential Palace and the president's residence. No tanks, no men in uniform, and no weapons on street corners, as the world would have expected to fill the streets of the Syrian capital on the day Hafez al-Assad died. The foreign minister's office was packed with men, busily debating something until I showed up at the doorstep. I walked in and asked Shara about the president's health. He did not give me a convincing answer, muttering a polite, "All is fine." I then noticed a paper on his desk, wrapped in a scroll like a university diploma, with the words "funeral preparations" printed on it as a header. I looked back at the minister with a blank expression on my face, shaking my head in disbelief while having a hard time holding back my tears. "Be strong, Bouthaina, you are a politician and you need to be strong," said Shara. He added, "This is God's doing and we can neither object to it, nor obstruct it. The President died this morning."

Notes

1. Indyk, *Innocent Abroad*, 275. "Shake-up of his regime" was a gross exaggeration on Indyk's part, as forming the new Miro cabinet was certainly no "shake-up."
2. Indyk, *Innocent Abroad*, 242.
3. Clinton, *My Life*, 903–904.
4. I eventually did take up the teaching offer, but only after the President's death in June 2000. The trauma of his passing was too much for me to bear, and I went to Michigan to escape the agony of being in Damascus in the months after his death.

Epilogue

IT IS NOW MORE THAN TWELVE YEARS SINCE THE FINAL EFfort in the Middle East peace process was held in Geneva between the late president Hafez al-Assad and President Bill Clinton on March 26, 2000. We can now reflect on two things: what happened during the Madrid peace process of 1991–2000 and the impact of what did and did not take place in those proceedings on our lives today.

I would like to stress that I am writing for posterity and that I consider myself to be a messenger for future generations. Although I am Syrian, I am not for or against any party in my assessment of the process. I write as an honest witness in the hope that the frustrating experience of those years will be a lesson for forthcoming generations to learn from, so that they do not repeat our mistakes.

Politicians have always surprised me by not saying things straight out and by rarely reaching a conclusion. They often convey an indirect message and leave it either to junior officials or to another time for their message to mature. As regards the peace process, there was an urgent need for the people concerned to be direct and to the point and to rehearse the agreement reached so that all parties should have the same clear understanding of what had been decided. This never happened. Unfortunately, the topics that absorbed most of the time and energy of the interlocutors were the venue, the dates of meetings, the best way to get in touch, and the dates of resumption of meetings. Substance and real progress were always deferred because the views expressed were so divergent and very complicated. Indeed, I have never witnessed such a systematic and deliberate waste of time at such a high level, for which a sizable cost had to be borne. In addition, the media were intent on conveying the impression that progress was being made, when in fact this was not the case—no real or definite progress was ever made. Vagueness was the key player, and anyone who tried to bring clarity to the proceedings faced obstacles and obstruction.

As the interpreter between President Assad and all his US interlocutors, I can testify that Hafez al-Assad always aimed for clarity. The people he talked to considered him to be intransigent because he did not accept any words put forward that were susceptible to various interpretations and that were not crystal clear. He often said, "I want to sign a peace agreement which future generations can defend long after I die," but that peace agreement was not to be reached. (Here it should be noted that the peace agreements reached between Egypt and Israel at Camp David, Jordan and Israel, and the Palestinians and Israel in Oslo did not create a true state of peace between Arabs and Israelis, which was why Hafez al-Assad was against these agreements. It was not because he was against peace in the Middle East, which is the way he has always been portrayed by the Western media.)

I myself took the cause of peace very seriously—at the expense of my family life and my career and future as a scholar of Shelley, as I had planned to do him and the Chartist poets justice in future books that unfortunately had to be delayed. At that time I was working on a book about Arab women novelists that was finally published under the title of *Voices Revealed* after a ten-year delay. Having given birth to my two daughters, Nahid and Nazek, in 1982 and 1985, respectively, I delayed having a third child until peace had been concluded. I thought that one day I would write about the suffering of Palestinian women once that suffering became history. But having traveled the extra mile for the sake of peace and having experienced three years of negotiations going nowhere, in 1994 I decided to become pregnant once again. I felt that since I was not able to twist the arm of history, perhaps having another child might be something worthwhile that I could do for my family and me. During my nine months of pregnancy, I never stopped working and traveling. My fetus and I witnessed the Barak-Shihabi negotiations and many of the Christopher-Assad sessions. I was not at all shy about being the only woman present—and very pregnant too—because I enjoyed being pregnant and considered it a blessing that God has granted us women this special privilege of nurturing human beings inside our bodies for nine months.

On July 15, 1995, I was interpreting for President Hafez al-Assad, who on that day was talking to the Australian foreign minister. After the meeting he said to me, "You look ripe for delivery; go home and rest."

I must have looked very swollen, but as my focus was totally on what I was doing, I did not pay much heed to what I looked or felt like. On Sunday, July 16, 1995, I stayed home, cleaned the flat, and cooked for my family. At dawn on July 17, I was taken to the hospital. After twelve hours of difficult labor, Reda was born at 4.45 P.M. on Monday, July 17, 1995. Next morning I called the palace, saying that I was fine and ready for work if I was needed.

What amazed me was that over the next two months, friends, neighbors, and relatives celebrated the birth of a baby boy in a way I had never experienced when I'd had my two lovely girls. I loved Reda and was very happy to give birth to him at the age of forty-two but hated the chauvinist attitude our society still embraces so deeply. I remember leaving Reda at a nursery to resume my work for peace when he was two months old. I cried and he cried, and I consoled myself by telling him that I hoped he would live in a better and more peaceful time. If peace prevailed, I thought, we would have achieved something worthwhile, both for my children and all our children. Now Reda is sixteen years old and we are living in a much more difficult time, but I was extremely fortunate to have given birth to him during the time we worked so hard and so long for peace, even though peace was never achieved.

I have worked on this book about the Syrian-Israeli peace process during the worst year of Syria's modern history. What the West has called the "Arab Spring" started in Tunisia, and after sweeping through Egypt and Libya, it arrived in Syria on March 15, 2011. More than a year later, we are left with over 10,000 people killed and kidnapped and over 50,000 people displaced, both in Syria and in neighboring countries. What I have learned from these terrible times is that the most important thing for all of us is to live in peace and harmony. The year has also shown beyond any doubt that the lack of peace in the Middle East is having an unpredictable impact not only on the Arab-Israeli conflict but also on the internal politics of Arab countries. There has never been any doubt in my mind that the establishment of peace is a worthy cause, but I feel that way now more than ever. The only alternative to peace is war, or many small wars that leave so many people killed and displaced.

I would like to stress, however, that the Oslo Accords brought no peace to the Palestinians and proved exactly what Hafez al-Assad predicted to Yasser Arafat: "that every item in this accord needs a separate agreement!" He added, "Nothing is final or crystal clear." The current state of the Arab-Israeli conflict proves that, beyond any doubt, Syria's position on the peace process was right, starting with Madrid in October 1991 and reaching up to Geneva 2000. Peace needs two main ingredients to succeed: it has to be just and it has to be comprehensive. As Hafez al-Assad often said: "The security of one side cannot be achieved at the expense of the other." Despite the loud media campaigns trumpeting both Camp David in 1978 and Oslo in 1993, the peoples of the region are very far from living in peace. There is a huge difference between trying to create a temporary buzz that implies a breakthrough and creating a sustainable peace that can last for years to come and brings justice and prosperity to the Middle East. US congressman Arlen Specter once said to President Assad: "If you sign a peace accord like Arafat, your picture will appear in all the world media." President Assad firmly responded: "I want to sign a peace accord that future generations can and will defend." People and posterity may well serve as a good compass for politicians.

While I write this epilogue, many Palestinian prisoners are on a hunger strike, protesting their prolonged and illegal arrest and the unashamed negligence of the international community. This plight and their resistance will undoubtedly continue until a just and comprehensive peace is reached for them in particular, and for the Arab world in general. Also on a personal note, I was blessed to see the birth of my first grandson, Najem al-Deen al-Saleh, while putting the final touches on this book. His birth gives me hope that my daughters, my son, and my grandchildren shall stay in the race for peace and for a better world. They know that I tried my best, although I did not win the race. We live a short life, after all, and what is important is to keep the torch alight and bequeath our values and tales to upcoming generations in order for them to continue trying for—if not achieving—the most noble of objectives, that being peace in the Arab World.

As I wrap up this epilogue in mid-2012, I have no idea what the Arab-Israeli conflict is going to look like one year from now. Nor do I have a clear vision of what kind of Arab world—Syria included—we are leaving behind for our children and grandchildren. What I do hope, however, is that they benefit from our mistakes and build upon our achievements, no matter how little those might be. That, after all, was exactly the objective behind my writing this book: a blueprint to build upon, learn from, correct, and develop.

APPENDIX 1

Letter from George H. W. Bush to Hafez al-Assad, May 31, 1991

THE WHITE HOUSE

WASHINGTON

May 31, 1991

Dear Mr. President:

I am writing you for the second time in a week, in this instance to share my thoughts about the Arab-Israeli peace process. Secretary Baker has reported to me on his many hours of conversation in Damascus. I have heard too from both President Mubarak and King Hussein about their recent meetings with you. I continue to believe that there is a real chance for making progress toward a comprehensive peace in the region. I believe just as firmly that it is in your interest as well as ours to seize that opportunity.

In this regard, I think we have reached a critical juncture in our efforts to put together a peace conference to make negotiations possible. We have tried to structure this process so the needs of all parties are taken into account in a fair and reasonable way.

As I see it, we have met fully all but two of your concerns. I understand your requirements, but the approach we have fashioned offers a way to address them -- both regarding the role of the United Nations in the process and the issue of reconvening the conference.

First, on the role of the UN, what we are proposing is a <u>package of elements</u> which will have a cumulative effect and should meet any reasonable requirements you might have for input from the UN. In addition, these elements, coupled with U.S. and Soviet sponsorship and European participation, meet both the test of "international legitimacy" and that of "appropriate auspices" embodied in UN Security

Council Resolution 338. Let me briefly lay out these elements:

(1) A UN observer will attend the conference.

(2) The process is based on UN Security Council Resolutions 242 and 338 and all parties agree to terms of reference calling for a "<u>comprehensive settlement based on 242 and 338</u>". This will be reflected in all conference documents and public statements.

(3) The parties and co-sponsors will deposit agreements with the UN and seek UN endorsement of the agreements;

(4) The co-sponsors will agree to keep the Secretary General informed of the progress of the negotiations.

Items three and four are commitments we were not in a position to make when Secretary Baker last met with you. Given the discussions the Secretary had in Israel, I am in a position to do so now.

Second, as you are aware, our position on reconvening the conference is that it be done by consensus. At the same time, I want to point out something additional that Secretary Baker was not able to convey to you in Damascus, namely that we intend our engagement throughout the negotiations to be significant. We and the Soviet Union will be a driving force behind the negotiations, taking on a special responsibility for making them succeed and cajoling and pressing the parties forward.

I want to make clear that we will be doing so on the only basis possible for a comprehensive peace: territory for peace applied to all fronts, including the Golan Heights. We will not change this fundamental policy position of ours; nor will we change our non-recognition of Israel's purported "annexation" of the Golan Heights. While Secretary Baker tells me he made these points to you, we both feel they deserve added emphasis and greater consideration by you.

In this regard, to increase the probability of a successful outcome on the Golan, I have even been willing to make the offer of a United States security guarantee of the border that Israel and Syria mutually agree upon. This would go beyond the assurances that the co-sponsors would give (as you requested) that the parties would carry out their agreements. This security guarantee -- which is unprecedented and far-reaching -- will affect the negotiations and their outcome far more than any symbols relating to the UN or a conference. My decision in favor of such a security guarantee was not an easy one to make. But I did so because I believe it offers the best chance for a peaceful resolution of the problems between Syria and Israel.

At this point, while I am not yet certain, I do believe that Israel is prepared to say "yes" to a conference based on the terms and modalities I have described. It is difficult for me to see how your interest could be served by saying "no" to this process.

The fact is we want Syria to participate because we seek a comprehensive peace. At the same time, we cannot agree that a process not proceed even if you choose not to come. Our bilateral relationship is dependent on many things; but as with other states in the region a critical part of that relationship depends on Syria's position on peace.

Mr. President, I want you to know that I remain personally committed to the principles I enunciated in my March 6 address to the U.S. Congress. Similarly, I cannot over-emphasize that the successful prosecution of the war in the Gulf has created new opportunities for progress in the peace process. These new opportunities may not come again and they ought to be seized.

4

As you can see, I think it is very important that Syria participate. Further, with respect to your two concerns, we are now in a position to offer assurances that we could not offer when Secretary Baker last visited you. With these additional assurances, our security guarantee, and the other elements of our proposal, we have gone as far as we can go and still produce a process. So, I need to know whether you are prepared to agree to this process, a process that is realistic and that is certain to be judged as reasonable by the international community.

If you will let me know that you are leaning toward participating in a peace conference along the lines described here and by Secretary Baker, I would be prepared to ask Secretary Baker to return to Damascus one more time to iron out the details.

Such a position on your part would, in my view, open historic possibilities for bringing peace to a part of the world that has too often known war. I hope the Middle East, and indeed the world, can count on your leadership and your commitment to peace.

Sincerely,

G. Bush

His Excellency
Hafiz al-Assad
President of the Syrian Arab Republic
Damascus

APPENDIX 2

Letter from Bill Clinton to Hafez al-Assad, May 27, 1993

```
                          Washington, D.C.
                          May 27, 1993
```

Dear President Asad:

Thank you for your letter of May 9, 1993 which I have read carefully. I appreciate your expressions of support for the role played by the United States in the Middle East peace process and the reaffirmation of Syria's commitment to achieving a just and lasting peace with Israel.

I have taken particular note of your commitment to work together to achieve a breakthrough to peace this year. As I noted in my previous letter to you, I believe we are at a critical juncture in the peace process. The bilateral negotiations, which just adjourned in Washington, made some progress. In each set of talks, papers have been tabled. The parties have moved into substantive consideration of many of the core issues. More, however, must be done.

Your efforts to help bring the parties back to the negotiating table are appreciated, and your engagement in public diplomacy earlier this month was a positive step that begins to build confidence and helps to create a positive climate in the negotiations. However, a comprehensive breakthrough this year will be enhanced if a way is found to move the Israeli-Syrian negotiations forward.

In my letter of April 8, 1993, I gave you my best judgment about the mechanism that would produce a breakthrough. I also emphasized that the United States is ready to facilitate the establishment of this mechanism, in accordance with our role as "full partner." Naturally, I was disappointed by your decision to put aside, for now, this approach. I continue to believe a private channel offers the best means for you and Prime Minister Rabin to test each other's intentions and determine whether the basis exists for an historic agreement between Israel and Syria.

I appreciate the confidence you express in the United States by suggesting that we verify the intentions and commitments of both sides. I also appreciate your willingness, in these circumstances, to provide me with appropriate responses. While I am prepared to consider such an undertaking, some important issues require clarification.

As I mentioned in my previous letter, I have begun to probe Prime Minister Rabin's positions and we have a clear sense of the direction of his thinking. It was on that basis that I recommended that you and he find a way to communicate through a private channel. But if you feel unable to take this step now, I will respect your position. At the same time, for us to play the role you suggest -- and to be effective in doing so -- we need to have a clear understanding of your views on the core issues of the content and timing of full peace and its relationship to the other critical elements of withdrawal, security and comprehensiveness.

If you feel able to provide us with your thinking on these core issues, I would be prepared to proceed along the lines you are suggesting.

Two points should be understood, however. First, our willingness to ascertain and, in your words, verify "the intentions and commitments of the two sides through private exchanges" is not a substitute for a private channel between you and the Israelis.

Secondly, while we are ready to help clarify and convey respective intentions and commitments to you and to Israel, we cannot guarantee or pledge to deliver such fundamental commitments, which need to be made directly between the parties. Our role as full partner is to facilitate this exchange, perhaps at first through the United States. Once that is done, and you are both reassured that the private channel will be productive, I believe that channel should then be established for the direct exchange of commitments. I make these points because I cannot guarantee commitments that I, alone, cannot fulfill; that is not in your interest either. Of course, I do not refer here to the border security arrangements which I reaffirmed to you in my last letter.

Time is short; forces opposed to peace will take advantage of failure to move ahead now. I am prepared, Mr. President, to move quickly on your suggestion, but this means we will need a clear understanding of Syria's key positions. I look forward to your response and to your views on how best to proceed. If you are prepared to engage with us on this basis, I would then be prepared to send Secretary Christopher to meet with you at the appropriate time.

I am convinced that an historic opportunity exists to achieve a peace which will transform the Middle East. It will require courage and vision from all sides to produce a "peace of the brave," but I am confident that working together we can overcome the past and build a new, better future for all the peoples of the region.

                      Sincerely,

                      /S/

                    William J. Cinton

His Excellency
    Hafiz al-Asad
        President of the Syrian Arab Republic,
            Damascus, Syria.

APPENDIX 3

Letter from Bill Clinton to Hafez al-Assad, July 4, 1993

THE WHITE HOUSE
WASHINGTON

July 4, 1993

Dear President Assad:

I am sending Special Middle East Coordinator, Ambassador Dennis Ross, to convey this message to you.

I remain dedicated to the objective of seeking a breakthrough to peace in the Middle East in 1993. I understand the importance of the negotiations between Syria and Israel to achieving this objective. Indeed, if we can find a way to break the deadlock in your negotiations it would have a dramatic impact on our efforts to achieve a comprehensive solution.

Through the exchanges Secretary of State Christopher and I have had with yourself and Prime Minister Rabin, I believe that both of you share our goal of achieving a just, lasting, comprehensive and real peace based on UN Resolutions 242 and 338 and the exchange of territory for peace.

We now need to establish an effective mechanism for converting this common commitment into negotiated agreements. This mechanism should allow us to probe the positions of both sides, convey the ideas of each side to the other at a political level, and thereby make it possible for you to gain greater confidence in the sincerity of each other.

In this way, we can facilitate and promote the exchange of commitments and play the role that only we can play: the role of full partner and honest broker. In this respect, Secretary Christopher has sent you ideas on addressing the

2

substance of territory, peace and security. And, as I have said in my earlier correspondence, at the appropriate time, I am ready to send Secretary Christopher to the region in fulfillment of this role.

I would greatly appreciate it if you would share your thoughts with Dennis Ross and our peace team on how best to proceed so that they can report back to the Secretary of State and me. We can then make a judgement about the next step in our pursuit of the noble cause of peace in the Middle East.

Sincerely,

Bill Clinton

His Excellency
Hafiz al-Assad
President of the Syrian Arab Republic
Damascus

APPENDIX 4

Letter from Bill Clinton to Hafez al-Assad, September 4, 1993

Washington, D.C.

September 4, 1993

Dear Mr. President:

We have reached an historic moment in our common search for a comprehensive and lasting peace in the Middle East. The announcement of agreement between Israel and the Palestine Liberation Organization on interim self-government, initially in Gaza and Jericho, and the agreement's provision that permanent status negotiations will lead to implementation of U.N. Security Council Resolutions 242 and 338 are dramatic achievements.

These are important steps forward for the Palestinians. If the agreement is used as a catalyst for progress towards a comprehensive settlement, it can help to offer hope to all the people of the region.

This agreement was negotiated directly by Israel and the PLO. Nevertheless, it could not have been achieved without the active commitment of all the other parties involved in the peace process. Indeed, without your historic commitment to the Madrid process there would not have been a breakthrough on the Palestinian-Israel track.

I am also encouraged by the recent progress made in the private exchanges between Prime Minister Rabin, Secretary Christopher, and yourself. Progress on the Palestinian track can pave the way for further progress on all the other tracks.

Mr. President, I am personally committed to achieving a breakthrough to a comprehensive peace in 1993. In particular, I am committed to working with you to achieve a peace agreement between Syria and Israel because of the powerful impact this would have on peace and stability in the region. In this context, I hope you will do whatever you can to support the agreement reached between Israel and the PLO because it will help to produce the comprehensive breakthrough we both seek. I also ask that you use your influence to restrain those Palestinian groups who are opposed to the agreement and may try to subvert it with violence. I am counting on your support. This is essential.

An opportunity for achieving a just, comprehensive and real resolution of the Middle East conflict is at hand. We must now redouble our efforts and not permit the enemies of peace to block us when we are so close to achieving our common objective. I am confident that, working closely together, we can ensure that the promise of peace for all is realized.

        Sincerely,

         /s/

        William J. Clinton

His Excellency
Hafiz al-Asad,
President of the
 Syrian Arab Republic,
Damascus

APPENDIX 5

Letter from Bill Clinton to Hafez al-Assad, December 2, 1993

THE WHITE HOUSE
WASHINGTON

December 2, 1993

Dear Mr. President:

I am asking Secretary Christopher to convey this letter to you as a manifestation of my continued commitment to achieving a real and comprehensive peace between the Arabs and Israel as soon as possible.

As you know, we had agreed that 1993 should be the year of breakthrough in the Middle East peace process. That breakthrough has indeed occurred. The Israel-Palestinian Declaration of Principles is an important step forward that should facilitate rapid progress on the other tracks.

We have not rested in our efforts to take advantage of that breakthrough. We have sought prompt and effective implementation of the agreement and we have urged others to do their part to create a conducive climate for further steps toward a comprehensive peace. Most importantly, we have focussed particular energy on reactivating the Syria-Israel negotiations because we understand that a breakthrough here is key to achieving our common objective.

As Secretary Christopher will explain to you, our efforts have been fruitful. I am confident you will agree that the foundation has now been laid for real progress. Given this foundation, Secretary Christopher will present some ideas to you on how we can best move ahead. I know you will give careful consideration to Secretary Christopher's proposals and I am looking forward to hearing his report on how you will work with us to facilitate the next steps.

As we proceed together toward the achievement of our common goal you can be certain that, as long as the parties remain sincere in their commitments, the pursuit of a just and lasting peace in the Middle East will remain one of my highest priorities.

Sincerely,

Bill Clinton

His Excellency
Hafiz al-Asad
President of the Syrian Arab Republic
Damascus

APPENDIX 6

Letter from Bill Clinton to Hafez al-Assad, October 12, 1999

THE WHITE HOUSE
WASHINGTON

October 12, 1999

Dear Mr. President:

I was glad to be able to meet with Foreign Minister Farouk Shara'a and saddened to hear about his illness. I hope he recovers quickly.

I am writing now because I believe we are approaching the moment of truth for you and Prime Minister Barak. Over the past weeks, we have conducted intensive discussions with both sides. My talks with you and Prime Minister Barak, Secretary Albright's discussions with both sides, the meetings in Bern, and the exchanges in the Washington area, have demonstrated to me that the requirements of both sides can be met. The exchanges have also very clearly crystallized the key differences between the two sides.

While the gaps are real, they are in my judgment narrow, and certainly resolvable. The actual determination of the borderline, the relationship between that borderline and control of key water resources, and the precise understanding on early warning are the key areas that in my view require decisions by the leaders at this stage if we are to conclude an agreement in a short period of time.

I have always expected that we would reach a point where decisions by the leaders would be required. Also, I have known that for me to be effective in helping both sides reach a mutually acceptable outcome, there would need to be direct meetings at a high political level between the two sides. There can be no substitute for that if there is to be an agreement.

I told Minister Shara'a that I would think about our discussion and make a proposal to you and Prime Minister Barak. After much consideration, I am convinced there is one logical pathway to reaching an agreement, and that is direct discussions between high level Syrian and Israeli representatives. We could host these discussions, and they could be unannounced and private. They should be at the political, not technical level. Their purpose would be to create a sufficient level of understanding on the key issues to allow Syria and Israel to conclude an agreement.

2

In light of the discussions that have now taken place, I fear that if we do not move to a political level and focus on the key decisions each side must make, we will miss this unique opportunity. Indeed, at this juncture, if the discussions remain indirect or direct but at a technical level, I believe that the process will be endless, with each side waiting for the other to make decisions and with an increased risk that other events will intervene to disrupt our efforts.

If I didn't believe that the gaps could be overcome, I would not make this proposal. I am fully aware of your needs. As I have previously told you, what Prime Minister Rabin deposited in my pocket remains and has not been withdrawn. From my conversations with Prime Minister Barak, I am convinced he will meet your needs in a way that satisfies you if it is clear that his needs will also be met. Without direct engagement at a political level, I do not see this happening.

I am prepared to do all in my power to help reach agreement on this track. But if I am to be in a position to do so, time is of the essence, and we now need an approach that will make my efforts worthwhile. I believe my proposal will do that.

Be assured, I will be making the same proposal to Prime Minister Barak and it is my hope the two of you will accept it. Such acceptance will signal your mutual readiness to make the decisions necessary to solve the key problems. I look forward to your response either in a phone call or, perhaps, through a personal envoy.

With determination and courage, I am convinced that we can together forge a peace with honor and dignity -- a peace that will be comprehensive, including Lebanon; a peace that will create a new strategic reality in the Middle East and one that is built on a new and important U.S.-Syrian relationship. Neither of us expected this would be easy, but now that peace may be within our grasp, I am asking you to accept my proposal. This will enable me to play my role and, I believe, ensure that we do not lose this historic opportunity.

Sincerely,

Bill Clinton

His Excellency
Hafiz al-Asad
President of the Syrian Arab Republic
Damascus

APPENDIX 7

Minutes of the Telephone Conversation Between Bill Clinton and Hafez al-Assad, January 18, 2000

CLINTON: Greetings Mr. President.

ASSAD: Greetings. I am happy and gratified whenever I see you or hear your voice in any phone call.

CLINTON: Thank you Mr. President. I thought a lot about our recent talks, and Secretary Albright briefed me of her talks with Foreign Minister Shara. As you know, Mr. President, after the first week of Shepherdstown, I was disappointed because the Israelis were not responsive to the issues on which you showed lenience. I made it clear to Prime Minister Barak that we needed to move if we wanted success, and that both Israel and Syria ought to take difficult decisions. Since you and I spoke last time, I obtained from Barak a reconfirmation of the Rabin Deposit, along with starting a process to mark the June 4 borders, along with other issues.

ASSAD: This is good.

CLINTON: I believe it answers your needs, as you have expressed them to me, and as they were outlined by Farouk al-Shara: beginning the marking of the June 4 borders. This answers your demands, but Barak also, has his own needs. He believes that marking the borders and confirming the Rabin Deposit can only move forward if talks begin on the Lebanese front days after Syria and Israel meet again. He wants us to announce that the Lebanese track will start days after resumption of Syrian-Israeli talks. He wants the world to know that when he finishes all of that, there will be a comprehensive peace that includes Lebanon. Mr. President: I think that his demand satisfies the needs of both parties. As for you, you would immediately get marking the June 4 borders, in addition to control over timing of the two tracks in the peace process. Barak would get the Lebanese track to start, and as for us, we can reach an understanding that the Lebanese and Israelis would not negotiate their borders unless you are satisfied with what you hear from the Israelis regarding the June 4 borders.

Based on that talks that I conducted with both parties, I am convinced that the differences between you, on all matters, are not great. I think we can reach a deal quickly if [we] follow the correct methods. I know for sure that you were disappointed, just as I was, that the Israelis did not show more lenience on June

4, during the first week of talks (at Shepherdstown). I think, however, that you ought not reach a conclusion that they are not interested in solving these issues in a manner that is satisfying to both parties. I think they are interested in solving all issues (in a manner satisfactory to both parties) and I think they want to do it with maximal speed. That is why I hope that you re-think this method, which secures for Syria reconfirmation of the Rabin Deposit, and marking the June 4 borders.

ASSAD: If I knew how to speak English, I would have spoken to you directly. I understand what you want to say. The agreement that was reached, through a third party, was that we send our delegation for talks, but our team got nothing in return. The Syrian delegation can go there now and stay for one or two months, and yet, get nothing in return. This of course, is bad, and is unacceptable for us. We cannot bear that, and we don't want to repeat it yet again.

CLINTON: I understand that Mr. President. What should have happened before was that the Israelis ought to have informed you and I beforehand that they were incapable of moving forward during the first week, due to their domestic problems. We would have been able to make different arrangements, and Syria would not have been placed in such a position, and therefore, would have handled affairs differently. I said this fully to Prime Minister Barak and he said that now, he is not only ready to start talks again, but to move forward and seal a deal at these negotiations. He is willing to mark the borders and solve all outstanding issues with maximal speed. I would have not brought the Syrian delegation here had I doubted that we were capable of achieving progress. I think that this is very important. I made it very clear to the Israelis that another week cannot pass that is like the first at Shepherdstown. I actually don't want them to come back if we are going to repeat what happened during the first week. They said that they understand and are willing to sit down for talks that solve all pending issues.

ASSAD: I conducted extensive talks during the past few days. The people here, and the state, have serious doubts that they are going to get what they want (from the peace talks). The best that we can do is let the border demarcation committee to meet and finalize the June 4 borders of 1967. When we and the Israelis agree on those borders, it would be safe to say that good progress was achieved. That is when Lebanon can resume its talks with Israel. That perhaps is more secure for everybody.

CLINTON: Mr. President, what you suggest spells out practical and political obstacles. Practically, what you have said takes a long time to achieve (demarcation of the border) and would show that this is the only thing we are negotiating. Politically, we cannot conduct talks over the demarcation of the border while shielding it from the news. When it is mentioned in the media this will create a real problem for Israel, because Barak would be negotiating the June 4 borders without even having starting the Lebanese talks. Having said that, I say again that the Syrian delegation is entitled to having doubts after what happened at Shepherdstown. Mr. Barak has promised me that this will not happen again, and that he is ready to re-confirm the Deposit. As for demarcation, Mr. President, these are difficult issues that cannot be solved by committees alone. At the end of the day, we need to achieve progress on the political front as well.

If we resume talks, I am confident that we will get assurances about the Deposit, and that the demarcation talks will start off with good intentions.

ASSAD: I repeat that we have great confidence in President Clinton. We cannot express this same confidence to anybody else, however. There are people who we don't trust. It was evident that the Syrian delegation was un-comfortable because the others did not seem eager about peace.

CLINTON: Mr. President; they did not want to move forward. Had I known, before the Shepherdstown talks, what I was later to learn while they were ongoing; that the Israelis will not show progress in the first week, I would have informed you of that, and said the same to Foreign Minister Shara. I would have told you not to show lenience during the first week because they were going to show none of it until the second. I regret that things didn't work out that way and I beg you not to reach big conclusions from that experience you had (at Shepherdstown). Barak is an unusual person and he has his special time considerations. Due to domestic Israeli constraints, he felt that he couldn't move forward during Week I of the talks. He is now committed, however, and I don't think you will get disappointed again if you return to the talks.

ASSAD: Our delegation will not return until adequate time has passed. As I said before, confidence is vital here and (it is now lacking) because they witnessed the experience first-hand (with the Israelis). Why did they refuse to negotiate the land factor? Are they afraid? They shouldn't be since the land is currently under their jurisdiction, until the treaty we are currently negotiating is signed. Even after it is signed, land would remain with them until the agreement is implemented. Meaning they can rest assured that they will keep the land until all of what they require is implemented. Honestly, I don't understand why they did not do that.

CLINTON: I think that the reason is the political atmosphere that exists in Israel, through which they operate. I have listened carefully to what you have just said in describing the process and understand how vital it is for the June 4 borders to be demarked properly. I have also listened carefully to the Israelis and they are saying that they would be willing to give up the Golan if their security needs are met. Obviously one of those security needs is Lebanon. They also realize that they need to reach a deal with you before commending on any talks with Lebanon. They cannot say: "We will do all of what Syria requires completely, and once we are done with that, move on to what we need as Israelis." At a minimum, they believe that they need to commence on all these issues simultaneously. Allow me to seek your help yet again Mr. President, and hope that you do not close the door shut before my suggestion. I do hope that you seriously consider my suggestion. Also please send your experts here (to the US) so that they make their comments about the American (peace) draft. Be sure Mr. President that all public remarks about what is happening will remain at a bare minimum since I don't want anything to obstruct the environment for peace, which is already, very strained and difficult. I feel that what I have proposed is the only we can reach a solution.

ASSAD: It is impossible to apply pressure on the Lebanese. We can influence our delegation indeed but we cannot force the Lebanese to do anything since they are an independent country and we have said that time and again. I don't know why you don't believe that? The Lebanese refuse to join the peace talks unless they see that Syria has achieved tangible progress. I personally tried to convince the Lebanese and they genuinely want to join the process and reach a peace deal with Israel. But why are the Israelis insisting on carrying out talks with them so quickly, before achieving nothing with Syria? It is something that arouses doubt, as far as I am concerned. As for media, you ask me to keep my comments to the press at a bare minimum. But the Israeli Prime Minister has conducted at least four television interviews whereas our Foreign Minister has not given even one. We always keep our promises but the problem is with the other party.

CLINTON: It is this kind of conversation that ought to take place between two parties. When we were at Shepherdstown, the Israelis would ask me: "Why don't the Syrians speak to us about all 'other' issues? All they speak about is borders because it is what matters to them."

ASSAD: Mr. President, our delegation put everything on the table at Shepherdstown.

CLINTON: I know that, but the Israelis did not clearly re-confirm the Deposit. They also did not agree to demark the borders. Now they have on both because they realized that nothing will be achieved unless these two points are agreed upon. This is something positive for Syria. All that they request in return is starting talks with the Lebanese. Mr. President I feel that such an agreement could have been reached in the first two days at Shepherdstown, before you lost your confidence in the Israelis. I completely understand, Mr. President, why you feel this way. All I ask is that you consider what I just offered you.

ASSAD: As you said Mr. President, something different should have happened at Shepherdstown. Nothing happened, however, because of the Israelis.

CLINTON: Mr. President I don't think Israel will sign a deal given the present conditions. I think that in order for them to start demarcation of borders, they need to give all parties (inside Israel) guarantees that at the end of the day, they will also be achieving a breakthrough and peace deal with Lebanon. That of course, would be only when Syria's requirements are all fulfilled. I must now end the conversation since I have to run off to two important meetings. And please allow me to stress that I have carefully studied the positions of both parties and I think that the gap can be bridged between Syria and Israel. I think that the conditions are ripe and the Israelis are ready to do that. I don't think that they want to see repetition of what happened during the Week I of Shepherdstown. Now they are ready to move forward.

ASSAD: Thank you Mr. President and I do wish you the best. I am grateful for your efforts and I do hope that they don't get wasted.

CLINTON: This opportunity will not get wasted Mr. President, because we are very close to reaching a deal. We have a government in Israel that is ready for an agreement and ready to mark the borders. We need to grab at this opportunity. I will continue to brainstorm for solutions and call you back at the nearest possible.

ASSAD: I thank you once again and I repeat: we gave you a heavy burden and we are grateful for all that you are doing.

CLINTON: Thank you Mr. President.

ASSAD: Thank you and see you soon.

Chronology of Key Events

August 2, 1990: Saddam Hussein invades Kuwait.

September 1990: US Secretary of State James Baker makes his first visit to Syria as part of a regional tour aimed at uniting Arabs against the Iraqi invasion of Kuwait.

January 12, 1991: President Hafez al-Assad addresses Saddam via Damascus Radio, asking him to withdraw from Kuwait and pledging full Syrian support if he does. The call is rejected by Saddam.

January 16, 1991: The Gulf War starts, with thirty-four countries (Syria included) joining forces with the United States to secure liberation of Kuwait. The war is "covered" by UNSCR 678 and gets the codename "Operation Desert Storm."

February 6, 1991: President George H. W. Bush personally contacts President Assad, for the very first time, by telephone, suggesting stronger Syrian-US cooperation in the Middle East. Assad welcomes the initiative to bring an end to the Arab-Israeli conflict.

March 13, 1991: Secretary of State Baker arrives in Damascus for his first postwar visit to Syria, where he discusses regional peace with President Assad.

March 16, 1991: President Bush addresses Congress, speaking about peace between the Arabs and the Israelis, along the same lines of his phone conversation with President Assad.

April 23, 1991: Baker arrives in Damascus, carrying a letter from President Bush to President Assad. The marathon meeting famously lasts for twelve hours nonstop, and Assad agrees to join the peace process, with the goal of restoring the June 4, 1967, borders and a clear US commitment to restore the occupied Golan Heights, in full, to Syria.

May 13, 1991: Meeting between Assad and Baker in which Assad stressed the important role of the Soviet Union.

July 18, 1991: Baker lands in Damascus to discuss a US- and Russian-sponsored Middle East peace conference with President Assad, seeking Syrian endorsement.

September 20, 1991: Baker visits Damascus to officially invite Assad to the peace Conference, and the Syrian leader accepts the invitation.

October 15–16, 1991: Baker comes to Damascus to discuss the points of reference of the peace conference and a venue that is suitable for Syria. Madrid is eventually agreed upon as a location.
October 30, 1991: The three-day Madrid Peace Conference starts in the Spanish capital, attended by a Syrian delegation headed by Foreign Minister Farouk al-Shara and an Israeli one that is chaired by Prime Minister Shimon Peres.
December 10, 1991: The first round of face-to-face talks in Washington takes place between Syria and Israel. They last until mid-December and fail to achieve any breakthrough.
January 13, 1992: The second round of the Washington talks take place between Syria and Israel, which also results in no breakthrough.
July 13, 1992: Yitzhak Rabin, an old foe of the Arabs, becomes prime minister of Israel, replacing the aging Yitzhak Shamir.
January 20, 1993: President Bill Clinton is sworn into office as the forty-second president of the United States. His election is welcomed by Syrian media and by President Assad personally, who sees promise in the young US president.
February 21, 1993: Clinton's new secretary of state, Warren Christopher, comes to Syria for his first round of talks with President Assad. The Clinton team reaffirms its commitment to Middle East peace, with Syria as a high priority.
April 8, 1993: President Clinton sends a letter to President Assad, emphasizing his strong commitment to Syrian-Israeli peace.
May 27, 1993: President Clinton sends a second letter to Assad, with further peace assurances.
August 1993: The third round of Washington talks takes place between Syria and Israel, this time under the auspices of the Clinton White House.
September 4, 1993: President Clinton sends his third letter of support to President Assad, saying that Syrian-Israeli peace is a high priority for the United States.
September 13, 1993: The Oslo Peace Accords are signed at the White House between Palestinian Liberation Organization chairman Yasser Arafat and Prime Minister Rabin. Syria denounces the accords, accusing Arafat of giving too much in return for less than half of historical Palestine from the Israelis.
September 23, 1993: The Oslo Accords pass in the Israeli Knesset with a 61–50 vote, with eight members abstaining.
October 7, 1993: President Clinton meets Foreign Minister Shara for the first time at the UN General Assembly. Clinton discusses Assad's commitment to Syrian-Israeli peace in light of Oslo.
December 2, 1993: President Clinton sends a fifth letter to President Assad.
January 16, 1994: The first Assad-Clinton summit takes place at the Intercontinental Hotel in Geneva, heralding a new phase in Syrian-US relations based on trust and mutual respect between Bill Clinton and Hafez al-Assad.
January 21, 1994: President Assad's oldest son Basel, age thirty-four, dies in a car accident on the Damascus Airport Highway. President Clinton telephones him to offer his condolences.

February 25, 1994: An Israeli settler named Baruch Goldstein, dressed in the military reserve uniform of the IDF, goes into a mosque in Hebron and opens fire on unarmed Palestinians during morning prayers. The Hebron massacre nearly dooms the peace process.

April 10, 1994: Secretary of State Christopher starts the first of ten visits to Syria in 1994. The last one takes place on December 6, 1994.

April 30, 1994: Secretary of State Christopher comes to Syria carrying the famous Rabin Deposit. President Assad refuses to commit to normalization, saying: "First we get our land back, and then we talk about everything else."

May 15, 1994: The US delegation returns to Syria after a quick visit to Israel, having briefed Rabin on Syria's initial response to the deposit.

May 18, 1994: Clinton sends Assad assurances that the deposit is in the "pocket" of the United States.

October 24, 1994: President Clinton holds a high-profile summit in Damascus with President Hafez al-Assad. It is Clinton's first visit to Syria, and the first for a US president since Richard Nixon came to Syria in 1974. Assad offers him an extended date for Israeli withdrawal from the Golan, in appreciation of his Damascus visit. The Syrian concession is turned down by Israel.

December 2, 1994: Informal talks take place at the home of Dennis Ross in Washington, attended by Syrian ambassador Walid al-Mouallem and Israeli ambassador Itamar Rabinovich. These informal talks last until mid-January 1995. Also in December, talks start in the United States, attended by Syrian Army chief of staff Hikmat Shihabi and his Israeli counterpart Ehud Barak at Blair House. They too fail to achieve any breakthrough, but they are appreciated by the United States, given that it was the first meeting between Syrian and Israeli military officials, which had been mandated by President Assad.

December 24, 1994: Chief-of-Staff Shihabi meets President Clinton at the White House for a one-on-one meeting.

January 1, 1995: Ammon Shahak replaces Ehud Barak as head of the IDF and continues talks, which result in no breakthrough, with General Shihabi.

November 4, 1995: Yitzhak Rabin, seventy-three, is assassinated in Tel Aviv by an Israeli extremist, and he is immediately replaced by Labor Party leader Shimon Peres. Syria is indifferent to the assassination, saying that it will not reengage in talks until it hears a firm commitment to returning the Golan Heights from Prime Minister Peres.

December 10, 1995: Warren Christopher comes to Syria, carrying a ten-point peace program from Israel's new prime minister, Shimon Peres.

February 1996: Four attacks by Palestinian extremists rock Israel in a period of nine days, nearly breaking the momentum of the Syrian-Israeli peace talks. The United States proposes an international conference to discuss and condemn terrorism and invites Syria to attend, but Damascus refuses. The summit takes place in the Red Sea city of Sharm al-Shaikh in March 1996.

April 11, 1996: The April War begins when the IDF strikes at South Lebanon with the declared objective of crushing Hizbullah. A land, sea, and air blockade is imposed over Lebanon, which is strongly condemned by Syria.

April 18, 1996: The IDF strikes a UN compound in Qana, South Lebanon, killing 118 Lebanese civilians.

April 19, 1996: Warren Christopher arrives in Israel for cease-fire talks and then travels to Damascus on April 20.

April 21, 1996: Christopher arrives in Damascus again, this time for an unannounced visit, returning from Israel. He is declined an immediate audience with President Assad, who was occupied with a scheduled meeting with Pakistani prime minister Benazir Bhutto.

April 26, 1996: The April Understanding is announced simultaneously between Lebanon and Israel, brokered by the Syrians and United States. The deal greatly increases the "chemistry" between Syria's Assad and President Clinton.

May 26, 1996: Israeli elections take place, resulting in Shimon Peres's defeat.

June 18, 1996: Likud heavyweight Benjamin Netanyahu takes over as prime minister of Israel from Shimon Peres, campaigning on a hard-line platform that refuses to accept Oslo and refuses to restore the Golan Heights to Syria.

July 7, 1996: Syria's top negotiator, Muwafak al-Allaf, who had handled peace talks since Madrid, dies at the age of seventy.

November 1996: President Clinton wins the US elections with 49.2 percent of the popular vote, defeating Ross Perot and Republican Bob Dole.

January 1997: Clinton begins his second term as US president.

August 7, 1998: American Jewish businessman Ronald Lauder arrives in Syria for secret talks with President Assad, mandated directly by Prime Minister Netanyahu. They too fail at reaching a breakthrough, given that Lauder is poorly informed on events in the Middle East.

June 23, 1999: An interview with President Assad is published in the pan-Arab daily *al-Hayat*, conducted by British journalist Patrick Seale. It carries a series of confidence-building messages for incoming Israeli prime minister Ehud Barak, whom Assad describes as "strong and sincere."

November 12, 1999: Lauder sends President Clinton a letter admitting that the "Syrian-Israeli peace draft" that he presented to the Americans in 1998 outlined some points that "were never accepted by the Syrians."

December 15, 1999: Ehud Barak and Foreign Minister Shara hold their first meeting at the White House, attended by President Clinton.

December 21, 1999: The United States announces that Shepherdstown, West Virginia, will host the upcoming round of Syrian-Israeli talks, attended by Foreign Minister Shara and Israel's new prime minister Ehud Barak.

January 3, 2000: The Shepherdstown talks begin in the United States amid high hopes that they will result in a breakthrough.

January 6, 2000: The new US secretary of state, Madeleine Albright, sits with Foreign Minister Shara and Bouthaina Shaaban to explain her new strategy vis-à-vis peace. A direct channel is opened between Shaaban and Albright, later known as the "Chick Channel."

January 13, 2000: The Israeli newspaper, *Haaretz*, publishes the entire draft text that Clinton had given Shara and Barak, with a report claiming that the Syrian foreign minister had granted more concessions to Israel than at any previous point during the Syrian-Israeli talks.

March 26, 2000: President Assad and Bill Clinton hold their last summit at the Intercontinental Hotel in Geneva, which also fails to achieve a breakthrough. It was based on the US assumption that Syria was willing to accept joint sovereignty over Lake Tiberius.

May 24, 2000: Israel withdraws unilaterally from South Lebanon, which is hailed in Syria as a thundering victory for Hizbullah.

June 10, 2000: President Hafez al-Assad dies in Damascus at the age of sixty-nine.

Cast of Characters

Syria

Abdel Raouf al-Kassem: Former prime minister (1980–1987) and national security adviser (1988–2000).
Adnan Makhlouf: Head of the Syrian Republican Guard under President Hafez al-Assad.
Ahmad Arnous: Bureau chief to Foreign Minister Shara.
Aleksandr Bessmertnykh: Soviet minister of foreign affairs in 1991.
Anissa Makhlouf: First lady of Syria, 1970–2000.
Basel al-Assad: President Assad's oldest son, and a Republican Guard officer.
Bouthaina Shaaban: Presidential interpreter, 1991–2000.
Bushra al-Assad: President Assad's daughter, a pharmacologist.
Farouk al-Shara: Foreign minister of Syria, 1984–2005.
Hikmat al-Shihabi: Chief of staff of the Syrian Army.
Ibrahim al-Omar: Member of the Syrian peace team.
Iskandar Luka: Notetaker and secretary to President Assad.
Mohammad Khodor: Syria's ambassador to London and member of the Syrian Peace Team to Madrid.
Mustapha Tlass: Minister of defense, 1972–2005.
Muwafak al-Allaf: Top Syrian diplomat, ambassador, and head of the Syrian Peace Team from the 1991 Madrid Peace Conference until 1996.
Rafiq Juwayjati: Syria's former ambassador to the United States and member of the Syrian Peace Team to Madrid and the Washington talks.
Riad Daoudi: Legal adviser to the Syrian Ministry of Foreign Affairs and member of the Syrian Peace Team.
Walid al-Mouallem: Syria's ambassador to the United States in the 1990s and member of the Syrian Peace Team.
Yusuf Shakkur: Former Army chief of staff and member of the Syrian Peace Team.

United States

Anthony Lake: National security adviser under President Clinton, 1993–1997.
Christopher Ross: US ambassador to Syria, 1991–1998.
Dennis Ross: Senior Middle East peace envoy under President Clinton.
Edward Djerejian: US ambassador to Syria, 1989–1991.

230 CAST OF CHARACTERS

Gamal Helal: President Clinton's interpreter.
James Baker: Secretary of state, 1989–1992.
Madeleine Albright: Secretary of state, 1997–2001.
Margaret Tutwiler: Spokeswoman for the US State Department under President Clinton.
Martin Indyk: US ambassador to Israel and assistant secretary of state for Near East affairs under President Clinton.
Ronald Lauder: An American Jewish businessman and heir to the Estée Lauder fortune, who engaged in Track II diplomacy with the Syrians at the request of Israeli prime minister Netanyahu in 1998.
Sandy Berger: National security adviser under President Clinton, 1997–2001.
Warren Christopher: Secretary of state, 1993–1997.

Israel

Amnon Shahak: Chief of staff of the Israeli Defense Forces, 1995–1998.
Benjamin Netanyahu: Prime minister of Israel, 1996–1999.
Ehud Barak: Prime minister of Israel, 1999–2001.
Itamar Rabinovich: Israeli ambassador to the United States.
Shimon Peres: Prime minister of Israel, 1984–1986 and 1995–1996.
Shlomo Yanai: Chief of planning in the IDF in the 1990s.
Uri Saguy: Director of Israeli military intelligence, 1991–1995.
Yitzhak Rabin: Prime minister of Israel, 1992–1995.
Yitzhak Shamir: Prime minister of Israel, 1986–1992.
Yossi Ben Aharon: Bureau chief to Yitzhak Shamir and member of the Israeli Peace Team.

Palestine

Ahmad Qurai: Senior Palestinian peace negotiator in the Oslo Accords.
Faisal al-Husseini: Jerusalem notable and member of the Palestinian Peace Team to Madrid.
Haidar Abdul Shafi: Head of the Palestinian Peace Team to Madrid.
Hanan Ashrawi: Spokeswoman for the Palestinian delegation to the Palestinian-Israeli peace talks and member of the Madrid Peace Team.
Saeb Erekat: Top Palestinian negotiator and member of the Palestinian Peace Team to Madrid.
Yasser Arafat: Chairman of the Palestinian Liberation Organization.

Lebanon

Antoine Lahad: Leader of the Israeli backed South Lebanon Army from 1984 to 2000.
Elias Hrawi: President of Lebanon, 1989–1998.
Emile Lahoud: President of Lebanon, 1998–2007.
Nabih Berri: Speaker of the Lebanese parliament, 1992–present.
Rafiq al-Hariri: Prime minister of Lebanon, 1992–1998.

Bibliography

Archives

The official archives of President Hafez al-Assad, Presidential Palace, Damascus, August 1990–June 2000.
The official archives of the Syrian Foreign Ministry, Damascus, August 1990–June 2000.

Books

Albright, Madeleine. *Madam Secretary: A Memoir*. London: Macmillan, 2003.
Aruru, Naseer Hasan. *Dishonest Broker: The US Role in Israel and Palestine*. Cambridge: South End Press, 2003.
Ashrawi, Hanan. *The Side of Peace: A Personal Account*. New York: Simon & Schuster, 1995.
Baker, James. *The Politics of Diplomacy*. New York: G.P. Putnam, 1995.
Beilin, Yossi. *The Path to Geneva: The Quest for a Permanent Agreement, 1996–2004*. New York: RDV Books, 2004.
Ben Ami, Shlomo. *Scars of War, Wounds of Peace: The Israeli-Arab Tragedy*. Oxford: Oxford University Press, 2006.
Ben Gurion, David. *My Talks with Arab Leaders*. New York: Third Press, 1973.
Blum, William. *Killing Hope: US Military and CIA Interventions Since World War II*. London: Zed Books, 2003.
Bregman, Ahron, and Jihan Tahri, *The Fifty Years' War: Israel and the Arabs*. London: Penguin Books, 1998.
Carter, Jimmy. *Keeping Faith: Memoirs of a President*. Toronto: Bantam Books, 1982.
Carter, Jimmy. *Peace not Apartheid*. New York: Simon & Schuster, 2007.
Chomsky, Noam. *Fateful Triangle: The United States, Israel, and the Palestinians*. London: Pluto Press, 1998.
Christison, Kathleen. *Perceptions of Palestine: Their Influence on US Middle East Policy*. Berkeley: University of California Press, 1999.

Christopher, Warren. *In the Stream of History: Shaping Foreign Policy for a New Era*. Stanford: Stanford University Press, 1998.
———. *Chances of a Lifetime*. New York: Scribner Press, 2001.
Churchill, Winston. *The Churchill-Eisenhower Correspondence, 1953–1955*. Chapel Hill: University of North Carolina Press, 1990.
Clark, Ramsey. *A Report on United States War Crimes Against Iraq: Report to the Commission of Inquiry for the International War Crimes Tribunal*. College Park, MD: Maissonneuve Press, 1992.
Clark, Richard. *Against all Enemies: Inside America's War on Terror*. New York: Free Press, 2004.
Clawson, Patrick. *Dollars and Diplomacy: The Impact of US Economic Initiatives on Arab-Israeli Negotiations*. Washington, DC: Washington Institute for Near East Policy, 1999.
Clinton, Bill. *My Life*. New York: Knopf, 2004.
Cobban, Helena. *The Israeli-Syrian Peace Talks, 1991–96, and Beyond*. Washington, DC: United States Institute of Peace Press, 1999.
Cordesman, Anthony H. *Israel and Syria: The Military Balance and Prospects of War*. Westport, CT: Praeger, 2008.
Eisenhower, Dwight. *Mandate for Change, 1953–1956: The White House Years*. London: Heinemann, 1963.
Guernsey, JoAnn Bren. *Hillary Rodham Clinton*. Breckenridge, CO: Twenty-First Century Press, 2005.
Human Rights Watch. *Civilian Pawns: Laws of War Violation and the Use of Weapons on the Israeli-Lebanon Border*. New York: Human Rights Watch, 1996.
Ilan, Amitzur. *Bernadotte in Palestine*. Oxford, UK: Oxford University Press, 1989.
Indyk, Martin. *Innocent Abroad: An Intimate Account of American Peace Diplomacy in the Middle East*. New York: Simon & Schuster, 2009.
Kissinger, Henry. *Diplomacy*. New York: Simon & Schuster, 1994.
Kurtzer, Daniel. *Negotiating Arab-Israeli Peace: American Leadership in the Middle East*. Washington, DC: United States Institute of Peace Press, 2008.
Majali, Abd al-Salam. *Peacemaking: The Inside Story of the 1994 Jordanian-Israeli Treaty*. Norman: University of Oklahoma Press, 2006.
Maoz, Moshe. *Asad, the Sphinx of Damascus: A Political Biography*. London: Weidenfeld and Nicolson, 1988.
———. *Modern Syria: From Ottoman Rule to Pivotal Role in the Middle East*. Brighton: Sussex Academic Press, 1999.
———. *Syria and Israel: From War to Peacemaking*. Oxford: Clarendon Press, 1995.
———. *Syria Under Assad: Domestic Constraints and Regional Risks*. New York: St. Martin's Press, 1986.
Miller, David Aaron. *The Much Too Promised Land: America's Elusive Search for Arab-Israeli Peace*. New York: Bantam Books, 2008.
Netanyahu, Benjamin. *A Place Among the Nations: Israel and the World*. New York: Bantam Books, 1993.
Nixon, Richard. *RN: The Memoirs of Richard Nixon*. New York: Grosset and Dunlap, 1978.

Peres, Shimon. *Battling for Peace*. London: Weidenfeld and Nicolson, 1995.
Qurei, Ahmad. *Beyond Oslo: The Struggle for Palestine: Inside the Middle East Peace Process, from Rabin's Death to Camp David*. London: I.B. Tauris, 2008.
Rabinovich, Itamar. *The Brink of Peace: The Israeli-Syrian Negotiations*. Princeton: Princeton University Press, 1998.
———. *The Road Not Taken*. New York: Oxford University Press, 1991.
———. *Waging Peace: Israel and the Arabs, 1948–2003*. Princeton: Princeton University Press, 2004.
———. *The War for Lebanon, 1970–1983*. Ithaca: Cornell University Press, 1984.
Ross, Dennis. *The Missing Peace: The Inside Story of the Fight for Middle East Peace*. New York: Farrar, Straus and Giroux, 2004.
———. *Statecraft and How to Restore America's Standing in the World*. New York: Farrar, Straus and Giroux, 2008.
Russell, Malcolm. *Syria Under Faisal I*. Minneapolis: Bibliotheca Islamica, 1985.
Sagie, Uri. *The Israeli-Syrian Dialogue: A One-Way Ticket to Peace?* Houston: James A. Baker III Institute for Public Policy, Rice University, 1999.
Said, Edward. *Culture and Resistance: Conversations with Edward W. Said*. London: Pluto Press, 2003.
Saunders, Bonnie F. *The United States and Arab Nationalism: The Syrian Case, 1953–1960*. Westport, CT: Praeger, 1996.
Savir, Ur. *The Process: 1,100 days That Changed the Middle East*. New York: Random House, 1998.
Seale, Patrick. *Asad: The Struggle for the Middle East*. London: I.B. Tauris, 1988.
———. *The Struggle for Syria: A Study of Post-war Arab Politics, 1945–1958*. London: I.B. Tauris, 1961.
Smith, Charles D. *Palestine and the Arab-Israeli Conflict: A History with Documents*. Boston: Bedford/St. Martin's, 2007.
Telhami, Shibley. *The Stakes: America and the Middle East*. Boulder: Westview Press, 2002.
Tucker, Spencer. *The Encyclopedia of the Arab-Israeli Conflict: A Political, Social, and Military History*. 4 Vols. Santa Barbara, CA: ABC-CLIO, 2008.
Van Dam, Nikolaos. *The Struggle for Power in Syria: Politics and Society Under Asad and the Baath Party*. London: I.B. Tauris, 1996.
Warshaw, Shirley. *The Clinton Years: Presidential Profiles*. New York: Facts on Files database, 2004. www.fofweb.com.
Weizmann, Chaim. *Trial and Error: The Autobiography of Chaim Weizmann*. New York: Harper, 1949.
World Almanac and Book of Facts. New York: World Almanac, 2009.
Wright, Lawrence. *The Looming Tower: Al-Qaeda and the Road to 9/11*. New York: Knopf, 2006.

Newspapers and Magazines

Al-Ahram (Cairo)
Al-Baath (Damascus)
Al-Hayat (London)

Al-Qudsi al-Arabi (London)
Al-Thawra (Damascus)
Annahar (Beirut)
Assafir (Beirut)
Guardian (London)
Haaretz (Tel Aviv)
The Huffington Post
Independent (London)
International Herald Tribune
L'Express (Paris)
Life
Los Angeles Times
Maariv (Tel Aviv)
Newsweek
New York Times
Time
Tishreen (Damascus)
Wall Street Journal
Washington Post
Washington Report on Middle East Affairs
Yediot Aharanot (Tel Aviv)

Index

Abbas, Mahmud, 71
Abraham, Daniel, 26
Abu Saleh, Majid, 40
Adwan, Kamal, 118
Albright, Madeleine, 177(fig.), 230; on Barak, 171–172; "Chick Channel," 180–184; Damascus visit, 180; Geneva Summit, 191–195; Lauder talks, 161; Shepherdstown talks, 176–178; Syrian peace on US terms, 190
al-Allaf, Muwafak, 229; failure of Washington talks, 56; Latakia meeting, 123–124; Madrid conference, 40, 46, 48; Washington talks, 50–52, 54–57
Allush, Raslan, 40
Amal Movement, 140
Amidror, Yaakov, 161
Ammura, Abdulfattah, 149(fig.)
April War and April Understanding, 139–147, 151–155
Arab Spring, 201
Arad, Uzi, 161
Arafat, Yasser, 20, 131, 163, 188, 230; Assad's opinion of, 75; Hebron massacre, 98; Netanyahu's view of, 160; Oslo negotiations, 70–77; "peace of the brave," 173; Shepherdstown talks, 174
Arens, Moshe, 25, 31–32, 47

Arms negotiations, 13; Lauder talks, 164; Syrian–North Korean trade, 43; US-Iraqi relations, 14; US shipments to Israel as topic of concern, 17, 22
Arnous, Ahmad, 40
Ashrawi, Hanan, 20, 53
al-Assad, Basel, 89–92, 95, 231
al-Assad, Bushra, 90–92, 231
al-Assad, Hafez, 96(fig.), 108(fig.), 109(fig.), 202–203; about-face on Madrid assurances, 26–27; Albright's visit to the Palace, 180; April 1991 meeting with Baker, 18–24; April War and April Understanding, 142, 142(fig.), 143–147, 151–155; Baker's hopes for US visit by, 125; Baker's peacemaking goals, 16–17; Bessmertnykh's meeting with, 30; Clinton's domestic troubles, 159; Clinton's working relationship, 67–68, 79–80; commitment to peace after Baker negotiations, 24–25; congressional delegation, 95; Damascus Summit with Clinton, 107–113; death of, 196–198; death of son Basel, 89–92; destruction of Qunaitra, 136(n19); education grant, 1–6; Geneva Summit, 80–89, 191–196; hard line on Golan

235

withdrawal, 69; health of, 188–190; Hebron massacre, 97–98; Iran-Iraq War, 14; Iraqi invasion of Kuwait, 9–10; Latakia meeting, 123–126; Lauder talks, 161–167; mother diplomacy, 86–87; new government, 187–188; Pakistani visit, 149(fig.); Peres's conditions for Syrian-Israeli talks, 132–134; political situation after Rabin, 131–133; preparing public opinion for Madrid, 41; pride and respect for General Azma, 130; Rabin Deposit, 97, 99–107, 110–112; Rabinovich proposal of partial withdrawal from the Golan, 117–118; response to Iraqi invasion of Kuwait, 10–15; response to Oslo Accords, 74–75; Seale biography, 173; second round of Washington talks, 66; Sharm al-Shaikh Summit, 138–139; snubbing Christopher, 148–151; struggle over Lake Tiberias, 127; UN and European representation in Madrid, 21–23; view of Barak, 173–174; Washington talks, 65
Atasi, Abdul Wadod, 40
al-Azma, Yusuf, 129–130
Azulay-Katz, Orly, 131

Baath Party, 196
Baker, James, 230; April 1991 meeting with Assad, 18–24; Assad's commitment to peace, 24–26; Assad's demand for Jerusalem, 27; Assad's hard line for peace with Israel, 20–21; Assad's withdrawal from Iraq's domestic politics, 31; Bessmertnykh's meeting with, 30; conference delegations and observers, 44; emigration of Syrian Jews, 105–106; hopes for US visit by Assad, 125; Israeli and Syrian positions on Lebanon, 31–33; Madrid conference, 41, 48; Palestinian issue at core of peace effort, 76; second round of Washington talks, 65; shuttle diplomacy, 16–17; Syrian response to Kuwait invasion, 11–13; UN Resolution 3379, 18
Balkan situation, 82
Bandar bin Sultan, 72, 189
Barak, Ehud, 232; April Understanding, 142–143; Assad's view of, 173–174; coalition and allies, 172; Geneva Summit, 89, 191–193; Lauder talks, 161; Rabin Deposit, 182–183; replacing Netanyahu, 171–172; Shepherdstown talks, 174, 176, 178, 184–185, 187; Shihabi-Barak meeting at Blair House, 118–123
Begin, Menachem, 154
Bekaa Valley battle, 176
Ben Aharon, Yossi, 41, 47–48, 51–52, 54–57, 63–64, 178, 230
Ben Gurion, David, 137
Berger, Sandy, 120(fig.), 159–161, 174–175, 190, 230
Bernadotte, Folke, 19, 46
Berri, Nabih, 82, 152, 230
Bessmertnykh, Aleksandr, 29–30, 229
Bhutto, Benazir, 148, 149(fig.)
Bhutto, Nusrat, 9
Bladder diplomacy, 24
Blair House, 118–123, 175, 177
Blitzer, Wolf, 88
Border contests: April Understanding, 147; Clinton's position, 159; Jerusalem, 27; Lauder talks, 163–164, 166–167; 1923 vs. 1967 borders, 127, 128(n16); Rabin Deposit, 99, 103, 105; Shihabi-Barak meeting at Blair House, 121
Bosnia, 146
Both Right and Left Handed: Arab Women Talk About Their Lives (Shaaban), 87
Burns, Nicolas, 140
Bush, George H. W.: advancing Arab-Israeli peace, 16; Gulf War, 15; ignoring land-for-peace formula, 44–45; "new world," 71–72; 1992 elections, 61, 66; opening the conference, 45; second round of

Washington talks, 65; Syrian response to Kuwait invasion, 11–12; Washington talks, 54–55, 63
Bush, George W., 31, 122

Camp David Accords (1978), 43, 47, 174, 200, 202
Carter, Jimmy, 12, 22, 27–28, 44, 122
Casualties: April War, 140–141; Arab Spring, 203; Gulf War, 16
Cease-fire talks, 141–148, 152–153
"Chick Channel," 180–184
Chirac, Jacques, 13–14, 142, 151
Christopher, Warren, 142(fig.), 200, 230; April War and April Understanding, 142–147, 151–153; Assad snubbing, 148–151; Clinton-Assad relations, 79; first Syria visit, 67; Geneva Summit, 81, 83–84; Lauder on, 162–163; Oslo Accords, 71, 73; Peres's conditions for Syrian-Israeli talks, 133–134; Rabin Deposit, 98–101, 103, 105–106, 110–112; representing Clinton during election months, 157; Sharm al-Shaikh Summit, 138–139; Shihabi-Barak meeting at Blair House, 118, 120–121; US view of Rabin government, 68–69
Clinton, Bill, 108–109(fig.), 123(fig.), 201; Assad snubbing Christopher, 150; Assad's relationship with, 13, 79–80, 96; attempt to arrange Syrian-Israeli talks, 188–190; Barak's resumption of Syrian talks, 172; Damascus Summit, 107–113; death of Assad's son, 91–92; domestic policies overshadowing Middle East process, 157–158; exclusion from Lauder talks, 161; foreign policy, 68–70; Geneva Summit, 80–89, 190–196; Hebron massacre, 98; Israeli-Syrian gatherings in Washington, 117; Lauder talks, 164, 166–168; mother diplomacy, 86–87; 1992 elections, 61, 66–67; Oslo Accords, 73, 76; Peres's conditions for Syrian-Israeli talks, 132; Rabin Deposit, 105, 110–112; Rabin's first meeting with, 69; Rabin's funeral, 131; Shepherdstown talks, 174–176, 178, 183–184, 187; Shihabi-Barak meeting, 120(fig.), 121–122; US response to Israel bombings, 138; working relationship with Assad, 67–68
Clinton, Hillary, 109, 122, 158
CNN interviews, 42
Communist Party, 181
Congress, US, 66, 95
Conspiracy theory, 158
Correction Movement, 1

Daaboul, Abu Salim, 197
Daoudi, Riad, 40, 42, 176, 178, 229
de Charette, Herve, 148
Demilitarized zones, 99, 166, 179
Diplomatic relations, 99, 166, 179
Djerejian, Edward, 18, 24, 26, 53–54, 63, 229
Dole, Bob, 22, 157

Early warning stations, 99, 121–122, 127, 164
Economic development, 134
Egypt, 117–118, 134
Erekat, Saeb, 44, 53, 70, 230
European presence, 44; April Understanding, 154; Assad's request for representation in Madrid, 21–23; 1923 borders, 179; Shamir's antipathy to, 19

Faisal I, 129
Foreign aid, 65–66, 134
France: April War and April Understanding, 151, 154; Hussein's relations with, 13–14; Maysaloun, Battle of, 129
Friedman, Thomas, 76

Gaza Strip. *See* Occupied Territories
Gemayel, Amin, 53
Geneva Summit: Assad's preparation and conduct, 80–86; closed session,

86–87; failed negotiations, 190–196; speculations over Assad's health, 188–189
Germany: Gulf War, 15
Gibran, Khalil, 134
Glaspie, April, 9
Golan Heights: Albright's view of, 183; Assad's hard line on withdrawal, 19, 28, 68–69, 80; Assad's victory in defeat, 130; Barak's compensation request for withdrawal, 172; Bush's failure to mention in Madrid, 45; Clinton's position, 159; destruction of Qunaitra, 134–135, 136(n19); diplomatic relations as condition for withdrawal, 179; Geneva Summit, 192–193; importance to Israeli security, 184; Lauder talks, 163; post-Madrid annexation of, 49; Rabinovich proposal for partial withdrawal, 117–118; Rabin's bargaining power, 88–89; Rabin's phased withdrawal plan, 83–85, 97; Sadat's pledge to restore, 30; settlements, 52; Shepherdstown talks, 178–179, 187; as sticking point for negotiations, 134; success or failure of the peace process, 29. *See also* Rabin Deposit
Golan Heights Separation of Forces Agreement, 69–70
Goldstein, Baruch, 97–98
Gorbachev, Mikhail, 25, 44
Gore, Al, 66
Gulf War: Arab opposition to Syria's participation, 16; Arafat's position, 72; Assad's withdrawal from Iraq's domestic politics, 31; Bush's approval ratings following, 61; coordination of, 15–16; Syrian response to Kuwait invasion, 12–13; US response to Kuwait invasion, 9–10

Haaretz newspaper, 88, 185
Habash, George, 51
Hamas, 138, 160
Hamidi, Ibrahim, 185
al-Hariri, Rafiq, 82, 141–142, 151–152, 230
al-Hayat newspaper, 185
Hebron agreement (1997), 76
Hebron massacre, 97–98
Helal, Gamal, 22, 81, 190–191, 230
Helsinki Declaration (1975), 23
Hirschfeld, Yair, 72
Hizbullah, 108; April War and April Understanding, 139, 141–142, 144–146, 151–153, 155; Assad-Baker meetings before Madrid, 32; Lahoud's efforts in Lebanon, 197; Lauder on, 163; Peres's conditions for Syrian-Israeli talks, 133; Qana massacre, 139–140
Hrawi, Elias, 32, 53, 82, 98, 138, 230
Hussein, Saddam: Assad's response to Kuwait invasion, 10–11; attacks on Israel, 20; Iraqi invasion of Kuwait, 9–10; US and Syrian perspectives on, 13
Hussein I of Jordan, 88
Hussein Ibn Ali, 104
al-Husseini, Faisal, 230

Indyk, Martin, 230; April War and April Understanding, 139; Geneva Summit, 88, 195; Hebron massacre, 98; Lake Tiberias question, 183; Lauder talks, 161; Netanyahu's position on borders, 166; Oslo Accords, 68, 74; Rabin Deposit, 111–112; Shepherdstown talks, 176; Syrian peace on US terms, 189
Innocent Abroad (Indyk), 69–70
Iran, 158, 188
Iran-Iraq War (1980–1988), 9, 14, 40, 188
Iraq, 31, 158
Iraq War (2003), 31
Islamic Jihad, 137–138, 160
Islamic Revolution (Iran), 188
Ismail, Zakariya, 40
Israel: annexation of Golan Heights, 49; April War and April

Understanding, 139–147, 151, 153–154; Assad's demands and concessions for Israeli borders, 21, 41–42; Assad's media interviews in Madrid, 42–43; Assad's military leadership in 1967, 130; Barak replacing Netanyahu, 171–172; Bessmertnykh's efforts for Madrid, 30; bilateral talks in Madrid, 44, 46–49; bombings after Rabin assassination, 137; destruction of Qunaitra, 134–135, 136(n19); failure of Washington negotiations, 56; Geneva Summit, 82–83, 88, 192; Hebron massacre, 97–98; Hillary Clinton's criticism of Palestine, 158; Hizbullah attack, 108; Jordanian debate with, 52–54; Latakia meeting, 125–127; Lauder talks, 161, 163–166; Lebanese conflict, 31–33, 139; Netanyahu's defeat of Peres, 159; 1923 and 1967 borders, 127, 128(n16); occupation of Palestine, 10; opening speech at Madrid, 45; Oslo Accords, 70–76; political situation after Rabin, 131–133; Rabin Deposit, 97–107; Rabin's hard line on Golan, 68; response to Assad's commitment to peace, 25–26; Sadat's negotiations, 13; Shamir's policy affecting peace process, 19–20; Shara's opening speech at Madrid, 45–46; Shepherdstown talks, 176–179, 184–185; Shihabi-Barak meeting, 118–123; Syrians' reluctance to negotiate with, 39–40; US arms shipments, 17; US view of Rabin government, 68–69; Washington, D.C., talks, 50–52, 54–55, 63. *See also specific individuals*

Israeli Defense Forces (IDF): April War and April Understanding, 139–141; Assad-Baker meetings before Madrid, 32; Barak's background, 118; exhumation of remains, 176; Oslo Accords provision, 71; Peres's background, 137; Syrian accusation of state terrorism, 52; terms of Lauder talks, 166

Jaber Al-Ahmad Al-Jaber Al-Sabah, 10
Jamil, Naji, 3
Japan: Gulf War, 15
al-Jazzar, Mohammad, 40
Jerusalem, 27–28, 71, 159–160
Jordan, 51–54, 65, 88
Jordan River, 163, 167, 179, 192
Juan Carlos, 44
Juwayjati, Rafiq, 40, 55, 229

al-Kassem, Abdel Raouf, 80, 229
Kelley, Virginia Cassidy, 86
Kennedy, John F., 79–80
Khaddam, Abdul Halim, 149(fig.)
al-Khatib, Fawzi, 40
Khodor, Mohammad, 229
Khury, Clovis, 40
Kissinger, Henry, 12, 22, 69–70, 181
Kozyrev, Andrei, 71
Kuwait: Baker's view of the destruction, 18–19; Gulf War, 15–16; Iraqi invasion, 9–10, 40; Syria's response to Iraqi invasion, 10–15, 188; US perspective on invasion, 13

Lahad, Antoine, 32, 36(n95), 230
Lahoud, Emile, 196–197, 230
Lake, Anthony, 81, 231
Land-for-peace formula: Assad-Baker meeting, 25–26; Barak's antipathy to, 172–173; Blair House meeting, 118; failure at Madrid, 48, 50; Geneva Summit, 192; Lauder talks, 163; Shamir's policy, 19–20; Shepherdstown talks, 176–178; Sinai Peninsula and the Golan, 30; Syrian conditions in Washington talks, 57. *See also* Golan Heights
Latakia, Syria, 41, 123–124
Lauder, Ronald, 160–168, 172, 230
Lebanese Communist Party, 140
Lebanon: April War and April Understanding, 139–147, 151–154; Assad and Arafat, 75; Assad-Baker meetings before Madrid, 32,

36(n95); Assad's decision to send troops, 188; Geneva Summit, 81–82; Israeli shelling of South Lebanon, 52; Lauder talks, 163; liberation of South Lebanon, 196–197; Madrid conference, 31–33; Operation Spring of Youth, 118; Qana massacre, 139–140; Sharm al-Shaikh Summit, 138; Shepherdstown talks, 177–178; unannounced helicopter flights, 150; Washington, D.C., talks, 52–53
Lewinsky, Monica, 157–159
Libya, 158
Luka, Iskandar, 18, 80–81, 229

Madam Secretary (Albright), 182
Madrid Peace Conference: Assad's conditions, 20–21; Assad's motivations for the peace process, 33–34; assessment of, 49–50; Bush's overtures to Assad, 16; choosing a venue, 28–29; the conference, 43–46; direct talks with Israel, 46–49; effect of Oslo Accords, 71–72; Lebanon as issue, 31–33; Palestinian representation, 20; Soviet role, 29–30; Syrian delegation, 40–43
al-Majali, Abdussalam, 53
Majid, Esmat Abdul, 21
Makhlouf, Adnan, 89, 229
Makhlouf, Anissa, 90, 229
The Man Who Could Not Win (Azulay-Katz), 131
Mandate Palestine, 179
Maysaloun, Battle of, 129
McMahon, Henry, 104
Media: Allaf interview quoting Shamir, 51; Clinton's domestic troubles, 158–159; Geneva Summit, 87–88, 195–196; Lauder draft, 167–168; Madrid conference, 42–43, 45; newspaper diplomacy, 173–174; Oslo Accords, 70–72; Shepherdstown talks, 175, 185; speculations over Assad's health, 188–189; Syria's concerns over Israel's use of, 46–47
Memorandum of understanding (MOU), 172
Miller, David Aaron, 63, 185
Miro, Mohammad, Mustapha, 187–188
Mordechai, Yitzhak, 161, 166
Mother diplomacy, 86–87
al-Mouallem, Walid, 44, 108(fig.), 229; April Understanding, 142(fig.); Israeli-Syrian gatherings in Washington, 117; Latakia meeting, 123–124; Lauder talks, 160–162; Madrid conference, 40, 42; Oslo Accords, 71, 76; second round of Washington talks, 63; Shepherdstown talks, 176; Shihabi-Barak meeting, 118, 120(fig.), 123
Mount Hermon, 179
Mubarak, Hosni, 138, 189
My Life (Clinton), 81, 194–195

Nader, George, 162
al-Najjar, Muhammad Youssef, 118
Nasrallah, Hasan, 108, 139
Nasser, Gamal Abdul, 27, 92(n1)
Nasser, Kamal, 118
National Security Council (NSC), 68
Naval blockade, 153
Naveh, Danny, 161
Netanyahu, Benjamin, 230; Barak's criticism of, 172–173; electoral victory, 159–160; Lauder talks, 160–168; Oslo Accords, 75–76; political demise and replacement by Barak, 171–172
Netherlands, 28–29
Newsweek magazine, 42
Nixon, Richard M., 12, 22
Nobel Peace Prize, 69, 131, 187
Normalized relations, 41, 65, 105, 166
Nour al-Din, Sati, 195–196
Novik, Nimrod, 185
Nuclear technology, 13–14

Oaker, Mary Rose, 26
Obama, Barack, 122
Occupation of Kuwait, 10–15

Occupied Territories: Israeli atrocities, 56; Jerusalem's inclusion in, 27; Oslo Accords provision, 71, 73–76. *See also* Golan Heights; Palestinian Territories; Settlements
Oil: French contract with Iraq, 14; Iraqi invasion of Kuwait, 9–10
Oil-for-food program (UN), 14
Olmert, Ehud, 155
Oman: Gulf War, 15
al-Omar, Ibrahim, 119, 176–177, 229
Omran, Adnan, 142(fig.)
Operation Accountability, 140
Operation Desert Storm, 15–16, 33, 188
Operation Grapes of Wrath, 139, 154
Operation Peace for Galilee, 154
Operation Spring of Youth, 118
Oslo Accords (1993), 69–77, 82, 119, 201–202
Owens, Wayne, 26

Pakistan, 148
Palestine War (1948), 127
Palestinian National Authority (PNA), 71
Palestinian Territories: commitment to the liberation of, 40; continuing resistance, 202; Hebron massacre, 97–98; Hillary Clinton's criticism of the conspiracy theory, 158; increasing hold by hard-line groups, 138; intifada of 1987, 56; Israeli occupation, 10; Lake Tiberias negotiation, 179; Madrid conference, 20, 27, 44; Operation Spring of Youth, 118; Oslo Accords, 70–74; Rabin's hard line, 69; Syria's role in Middle East peace, 19; Washington, D.C. talks, 51, 53, 63–64
Pan-Arabism, 181
"Peace of the brave," 173
People's Palace, Damascus, 180
Peres, Shimon, 230; April Understanding, 142–143, 152; bombings in Israel, 137; conditions for Syrian-Israeli talks, 133–134;
Netanyahu replacing, 171; Netanyahu's victory over, 159–160; Oslo Accords, 71, 73; political situation after Rabin assassination, 131–132; Qana massacre, 140; Sharm al-Shaikh Summit, 138–139
Perot, Ross, 61, 66, 157
The Politics of Diplomacy (Baker), 11
Popular Front for the Liberation of Palestine (PFLP), 51
Posterity: Clinton on, 66–67
Powell, Colin, 69

Qabbani, Sabah, 173
Qaddour, Nasser, 142(fig.)
Qana massacre, 139–140
Qatar: Gulf War, 15
Quayle, Dan, 66
Qunaitra (Golan Heights), 134–135, 136(n19)
Qurai, Ahmad, 72, 230

Rabin, Lea, 132–133
Rabin, Yitzhak, 171, 230; assassination, 130, 137–138; Geneva Summit, 82, 85, 88; intifada of 1987, 56; Latakia meeting, 126; 1923 vs. 1967 borders, 128(n16); opinion of Assad, 96; Oslo Accords, 73; partial withdrawal from the Golan, 117–118; political situation after the assassination of, 131–132; replacing Shamir government, 64, 68; Shamir Plan, 47; Shihabi-Barak meeting, 118, 123
Rabin Deposit: Assad's stance on, 180; Barak's ignorance of, 121; Barak's stance on, 172, 177–178, 184–185; concealment of, 126; Israeli response to Syrians, 105–107; Lake Tiberias, 127; Netanyahu's position on, 160; Peres's succession, 131; Shepherdstown proposal, 183–184; Syrian peace on US terms, 190; Syrian response, 110; Syrian view of, 100–104; terms of, 98–99; US draft agreement for Shepherdstown,

174–175; US involvement in, 100, 104–105
Rabinovich, Itamar, 68, 100, 117, 119, 173, 230
Racism: Zionism as, 17–18, 56
Ramadan, 176
Reagan, Ronald, 28, 124, 162
Refugee problem, 47, 71
Religion, 178
Rizq, Elias, 40
Rød-Larsen, Terje, 72–73
Ross, Christopher W. S., 229; Assad snubbing Christopher, 150; Assad-Baker meeting, 26; Clinton-Assad relations, 79–80; Qana massacre, 139; second round of Washington talks, 65; Shara-Ross meeting, 49–50; situation after Rabin assassination, 130–131
Ross, Dennis, 229; April War and April Understanding, 142–147, 151–153; on Assad and Arafat, 160; Assad-Baker meeting, 26; Assad-Clinton press conference, 113; Assad-Clinton relations, 79, 96; Assad's land-for-peace formula, 28; failure to schedule Shihabi-Shahak meeting, 122–123; Geneva Summit, 81, 83–84, 88, 191–192, 194–195; Hizbullah attack, 108; Latakia meeting, 123–127; Lauder talks, 161, 167; Oslo Accords, 73; Peres administration, 159; Peres's conditions for Syrian-Israeli talks, 132–133; Rabin assassination, 106, 130; Rabin Deposit, 100–101, 103–105, 110–111; Shepherdstown talks, 174–176, 178–179; Shihabi-Barak meeting, 120(fig.); struggle over Lake Tiberias, 128; on Syrian women, 181–182; US response to Israel bombings, 137–138; Washington talks, 117
Roth, Allen, 162
Russia: Geneva Summit, 81–82

al-Saadawi, Khalil, 4
al-Sadat, Anwar, 13, 43, 174
Saguy, Uri, 176, 230
Sankar, Salha, 90
Saud al-Faisal, 138
Saudi Arabia, 15, 53, 138
Schweid, Barry, 87–88
Scud missiles, 20
Sea of Galilee. *See* Tiberias, Lake
Seale, Patrick, 84, 154, 173
Security: Assad's view of responsibility for, 17; Golan Heights ensuring Israeli security, 84, 193; Lauder talks, 164; Shihabi-Barak meeting, 121–122
Security zones, 75–76, 145–146, 177, 179
Settlements, 45, 52, 57, 64, 66, 75, 99, 101
Shafi, Haidar Abdul, 20, 53, 70–72, 230
Shahak, Amnon, 122, 140, 230
Shakkur, Yusuf, 175–176, 229
Shalit, Gilad, 77, 78(n38)
Shamir, Yitzhak, 230; Allaf interview quoting, 51; Bessmertnykh's meeting with, 30; decay of coalition, 64; Madrid conference, 41, 44–45; Palestinian policy affecting peace process, 19–20; peace conference venue, 28; Rabin replacing, 68
Shamir Plan, 47, 50
Shappira, Shimon, 161
al-Shara, Farouk, 96(fig.), 229; April Understanding, 142, 142(fig.), 145–146; Assad-Baker meeting, 18; Assad's death, 198; culture of resistance, 130; Geneva Summit, 80–81, 192, 195; Hizbullah disarmament, 32; Jerusalem's inclusion in Occupied Territories, 27; Latakia meeting, 123–124; Lauder talks, 160; Madrid conference, 40–41, 44–46; Rabin Deposit, 102, 110–111; response to Oslo Accords, 76; Ross-Shara meeting, 49–50; Shepherdstown talks, 174, 176–179, 182–184; struggle over Lake Tiberias, 128;

Syria's response to Kuwait
  invasion, 10; Yusuf al-Azma, 130
Sharm al-Shaikh Summit, 138
Sharon, Ariel, 166–167, 184
Shas Party, 172
Shepherdstown: Albright's faith in,
  184–185; "Chick Channel," 180–
  184; choice of venue, 174–175;
  Lake Tiberias question, 192;
  personnel and objectives, 176–177
Shevardnadze, Eduard, 29
al-Shihabi, Hikmat, 118–123,
  120(fig.), 126–127, 171, 229
Shultz, George, 12
Shuttle diplomacy, 16–17, 150–151
Sinai Peninsula, 30, 47–48
Soviet Union: importance to Syrian
  peace negotiations, 17; role in the
  pre-Madrid negotiations, 29–30
Stephanopoulos, George, 138
Suicide bomb, 107–108
Summit of the Peacemakers, 138–139
Switzerland, 28, 80. *See also* Geneva
  Summit
Sykes-Picot Agreement (1916), 27, 82
Syrian Social Nationalist Party
  (SSNP), 140

al-Tabba, Farouk, 40
Taif Accords, 32, 82
Tange, Kenzo, 110, 114(n42)
Tayara, Adnan, 40
Terrorism: Assad's accusations of
  Israel, 113; Baker and Assad
  defining, 18; freedom fighters vs.
  terrorists, 51–52; Netanyahu's hard
  line, 160; response to Israel
  bombings, 138; Shamir's
  accusations of Syria, 45; suicide
  bomber, 107–108; US list of state-
  sponsored terrorists, 34; US view of
  Iraq, 14
Tiberias, Lake, 127, 163, 179, 183, 192
Tishreen newspaper, 51
Tlass, Mustapha, 102, 231
Tourism, 117
Trade: Iraqi-French relations, 14
Truman, Harry, 127

Trust, importance of, 13
Tutwiler, Margaret, 26, 232

United Arab Emirates: Gulf War, 15
United Arab Republic, 92(n1)
United Nations: Assad's request for
  representation in Madrid, 21–23,
  25; basis for Madrid process, 29;
  Gulf War, 15; oil-for-food program,
  14; Qana massacre, 139–140;
  Syrian mandate for peace with
  Israel, 19; Zionism as racism, 17–
  18, 56
United States: approval of Barak's
  administration, 172; April War and
  April Understanding, 143–147,
  151–155; Assad snubbing
  Christopher, 148–151; Assad's
  impatience with failure to achieve
  peace, 21–22; Assad's interest in a
  relationship with, 33–34; Assad's
  media interviews in Madrid, 42–43;
  Assad's withdrawal from Iraq's
  domestic politics, 31; commitment
  to peace after Baker negotiations,
  25; direct talks in Madrid, 48; draft
  agreement for Shepherdstown, 174–
  175; Gulf War, 15–16; Israel's
  desire for direct negotiations with
  Syria, 50; 1992 elections, 61, 63,
  66; Oslo Accords, 70–72; Rabin
  Deposit, 98–103, 105–107;
  response to Iraqi invasion of
  Kuwait, 11–13; response to Israel
  bombings, 137–138; second round
  of Washington talks, 63–66; Shara-
  Ross meeting, 49–50; Shara's
  opening speech at Madrid, 46;
  Sharm al-Shaikh Summit, 139;
  Shihabi-Barak meeting, 118–123;
  speculations over Assad's health,
  188–190; stalemate in Washington
  talks, 57; stance on Israeli occupied
  territories, 27–28; view of Rabin,
  68–69; Washington talks, 50–52;
  Zionism as racism, 17
UN Security Council Resolution 242,
  27–28, 44, 47, 49, 51, 55, 57, 63

UN Security Council Resolution 338, 28, 44, 47, 49, 51, 63
UN Security Council Resolution 425, 53, 143

Velayati, Ali Akbar, 148
Venue, choosing, 28–29, 51, 63–64, 80, 174
Vilnai, Matan, 139–140

Waldheim, Kurt, 46
Washington, D.C.: Israeli-Jordanian talks, 52–54; Israeli-Syrian talks, 50–52; pessimism about second round of talks, 62–63; second round, 54–55; Syrian conditions for negotiation, 55–58
Water rights, 70, 127, 166
Watergate, 22
Wehbeh, Mikhael, 142(fig.)
West Bank. *See* Occupied Territories
Western Wall Tunnel, 160
Women, 180–184, 200

Yanai, Shlomo, 176–177, 230
Yeltsin, Boris, 81–82

Zardari, Asif, 148–149, 149(fig.)
Zionism as racism, 17–18, 56
al-Zoubi, Mahmud, 149(fig.), 187–188

About the Book

BOUTHAINA SHAABAN WORKED CLOSELY WITH SYRIA'S PRESIdent Hafez al-Assad from 1990 until the time of his death, serving as both official interpreter and adviser. Her new book, part memoir and part historical account, takes the reader behind the closed doors of the Syrian Presidential Palace to provide uniquely Syrian perceptions of the failed Arab-Israeli peace talks.

Sharing firsthand stories of relationships (her own and Assad's) with members of the Bush and Clinton administrations and drawing on previously unavailable minutes and other documents from the Syrian presidential archives, Shaaban takes us from the early Syrian-US engagement in 1990–1991 to the three Assad-Clinton summits in 1994–2000. In the process, she includes intriguing revelations about the Rabin Deposit, the April Understanding on Lebanon, and the 1998 Track II effort with Israeli prime minister Benjamin Netanyahu.

Shaaban offers the first account of these negotiations to come from a Syrian insider—an essential contribution to our understanding of the enduring conflict in the Middle East.

BOUTHAINA SHAABAN has been professor of English literature at Damascus University since 1985. In the 1990s, she served as principal interpreter for President Hafez al-Assad and was an active participant in the Middle East peace process. Dr. Shaaban's life and work are the subject of Ziad Hamzeh's film *Woman*, which was awarded the Golden Palm for best film at the 2008 Beverly Hills Film Festival.

RECEIVED MAY 3 0 2013 5500